Class Meets Land

INTERNATIONAL JOURNAL OF URBAN AND REGIONAL RESEARCH

IJURR STUDIES IN URBAN AND SOCIAL CHANGE BOOK SERIES

The IJURR Studies in Urban and Social Change Book Series has been a cornerstone in global urban studies since its founding in 1992 and has pushed the boundaries of critical, interdisciplinary, and theory-driven urban research. Contributors have conducted pathbreaking, theoretically informed empirical studies on inequality, informality, politics, environmental justice, gentrification, and segregation across the Global North and South. The common thread underlying these diverse interventions has been to respond to the urban question, How are cities both sites of significant inequality and repression and incubators of transformative cultural and political movements? Partnering with University of California Press since 2024, the IJURR Book Series continues to be a central intellectual hub for understanding the complex challenges facing cities in the twenty-first century.

Series Editorial Board:

Walter Nicholls, Editor-in-Chief

Manuel Aalbers

Talja Blokland

Dorothee Brantz

Patrick Le Galès

Jenny Robinson

Class Meets Land

THE EMBODIED HISTORY OF LAND
FINANCIALIZATION

Maria Kaika and Luca Ruggiero

UNIVERSITY OF CALIFORNIA PRESS

University of California Press
Oakland, California

© 2025 by Maria Kaika and Luca Ruggiero

Library of Congress Cataloging-in-Publication Data

Names: Kaika, Maria, author. | Ruggiero, Luca, author.
Title: Class meets land : the embodied history of land financialization /
   Maria Kaika and Luca Ruggiero.
Other titles: IJURR studies in urban and social change book series.
Description: Oakland, California : University of California Press, [2025] |
   Series: IJURR Studies in Urban and Social Change Book Series |
   Includes bibliographical references and index.
Identifiers: LCCN 2024030671 | ISBN 9780520410077 (hardback) |
   ISBN 9780520410084 (paperback) | ISBN 9780520410091 (ebook)
Subjects: LCSH: Social conflict—Italy—Milan—History. |
   Financialization—Italy—Milan—History. | Capitalism—Italy—Milan—
   History. | BISAC: SOCIAL SCIENCE / Sociology / Urban | SOCIAL
   SCIENCE / Human Geography
Classification: LCC HN488.M5 K35 2025 | DDC 306.0945/211—dc23
   /eng/20240806
LC record available at https://lccn.loc.gov/2024030671

Manufactured in the United States of America

33 32 31 30 29 28 27 26 25 24
10 9 8 7 6 5 4 3 2 1

For Athanasios Kaikas and Androniki Kaika
(Αθανάσιος Καΐκας & Ανδρονίκη Καΐκα), sources of
inspiration and drive to create a better world. Thank
you for all those years of waking up at 4:30 for factory
shifts and household work, hoping you could give us a
better life. You did; and you taught us to do the same
for many others—MK

For Vittoria and Vittorio, thank you; it is from you that
I learned to put passion, commitment, and dedication
into my research work—LR

Contents

List of Illustrations ix

Acknowledgments: The Academic Manuscript as
a Collective "Labor of Love" xi

Introduction: A Timeful Analysis of Class Struggle
as a Force of Spatial Production 1

**PART I. CITY OF INDUSTRY: LAND AS THE MEANS
TO FORGE A NEW ANTHROPOLOGICAL TYPE OF
WORKING MEN AND WOMEN (1880–1939)**

1. Class Meets Land: Turning Flexible Peasantry into
Disciplined Industrial Labor (1880–1922) 23

2. Land as Catalyst for Forging Class Consciousness
(1922–1939) 45

**PART II. CITY OF WORKERS: LAND AS SPACE FOR
COMMONING AND RADICAL POLITICAL ACTION
(1939–EARLY 1970S)**

3. Land as Citadel of Workers' Anti-Fascist Resistance
(1939–1945) 67

4. "Italy's Stalingrad" and the "Years of Lead": Radicalizing
Social Claims over Industrial Land (1945–Early 1970s)   81

PART III.   CITY OF TECHNOLOGY: LAND REVANCHISM AS
A MEANS OF TRANSITIONING TO HIGH-TECH
CAPITALISM (EARLY 1970S–EARLY 1990S)

5. Land Revanchism and the Unmaking of the
Working Class (Early 1970s–1985)   107

6. The Eureka Moment: "Discovering" Industrial Land
as Asset (1985–Early 1990s)   118

PART IV.   CITY OF FINANCE: LAND AS PURE FINANCIAL
ASSET (EARLY 1990S–2020)

7. Land Financialization as a "Lived" Process: From
Industrial Commodity Production to the Production
of Land as Financialized Asset (Early 1990s–2000)   137

8. Decaffeinated Urbanity: Financialized Land as
No-Man's-Land (2000–2020)   155

Epilogue: Financialization as "Lived" Process:
Moving the Field Forward   167

Notes   173
References   175
Index   193

Illustrations

FIGURES

1. Umberto Boccioni sketch for *La città che sale* (The city that rises), 1910 — 24

2. The Bicocca factory and the workers' village — 40

3. The Pirelli company in 1922 — 51

4. Contemporary view of one of Borgo Pirelli's homes for workers — 58

5. Contemporary street view of the Pirelli Tower, constructed in the 1950s and officially opened in 1960 — 77

6. The iconically designed workers' refectory at Bicocca — 79

7. Claiming the city center: workers protesting in front of the Pirelli Tower in Milan, October 9, 1969 — 95

8. Milan's urban boundaries in 1936 versus the 1980s, showing urban growth in relation to Bicocca's geographical position — 122

9. Bicocca's influence on Milan's post-Fordist development geographies — 124

10. Structure of the Pirelli Group in 1993 — 149

ILLUSTRATIONS

11. The old Pirelli concrete cooling tower, now functioning as a conference hall, is "engulfed" by the new glass and steel headquarters building 158

12. A ruptured urbanity. Bicocca's village, on the left, juxtaposed to the contemporary office and residential buildings 160

13. Monumental architecture and "decaffeinated" urbanity 161

TABLES

1. Minimum and maximum permissible gross floor areas (GFAs) per land use for Bicocca Technocity 129

2. The international market shares of the tire industry in 1990 140

3. Pirelli Group finances, 1991–93 145

Acknowledgments

THE ACADEMIC MANUSCRIPT AS A COLLECTIVE "LABOR OF LOVE"

This book is a "labor of love" (Boudreau & Kaika, 2013), like the coauthored articles that preceded it. What we mean by this is that the labor necessary for materializing it was contributed "in excess" of labor recompensed by academic institutions and "over and above" labor recompensed by funding bodies. Our fieldwork and travel were originally funded by a British Academy research grant (SG: 45263) and later by small funds from the School of Geography and the Environment at the University of Manchester, the University of Catania, and the Centre for Urban Studies and the Urban Planning Group at the University of Amsterdam. But the intensity of our intellectual dialogue, the involvement with local actors that kept pulling us back to Milano Bicocca, and the visits and intricate exchange of documents, articles, book chapters, maps, emails, and phone and skype calls between Catania, Oxford, Milan, Amsterdam, Thessaloniki, and Manchester stretched into weekends and "holiday" periods over fifteen years.

It was pure joy, as this work was as close to unalienated labor as work can get. Books as a labor of love are becoming rare during these times of massive funding cuts and intensification of work for public academic institutions.

xii ACKNOWLEDGMENTS

However, the labor of love that went into this manuscript was not ours alone. Our research received support, feedback, and access to archival material from a number of academic and nonacademic individuals and organizations. Special thanks are owed to Serena Vicari Haddock, Frank Moulaert, Raffaele Cercola, Roberta Sollazzi, Erik Swyngedouw, Matteo Bolocan Goldstein, Tom Bailey, Marianna D'Ovidio, Cabirio Cautela, Lorenzo Coccoli, and Ioannis Iliopoulos for their academic input. Our colleagues at the Universities of Oxford, Manchester, Amsterdam, and Catania were very supportive. The British Academy funded the initial fieldwork phase (2007–12). We owe many thanks to the following archives for giving us access: Istituto per la Storia dell'Età Contemporanea (ISEC); Archivio Civico in Milan (ACM); Biblioteca Sormani; Biblioteca dell'Università Commerciale Luigi Bocconi; Biblioteca del Politecnico of Milan; and Archivio del Lavoro-CGLI Milano. Special thanks to Eleonora Cortese at the Archivio del Lavoro-CGLI Milano, Cesare Maiocchi at Pinacoteca di Brera, and the Treviso, Museo Nazionale Collezione Salce, Direzione regionale Musei Veneto, for facilitating copyright permissions. Special thanks to Fernando Schrupp Rivero and Chiara Ricci for offering us copyright of their beautiful designs and to Graham Bowden for the cartographic work. Many thanks also to the editors and referees of the journals *European Urban and Regional Studies* and *Antipode*, who published early versions of our theoretical argument and some of the empirical material presented here (Kaika & Ruggiero 2015, 2016, 2018). A big thanks is owed to the editors of the IJURR SUSC book series, particularly Walter Nicholls and the anonymous reviewers who offered excellent comments on our first draft. We also owe many thanks to the excellent publishing team at the University of California Press, and in particular to Kim Robinson, Aline Dolinh, and Jessica Moll; to Teresa Iafolla and the UCP's FirstGen program; to Elisabeth Magnus for the excellent copyediting; to P. J. Heim for indexing; and to Griffin Stoss for proofreading.

A most significant contribution to this collective labor of love came from nonacademic actors: people whose lives were caught up in the histories of class struggle over land and land financialization that we narrate in the book. These include industrial workers who themselves engaged in class struggle over land, as well as industrial managers, architects, and planners who were heavily involved in the production of space. These key research informants with whom we had the pleasure and honor to engage offered their time and opened their personal archives with great generosity. We would like to mention here two people in particular, who sadly are not with us any longer: the late Vincenzo Berardi (pseudonym, †2015) and the late Giovanni Nassi (†2010). Nassi explicitly expressed his wish to be named in our publications, while Berardi wished to remain anonymous. Berardi was a former industrial worker and one of the main leaders of the 1968–71 workers' movement in Italy. With great passion and emotional investment, he gave us granular qualitative data regarding important pages of industrial history, particularly the 1960s and 1970s, as well as access to his personal archives. Nassi, the son of an industrial worker, who became manager and CEO in the 1980s and 1990, was equally very generous with his time. He gave us access to his archive and picked up the story of class and land from where Vincenzo Berardi left it. He gave us a detailed account of how in the 1980s and 1990s he had pioneered new real estate strategies for industrial land that became instrumental for finally turning it into a financial asset.

This book would not have been written without the contribution of all the people and institutions mentioned above. And writing this book would not have been possible without the enduring and continuous support of Licia Larocca and Erik Swyngedouw. Thank you.

Introduction

A TIMEFUL ANALYSIS OF CLASS STRUGGLE AS A FORCE OF SPATIAL PRODUCTION

In her book *Timefulness*,[1] geologist Marcia Bjornerud (2018) discusses how our lives are shaped by deep (geological) time and processes that vastly predate us but that we rarely problematize in our everyday life. She introduces the term *timefulness* to instigate a way of "seeing things not merely as they are now, but also recognizing how they evolved over time" (p. 1). Our monograph offers such a timeful way of approaching the central role that the class struggle of working women and men over land has played—and still plays—in choreographing each moment of transformation of global capitalism, from the late nineteenth century to the early twenty-first century. In doing so, the book reveals something that is almost counterintuitive: namely, that the dynamics of nineteenth-century class struggles over land are deeply implicated in the transition to twenty-first-century financial capitalism.

The timeful analysis we present here is woven into side-by-side narratives of the close-knit, one-and-a-half-century-long histories of Milan's working-class men and women (leagued in class struggle and anti-Fascist resistance), the district of Bicocca (one of Italy's first industrial areas, northeast of Milan), and one of Italy's oldest industries (Pirelli).

2 INTRODUCTION

The tumultuous histories of the company, the workers, and the land that we present here are intertwined with the political, social, economic, and spatial transformations of Milan. But they also stand as emblematic case studies of the wider socio-spatial, economic, and political transformations that marked the conflict-ridden history of capitalism in the twentieth and early twenty-first centuries. The book's front cover, a 1915 advertisement for the Italian tire industry, captures this intimate relationship between urbanity, industry, a particular imaginary of the industrial worker, the fantasy of progress through industrialization, and, above all, the central role of land and space in catalyzing the socioeconomic transformations that mark the relentless unfolding of capitalist socio-spatial relations.

Inserting the production of space and the assetization of industrial land into the analysis of class struggle right from the beginning of industrial capitalism enables us to demonstrate that land assetization and financialization are not recent phenomena: they are timeful processes, intimately sculpted by social struggle over a long period of time. The timeful approach we introduce here distinguishes this book from previous research[2] on land and class struggle, which examines single case studies only at particular historical moments, with few notable exceptions[3] (Thompson, 1964; Castells, 1984; Tilly, 1986; Katznelson, 1992; Gould, 1995; Mitchell, 1996, 2012). Despite past and recent calls for historically sensitive research,[4] the lack of engagement with processes over a longer historical time span persists and deprives scholarship of the ability to assess how historical changes in broader political economic, social, and cultural relations precipitate new roles for land and spatial strategies in the struggle for class power that drives capitalist transformations. This book's timeful analysis generates a number of new insights.

First, it makes possible the development of a multifaceted conception of land, which transcends dominant mono-dimensional theorizations often found in critical scholarship. Here we show that land has never been "only" an unproductive asset or "simply" a condition of production. Right from the beginning of industrialization, land was promptly "discovered," claimed, and effectively mobilized by *both* capital and labor as a class ally, an asset that could perform a range of social, symbolic, and material roles in production and reproduction.

INTRODUCTION 3

Our narrative foregrounds the parallel existence of these different and often-conflicting material and symbolic roles that land played for capital and for labor over the course of one and a half centuries. From early industrial accumulation all the way to financialization, industrial land was planned, designed, and organized by capital as a condition of production, an accumulation strategy, an asset, a tool for labor control, and an accessory in turning the workforce into the anthropological type that production demanded at any given moment: first disciplined, then flexible industrial laborers, and, more recently, unskilled precarious workers switching between industrial production and the service economy. Simultaneously, however, the same land has been equally effectively and continuously mobilized by labor: as an accessory in struggles for empowerment and resistance, as the means to ground class rights into everyday life and spatial practices, and as a strong social/political ally to formulate demands for labor rights and unionization.

Our book tells the story of how each new phase of capitalism demanded the destruction of old and the production of new symbolic and material class roles for land. The book also shows that these roles were never predetermined or mono-dimensional: each time, a plurality of—often contradictory—new imaginaries for the material and symbolic role of land (for production, reproduction, profit, socialization, and empowerment of working women and men) were created *in parallel* by both capital and labor and were claimed and fought over through intense class struggle.

Second, our narrative reveals that the historical persistence of class struggle over the preservation of old and the production of new material and symbolic roles for land generated space-specific forms of class consciousness for *both* capital and labor—not only during early industrialization but continuously, and all the way to the most recent phase of financialized capitalism. We argue that the ever-shifting and multifaceted symbolic and material meanings of land for both labor and capital gave rise to a plurality of identities, loyalties, and senses of belonging: for workers (to the factory, the family, the workers' communities, the workers' movement, the feminist movement, and trade unions) and for capitalists alike (to profit making first and foremost, but also to the factory, the city as a whole, the workers, and the social spaces they patronized).

4   INTRODUCTION

Third, these multifaceted loyalties and this spatially grounded class consciousness became deeply implicated in transitions from one mode of accumulation to another: from high-tech restructuring to recent financialization practices. But our analysis also shows that local industrial working-class populations, traditional elites, and institutions were never passive recipients, merely subjected to global capital restructuring and later financialization. They were, in fact, key protagonists. Their continuous socially embodied struggles that renegotiated changes in the material, economic, and symbolic value of land that postindustrial and financial capitalism needed were not the *outcome* but the *necessary means for* the transition from industrial to high-tech and later financialized capitalism.

Land assetization, and more recently land financialization, performed not simply a *coordinating* but a key *transformative* role. The socially embodied mobilization of land as a financial asset acted as catalyst for the "capital-switching" process from the "real" economy of goods and services to financialized forms of global capital accumulation. Mobilizing industrial land as a real estate asset was an act that not only enabled local traditional elites to survive the deep crisis of industrial capitalism but also allowed them to morph into protagonists of a new financialized phase of global capitalism. However, turning land into real estate asset required a violent revanchist act that claimed back what had historically become the working people's social spaces. The loss of these spaces, in turn, played a key role in morphing the labor force into what capital required as it entered a new accumulation phase: first flexible, and finally precarious.

But the intense class struggle over land ensured that even this final revanchist act was not monolithic. Land is a reluctant participant in these transformations. Our analysis highlights the cracks, the less-than-perfect transitions, in land's symbolic and material ownership and depicts capitalism as a less-than-perfect system that never fully breaks with the past but continuously absorbs components of the previous modes of production in the way it functions, develops, and plans for its future survival.

Fourth, the actors and histories that this book brings to light enable us to develop a novel understanding of land financialization as a "lived" process:[5] namely, a "slow-burning," deeply historical, local, and socially embodied process through which land rent became enrolled *simultaneously* in historical cycles of local class struggle and circuits of global (financial) capital

INTRODUCTION 5

accumulation and circulation. Shifting focus away from the usual suspects of financialization (global financial, banking, real estate, and governance elites) and foregrounding traditional local industrial elites and workers' organizations demonstrates that they are not so much "parochial" and local agents, as customarily depicted, but rather central actors and intermediaries in remodeling the architecture of the global financial sector.

We show that the recent production of land as a financial asset is not an ahistorical, unanticipated, top-down process, driven by some abstract global actors in response to a recent moment of crisis in capital accumulation; rather, it is the outcome of historical class struggle over land between traditional elites and workers. This struggle was central for the transition to the more recent financialized phase of capitalist accumulation. Our embodied and historically grounded reading of land financialization as a lived process puts "flesh and bone" on the disembodied data and debates that characterize much of the land financialization literature and challenges the dominant and often socially vacuous macroeconomic or governance-centered analysis of land financialization. This approach sets this monograph apart from other contributions to land financialization.

Fifth, we affirm that, even when land is fully embedded in global capital markets as a financial asset, its value still needs to be produced at the local level. Our approach demonstrates how the significant changes enacted by governance regimes to facilitate the financialization of the economy were not a response to the demands of some abstract "global" forces or international elites; governance regimes responded mainly to the needs of locally embedded traditional elites that desperately tried to reimagine their role, reassert their position in global markets, and explore new forms of capital accumulation.

Claiming the social spaces of industrial land back from workers and turning them into real estate, high-tech, or financial assets was instrumental not only for changing irrevocably capital's social deal with workers but also for transforming capital's social deal with local authorities over the production of urban space. It was precisely this change, we argue, that enabled traditional elites to remain competitive and relevant in a changing (global) economy.

Finally, our call for a timeful, socially embodied, and geographically embedded scholarship is a form of resistance against the ever-growing

6   INTRODUCTION

(institutional and market) demands for accelerating the production and turnover time of academic publications. The pressure to publish ever more and faster spurs the production of "timeless" scholarship: namely, a scholarship that can be rigorous and critical only if it sacrifices deeper historical analysis, focuses on processes over shorter periods of time and things as they "appear in the current temporal plane," and neglects to examine "the paths through time that shaped what they are now, and what they may become in the future" (Bjornerud, 2018, p. 1).

In the current context it is more difficult, but also more important than ever, to resist timelessness and insist on taking a timeful approach to scholarship. This can become transformative not only for producing knowledge in general but also for better understanding the current phase capitalism is in and, more importantly, for better linking academic knowledge to political praxis.

HOW THE STORY UNFOLDS

The book is structured in four parts, each containing two chapters. Part I, "City of Industry: Land as the Means to Forge a New Anthropological Type of Working Men and Women (1880–1939)," examines the role that industrial land acquired during early industrialization in catalyzing the production of a new anthropological type of disciplined worker that industrial production demanded at the time, but also in forming class consciousness. Part II, "City of Workers: Land as Space for Commoning and Radical Political Action (1939–Early 1970s)," chronicles how, in a beautiful stroke of irony, the spaces that were produced during early industrialization to control, stabilize, and anesthetize "the insubordinate spirit of the workforce" turned, after the 1930s, into launching pads for radical forms of class struggle. This part documents the complexification of the material and symbolic roles of industrial land as this turned into a space for workers' communal practices and radical political action. The socialization of land was instrumental for mobilizing Bicocca as a stronghold of anti-Fascist activism during World War II, and later as a key space of encounter and exchange between workers, feminists, students, and the *Operaismo* movement, but also as a hub for more radical and violent

INTRODUCTION 7

forms of industrial action (1960s–early 1970s). Part III, "City of Technology: Land Revanchism as a Means of Transitioning to High-Tech Capitalism (Early 1970s–Early 1990s)," explains how the combination of a weakened workers' movement and a crisis in industrial production during the 1970s and 1980s inspired and facilitated what we call "land revanchism": a process whereby capital forcibly claimed back the land and spaces it had "lost" to workers over the previous decades. The spaces that for decades had been perceived and had functioned as workers' social spaces were violently reclaimed and returned to capital. This, in turn, was the origin of reimagining and eventually producing land as an asset, restructuring labor relations and nurturing a new urban economy. Part IV, "City of Finance: Land as Pure Financial Asset (Early 1990s–2020)," documents how the most recent history of mobilizing land as a financial asset is a lived and embodied process, rooted in the history of one and a half centuries of class struggles over land. After a new wave of crisis in the late 1990s to early 2000s, capital discovered that mobilizing industrial land as a financial asset could not only save traditional industrial elites but also help them enter a new phase of financial speculative capitalism.

Turning Flexible Peasantry into Disciplined Industrial Labor (1880-1922)

The book's first chapter asserts the important material and imaginary role that land played during the first phase of industrialization. We show how this so-called "unproductive asset" nevertheless played a key role in producing a new anthropological type of disciplined women and men out of the "flexible" and "unruly" peasantry. It was no easy task to turn peasants into disciplined industrial labor. All industrialists were struggling, and Giovanni Battista Pirelli, who had just established his new rubber products company, was shrewd enough to deliberately seek out and employ soldiers, freshly discharged from the Italian army, since these young men had already been trained to follow hierarchy and discipline. However, the rhythm by which the army discharged men could not keep up with the industry's growing appetite for disciplined labor. Soon production intensification, combined with low wages, and deteriorating living conditions, plunged the industrializing world into widespread class conflict. In Italy,

8   INTRODUCTION

after the "bloody Milan riots" of May 1889, the first calls were made for welfare provision at factories to pacify the workforce. Again, Giovanni Battista Pirelli was among the first to respond. When, in 1906, he acquired Bicocca, a large piece of agricultural land northeast of Milan, this land became the means to embrace both industrial paternalism and Taylorism in one move. Pirelli hired the best architects, under the mandate to design industrial spaces that would be didactic about disciplined factory work. The aestheticization of industrial discipline extended from the design of buildings to rules about the attire and manners of men and women on the shop floor. At the same time, the new industrial landscapes also started featuring spaces dedicated to welfare and social activities for workers and their families (schools, crèches, health services). The combination of discipline and community spirit that these spaces propagated became instrumental for forging the new anthropological type of worker that industrial capitalism needed: a disciplined human being, with body and life bound to production spaces, willing to be part of a "solidarity network" between entrepreneurs and workers. By 1913, Pirelli's plants at Bicocca employed 3,725 workers. As production and welfare provision was expanding, and as more industries were locating northeast of Milan, this area morphed into a dense industrial district. The district was thus aptly nicknamed "the City of Factories." However, as the production of space in and around these factories intensified, the material and symbolic roles that land played complexified and became multifaceted: from a condition of production, industrial land was becoming simultaneously a pacifier of class conflict and a social and family space for working men and women, and it would soon also become a par excellence terrain for class struggle.

Land as Catalyst for Forging Class Consciousness (1922–1939)

During the first two decades of the twentieth century, the production of welfare and social spaces on industrial land became a widespread practice in Italy and across the industrializing world. As factory owners became increasingly involved in the production of space in and around industrial land, they developed a mutually beneficial relationship with state institutions that would last for decades to come. However, when Mussolini came to power in 1922, industrial land in Italy acquired a heightened sociopo-

INTRODUCTION 9

litical role. The Fascist ideology of *Corporativismo* banned strikes and workers' meetings, but at the same time it demanded welfare provision at the factories as proof of loyalty to the regime. Industrialists obliged, and factory towns proliferated. By the 1920s, Pirelli had added housing, sports grounds, and schools at Bicocca, and the industrial land now resembled a miniature village that was named the Borgo Pirelli. Now spatial arrangements managed not only the bodies of men and women working on the shop floor but also their entire families' bodies during schooling, shopping, and recreation.

The success of factory-based welfare practices in forging disciplined and loyal workers was such that many generations of critical scholars blamed factory welfare for "corrupting" class consciousness. But in this book we turn this argument on its head. The original material and analysis we present shows that, contrary to "corrupting" class consciousness, the new symbolic and material roles that industrial land acquired under paternalism became a strong ally in *forging* class consciousness for both labor and capital. The spaces that were created to pacify the workforce soon became catalysts for launching a fierce class struggle. Although the Borgo Pirelli was conceived and produced as a homage to the company's legacy and growing power, for the workers the same village was perceived and lived as their very own social space. As population density, gender diversity, and class homogeneity increased in factory villages, workers started perceiving industrial land as a space they could—and soon would—claim not only symbolically but also materially as their own. This spatially engrained formation of class consciousness was deepened as company welfare expanded to comfortable housing, crèches and schools in palatial historical buildings, purpose-built healthcare facilities, and, later, access to magnificent lakeside holiday resorts. Working men and women did become loyal—but not to capital or management. Their loyalty lay with the new socio-spatial arrangements around their everyday lives and reproductive activities that accompanied the relations of production; their class identity formation became intertwined with the imaginary of a collective ownership of the industrial land that hosted their socio-spatial practices—an imaginary that, for a brief moment in time, would become material. Class identity formation was so deeply inscribed into spatial arrangements that soon the spatial claims of workers extended from halls dedicated to union meetings

10   INTRODUCTION

to the allocation of land for personal allotments, gardens, and recreational spaces. In these early years of industrial paternalism, the company itself supported the symbolic construction of factory space as the workers' own, through references to workers as "the barons in overalls" and to workers' families as "the Pirelli dynasties." Workers were forming a *multiplicity* of loyalties: not just to production spaces but also to spaces hosting their reproduction, their communities, unions, homes, families, and social life. Importantly, however, these intermingled loyalties were not unranked: they had a *hierarchy* that would become starkly clear during the Second World War when Bicocca's land became a hub for anti-Fascist resistance, and later, for the initiation of radical forms of class struggle.

Land as Citadel of Workers' Anti-Fascist Resistance (1939–1945)

During the Second World War, under the dark shadow of Fascism, industrial land in Italy took on an additional and unexpected sociopolitical role. Chapter 3 focuses on how the material and symbolic appropriation of factory spaces as the workers' own social spaces in the years that preceded the war made it possible for Bicocca and other factory towns to become a haven for anti-Fascist resistance. Between September 1943 and April 1945, Bicocca became the stronghold of the National Liberation Committee (Comitato di Liberazione Nazionale, CLN), an outlawed anti-Fascist resistance group. The sense of belonging and emancipation that was forged in Bicocca during the years of the Great War was such that after the end of the war, when Pirelli's managers relocated to Switzerland for a while, the CLN and the working men and women of Pirelli resolved to run and manage the factories by themselves. The workers' claims to ownership of the means of production expanded from land and social spaces to the factory shop floor, machinery, and management. The radical imaginary that land belonged to workers (cultivated in previous decades) was very important for this change. When Pirelli's management returned, they seized back control of the means of production but for a brief period allowed workers to continue being involved in decision-making and factory management. During this period, they also instituted the Pirelli Cultural Center and the *Rivista Pirelli* magazine, which became important in Italian political and cultural life, and ensured the continuous presence of Bicocca as a space of radical social and political thought and praxis whose sociopolitical role expanded beyond the community of Pirelli's workers. So although workers handed back the means of production to factory owners after the Second World War, the cultural and social projects that the company offered in return stimulated the exchange of ideas between workers and the Italian left intelligentsia. This was important for sustaining the imaginary of Bicocca's land as an important hub for social struggle and contributed to radicalizing workers' claims in the years that followed.

"Italy's Stalingrad" and the "Years of Lead" (1945–Early 1970s)

The brief honeymoon period between capital and labor that characterized the years immediately after the war ended abruptly, when repeated crises in industrial production and capital accumulation led to wage cuts and redundancies. This period accentuated class struggle and complexified further the role industrial land played in socioeconomic and political praxis. In a stroke of irony, the spaces that had been originally designed and produced to control, stabilize, and anesthetize the "insubordinate spirit of the workforce" became the breeding ground for radical forms of class struggle. Chapter 4 depicts the 1950s, '60s, and early '70s, when Pirelli's workers (now counting over twelve thousand) forged strong links with Italy's *Operaismo*, feminist, and student movements, and Bicocca became a laboratory for more radical and innovative forms of social struggle, whose aims expanded beyond the social relations of production on the factory shop floor. The living memory of the years of anti-Fascist resistance and appropriation of the means of production by workers were crucial for radicalizing workers' claims. Wildcat strikes, sabotage, and continuous protests extending to Milan's city center were combined with more symbolic forms of spatial appropriation, such as giving the names of partisan leaders to streets and erecting urban monuments to resistance heroes. The militancy of men and women working in factories northeast of Milan during this period was such that this area was promptly nicknamed "Italy's Stalingrad." However, all this was taking place at the beginning of a period that became known as the "Years of Lead" (*Anni di Piombo*, 1960s–1980s), one of the most troubled periods in recent Italian history.

12   INTRODUCTION

The combination of economic crisis and sociopolitical turmoil fed into violent social clashes and acts of kidnapping, bombing, arson, and murder that terrorized Italian society. Often these acts (also known as the "Strategy of Tension") remained anonymous, and allegations were made against emerging far-right, far-left, and neo-Fascist groups, but also against the official state. It was not long before parts of the media also started associating the workers' militancy with terrorist acts. Although these allegations were never proven, they started denting social support for workers, dividing the unions internally, and weakening the labor movement. This, in turn, made it easier for capital to perform the violent act of "land revanchism" during the following decades, which would catalyze the transition to new forms of capital accumulation.

Land Revanchism and the Unmaking of the Working Class (Early 1970s–1985)

The book's fifth chapter moves on to examine what we term "land revanchism," a process whereby capital used land as a lever to claim back power from workers at the dawn of the deindustrialization for Western economies. We show how reclaiming space from workers and producing new symbolic and material roles for industrial land would, in turn, catalyze deindustrialization and the transition to new forms of capital accumulation. The industrial production crisis and broader socioeconomic turmoil of the late 1970s intensified capital's efforts to offset profit losses onto labor with wage cuts and layoffs. But these were met with fierce opposition. The industrial land and spaces that had become par excellence workers' insurgent spaces at "Italy's Stalingrad" served as the perfect lever for launching radical forms of class struggle. But now capital decided to use the same lever to gain back power; Pirelli responded to workers' radical class claims with the equally radical proposal to shut down most units at Bicocca and disperse production across Italy into smaller "flexible" units. Freed from industrial production, Bicocca's land would now be transformed into a Technocity, a research and technology center that could showcase Pirelli's intention to become a leading player in the international high-tech tire sector. This land revanchism would eliminate two internal "evils" in one strike—labor militancy and the lackluster pace of technological innovation. Inevitably, the proposal

INTRODUCTION 13

initiated a new round of class struggle. Workers fought hard to maintain control over their working, living, and communal spaces. However, the "Years of Lead" and the "Strategy of Tension" had already started weakening social support for the labor movement and had divided unions. Workers were now openly opposed not only by capital but also by local and regional authorities, who saw in the Technocity proposal an opportunity to mitigate the consequences of deindustrialization and reinvent Milan as an international technological innovation hub. The struggle over industrial land, which now involved in earnest three parties (workers, industrialists, and state institutions), resulted in a Pyrrhic victory for Pirelli's working men and women: in order to secure their jobs, they had to literally "hand back" the land that had become the centerpiece of their personal, family, communal, and political life, and the stronghold of their class identity and struggle. Only one production line would remain operational at Bicocca, and only a few hundred Pirelli workers and their families could continue living there. All the rest of the land was handed over to Progetto Bicocca, a daughter company that Pirelli established to manage the transformation of industrial and social spaces into offices and research and technology centers. The violent act of land revanchism that dispossessed workers became the catalyst for reallocating Milan's heroic working class into the growing ranks of a global "underclass" favored by neoliberal capitalism. As one veteran Pirelli worker put it, "They decided it was time to end class struggle," and the appropriation of land was crucial for making this happen. But land revanchism also became the precondition for reimagining, and eventually producing, land as an asset. This, in turn, became key to producing the new urban economies of the 1980s and 1990s.

The Eureka Moment: "Discovering" Industrial Land as Asset (1985–Early 1990s)

Chapter 6 analyzes the conditions under which industrial capital reimagined and materially produced industrial land as an asset, a means of accumulation in its own right. The land revanchism that preceded was key in activating this moment. Once again, Pirelli presents an emblematic case. In the late 1980s, the company's accounts were in the red as it could not overcome international competition. This was Pirelli's Eureka!

moment when company management realized that its industrial land could be reimagined, and accounted for, as a real estate asset that would provide the cash flow necessary to rescue the ailing company. Until that moment, industrial land had featured in Pirelli's accounts at zero value, as an investment that was depreciating over time. But now, for the first time, the same land was brought into the company's accounts as an asset whose value was not depreciating but increasing, if calculated according to speculative international real estate prices. The effect was immediate: Pirelli's accounts were balanced. For the time being, this was a "simple" act of creative accounting, but it also signaled the beginning of materially and socially producing industrial land as a real estate asset, and later as a financial asset.

Land Financialization as a "Lived" Process (Early 1990s–2000)

Although land financialization is often examined as a contemporary, macroeconomic phenomenon, driven by global financial elites, in chapter 7 we show land financialization to be a deeply historicized, embodied, and spatially embedded process that owes as much to the local histories and specificities of class struggle of men and women over land as to macroeconomic processes and global real estate capital flows. Shifting focus away from global financial elites and macroeconomic data, we demonstrate how, before land could be enrolled in circuits of global real estate markets, land rent had to be produced, first locally, by turning production and reproduction spaces into real estate values. For Pirelli's land at Bicocca, this happened during the 1990s when the company was desperately struggling to become an international player in high-tech rubber production. It was caught between two interrelated forms of class conflict: first, an international, interclass conflict among industrial elites, involving aggressive antagonism and hostile takeovers, and second, a local, more "traditional," form of class conflict involving further redundancies, factory closures, strikes, and demonstrations. During this period, Pirelli attempted a hostile takeover of its German competitor Continental, which turned out to be a disastrous failure. Pirelli was forced into public administration, and for the first time in the company's history the CEO ceased being a Pirelli family descendant. However, the failure to launch itself as a leader in the global high-tech industrial sector became a decisive

INTRODUCTION   15

push for local industrial capital to launch itself into a new, postindustrial, accumulation phase, focused on services and real estate speculation. Once again, industrial land became a key interlocutor in this process. While Pirelli was being forced into public management, its daughter company, Progetto Bicocca, delivered the first Technocity office building, which yielded unexpectedly high profits. The Technocity project that was expected to return revenues from local high-tech industrial innovation was returning profit from global land markets instead. Pirelli's new management seized the opportunity and turned real estate into a core business for the troubled company. This time, however, reimagining new roles for industrial land was not simply an accountancy exercise to support core industrial business. Now all plans for production recovery were shelved, and even the Technocity project was eventually abandoned. "Freed" from workers' claims and from every demand to host production, industrial land could now become a real estate asset in its own right. Thus Pirelli launched a plan for redeveloping Bicocca as Milan's new luxury "Historical Suburb," a highly speculative real estate venue mixing residential, office, cultural, and retail spaces. Importantly, the new imaginary and plans for the old industrial land were packaged as a financial asset whose stocks and shares were floated on the global market. The sales were promoted by a travelling international exhibition showcasing Bicocca and Milan as a pioneer of the new postindustrial urban economy. Under the speculative investment fever that followed, Pirelli made spectacular profits. And as its industrial land became core business, the company acquired a new branch: Pirelli Real Estate (Pirelli-RE).

However, the lesser-told story behind Pirelli's real estate success is that those rent values that became enrolled in global capital markets as financial assets, attracting new waves of investment to Pirelli and Milan, still had to be produced locally. Land financialization could not have happened without revising—once again—the social deal between capital, labor, and local authorities. The production of industrial land as a financialized real estate asset was predicated upon three violent acts. First was the act of value creation through discharging land from the multiplicity of social roles it had acquired over time: this meant shutting down the final remaining production lines, and a final round of layoffs. Second, the production of industrial land as financial asset was predicated upon the value added

16   INTRODUCTION

to the project by local authorities, who instituted special, site-specific, "flexible" planning regulations, delivery deadlines, and permissible total floor spaces. Finally, the success of land financialization was predicated upon the demise of any expectations from capital to assume a certain responsibility toward the city and citizens-workers from whom value was extracted. Globalized land financialization demanded the revision of the local historical relationship not only between capital and labor but also between institutions and capital. The mutually beneficial relationship between Pirelli and local and national authorities that had been firmly established under industrial paternalism, and was sustained under Fascism and during Milan's Fordist years, had to be radically revised in order to launch Milan's elites and the Milanese economy into a post-Fordist globalized era. Entering the more recent phase of footloose financial capitalism, local elites still demanded from local authorities to act as de facto facilitators for producing value and profit but did not give concrete promises in return to the city or its workers and citizens. These new values of neoliberal capitalism became inscribed into Bicocca's new spaces as it morphed into a Historical Suburb with luxury offices and housing.

Decaffeinated Urbanity: Financialized Land as No-Man's-Land (2000–2020)

The book's final chapter focuses on the socio-spatial implications of discharging industrial land from the multiplicity of social roles it had acquired over time in order to reinvent it as a financial asset. The reinvention of Pirelli's land as a financialized real estate asset successfully eradicated (materially and symbolically) the spatial imprints of one and a half centuries of struggles of men and women that produced and emblematized the multifaceted, intermingled, and coexisting imaginaries and uses that this industrial land acquired over time: City of Workers and showcase of industrial paternalism in the early twentieth century; hub for anti-Fascist resistance during the Second World War; exceptional case of appropriation of the means of production by workers after the war; "Italy's Stalingrad" and living laboratory for the *Operaismo*, feminist, and student movements in the 1960s and 1970s; exemplary case of land revanchism in the 1980s. The monumental architectural and urban design interventions that replaced

INTRODUCTION 17

the old industrial spaces formed what we call a "decaffeinated" urbanity, an urbanity "freed" from the requirement to serve industrial production but also "cleaned" from the imprints of the rich history of class alliances and conflicts that originally produced it. In this new urbanity, use and access rights are no longer up for grabs; they are granted only on the basis of property rights. Bicocca's new architecture, its residential and office buildings, the new university complex (Milano Bicocca), the opera, theater, and art gallery, perform a clear rupture from the working-class history that had produced multilayered imaginaries and materialities for this land over time. The original buildings that remain standing are either—literally—engulfed inside new office buildings (the old cooling tower), segregated away from key new functions (the few remaining workers' housing units), or cleared of references to the industrial production they once hosted (the Hangar Bicocca Gallery). The resentment and nostalgia are palpable in the old residents' narratives. But equally, Bicocca's new users (residents, office workers, university staff and students, cultural visitors) share the feeling that this is an alienating urbanity: a kind of "no-man's-land," a place where nobody feels quite at home. As in other similar redevelopment projects across the world, the eradication of the history and memory of class struggle that originally produced the Bicocca was key for the economic success of land assetization and financialization. A new decaffeinated urbanity was born.

In the next pages, we begin our detailed narrative of the tumultuous backstory of land financialization. We hope that the empirical and theoretical insight this timeful and embodied analysis brings will provide a perspective to enact future possibilities for an emancipatory social and political project that acknowledges the importance of reclaiming land as a social resource and a communal asset.

NOTE ON METHODS

We conducted field research during seven periods: February–March 2007; November–December 2007; October–November 2008;

September–October 2009; March–May 2019; November–December 2021; and October 2023. To support the book's timeful approach and longitudinal analysis, we combined archival research (for the period 1880s–2024) with life histories and semistructured open-ended interviews with key informants for the period that was still within living memory (1930s–2010). This material was supplemented with field visits guided by experts (architects and academics), direct observation, extensive analysis of policy documents (Milan City Council strategic planning documents, 1980s–2000), historical photographic documentation (1880s–2024), newspaper articles (1930s–2024), leaflets and pamphlets produced by workers' organizations (1940s–1970s), trade unions' official publications (1950s–1990s), official industrial annual reports and balance sheets (1970s–2010), and official advertising material and photographs (1910s–2024). The extensive life span of the research project made possible direct observations and mapping in situ of Bicocca's sociospatial transformations over the last fifteen years.

Archival material for the period 1880s–2024 was collected at the Archivio del Lavoro CGIL (Sesto San Giovanni), the Istituto per la Storia dell'Età Contemporanea archive (Sesto San Giovanni), the archives of the Biblioteca Sormani (Milan), Biblioteca dell'Università Commerciale Luigi Bocconi (Milan), and Biblioteca del Politecnico (Milan). In addition, the archives of the newspapers *Il Manifesto*, *Il Corriere della Sera*, *La Repubblica*, *Il Sole 24 Ore*, and *L'Unità* were consulted. Giovanni Nassi, who had held key managerial roles at Pirelli Bicocca, gave us access to his personal archive with material concerning mainly the period 1970s–1990s. Previous academic work on Bicocca and Pirelli, the online Historical Archive of Pirelli, and the published memoirs of four generations of Pirelli family members and company managers (A. Pirelli, 1946, 1984; P. Pirelli, 1930; G. Pirelli, 1990; B. Pirelli, 2002; G. Manca, 2005) were also valuable resources.

For the interviews and life histories, we mobilized a "polyvocal" methodological approach (Llewellyn, 2003), considering people who live and work in the spaces under study to be as important actors and informants as architects, planners, and developers. Therefore, it was important to identify (through snowballing) not only interlocutors from different generations who inhabit or have inhabited, work or have worked in the Pirelli-

Bicocca area, but also people from different positions and with different relations to the space and to the different groups of interest, who still held first- or secondhand living memories of the factory and the surrounding area. The living memory material we collected covered the period from the 1930s to 2010. Life history interviews were conducted with people who had lived and worked in the Bicocca. In-depth semistructured interviews were also conducted with trade union leaders and representatives of the period 1960s–1980s; with a manager and an architect directly involved in designing and delivering the most recent transition of Bicocca from industrial land into a mixed-use suburb for Milan (1990s); with local politicians and planners; with current residents of Bicocca; and with students and academics at the new Milano Bicocca University. We also tried long and hard—with numerous attempts and requests over a long period of time—to hold an interview with Pirelli's current management team; unfortunately, up to the moment our manuscript went to print, these requests were never answered.

The life histories of retired workers were collected during several meetings, each lasting several hours, and each establishing increasing levels of trust between interviewer and interviewee. All interviews were recorded and anonymized (unless the interviewee explicitly requested and gave permission to use their real name in the final publication). The interviews took place on sites chosen by the interviewees; often, these sites had been significant for the history of the workers' movement in Bicocca. We posed few questions and allowed the interviewees to "lead the interviewer-as-listener" (Hall, 2023, p. 2). We consider these life histories of workers to be a very significant contribution of our research, as they give voice to people who were silenced and marginalized for years (Gluck & Patai, 1991; Riley & Harvey, 2007; Rimoldi, 2017; Rohse et al., 2020). Thanks to the unique insight that this material gave us, we could develop our theoretical analysis and timeful approach. Our theory is grounded in, and filtered through, the memories and narratives of men and women concerning the central position of Bicocca's land in social struggles over production, reproduction, work, life, the economy, and the making of urban space. Thanks to this material and these actors, this book, we believe, makes a step toward bridging the gap between oral history and geographical research (Hall, 2023; Riley & Harvey, 2007).

20   INTRODUCTION

We did everything we could to double- and triple-check all dates and facts for the 150-year time span that the research material covers. When there were discrepancies between archival and interview material, we triangulated with further archival work and further interviews. For (very few) pieces of information, triangulation was not possible because of lack of additional data, or lack of availability or willingness of additional informants to engage or comment (e.g., Pirelli's current management). We demarcate these pieces of information as opinions rather than as facts (e.g., "according to X"). Unless otherwise stated, all translations from Italian are the authors' own.

PART I # City of Industry

LAND AS THE MEANS TO FORGE A NEW
ANTHROPOLOGICAL TYPE OF WORKING
MEN AND WOMEN (1880–1939)

1 Class Meets Land

TURNING FLEXIBLE PEASANTRY INTO DISCIPLINED INDUSTRIAL LABOR (1880–1922)

Starting to unfold the historicized process that led to land financialization, this chapter examines how industrial land, supposedly an "unproductive asset," nevertheless played a key material and imaginary role during the first phase of industrialization in producing a new anthropological type of disciplined male and female worker that was essential for industrial capitalism to thrive. The chapter follows the early history of Pirelli's industrial land from 1872, when the company was founded by Giovanni Battista Pirelli, until the first expansion of industrial production in the 1920s when G. B. Pirelli acquired Bicocca, a two-hundred-thousand-square-meter site northeast of Milan. The chapter explains how the expansion of the material and social role of industrial land during the early twentieth century was closely linked with mitigating class conflict and with turning flexible peasantry into disciplined industrial labor.

THE CITY OF FACTORIES RISES: LAND AS UNPRODUCTIVE ASSET

In 1910, Umberto Boccioni, one of the pioneers of the Italian *Futurismo* movement, painted *La città che sale* (The city that rises) (figure 1). The

Figure 1. Umberto Boccioni sketch for *La città che sale* (The city that rises), 1910. ©Pinacoteca di Brera, Milano—MiC; reproduced with kind permission.

painting captures what Boccioni was witnessing—awestruck—at the time: an entirely new industrial district rising out of an ancient agricultural landscape northeast of Milan, with unprecedented speed and force. *La città che sale* depicts an explosive, delirious melee of scaffolds reaching for the sky, factory chimneys rising next to houses, locomotive engines powered by a blend of human and animal sweat and labor, all interspersed with fire and covered in thick smoke. The painting conveys the mixture of apprehension and expectation that rapid industrialization and urbanization brought about, but also the widespread optimism that this process would bring economic, social, and cultural prosperity to Milan and to the entire country. The name of the brand-new industrial area that was sweeping away the ancient agricultural landscape in front of Boccioni's eyes was La Bicocca, and it was purposefully built to host the new factories of Pirelli, one of Italy's oldest companies, which at the time was manufacturing rubber products.

The industrial history of the city of Milan and the history of the Pirelli company go hand in hand. Pirelli today is a multinational giant with diversified production in a wide range of sectors, whose net annual global turnover in 2010 was on the order of 4.8 million euros (Pirelli & C., 2010). But Pirelli had humble beginnings; its history goes back to 1872, when Giovanni Battista Pirelli, an entrepreneurial young engineer, persuaded a group of investors in Lombardy to fund his project for a small factory to manufacture rubber products (A. Pirelli, 1946; Colli, 2001).

The founder of Pirelli was the eighth of the ten children of Rosa Riva and Santino Pirelli, a baker who died when Giovanni was only eight. After graduating with an engineering degree from the Polytechnic of Milan, Giovanni Battista Pirelli won the Kramer-Berra prize and—with the help of Giuseppe Colombo, an Italian entrepreneur who was also his professor and mentor—was sponsored to travel across Germany and France to acquire knowledge and technical expertise on manufacturing with a particular focus on the then-young rubber industry, which did not yet exist in Italy. Giovanni Battista's dream was to bring the secrets of the new industry home and establish his own company. His son, Alberto Pirelli, recounts in his memoirs the climate of great skepticism toward developing this type of industry in Italy. At that time, Italy was perceived mainly as an agricultural economy. Manufacturing was in its infancy, and the lack of local expertise in management, technicians, and workers meant that investors were not confident about investing in the country's industrialization (A. Pirelli, 1946). However, the valuable experience Giovanni Battista recorded in his diaries and brought back to Italy (Polese, 2003) helped him persuade a group of investors in the Lombardy region to fund his initial venture. The investors included successful textile entrepreneurs Visconti di Modrone and Eugenio Cantone (Colli, 2001).

In 1872 Pirelli established a small limited company (*società in accomandita semplice*) for manufacturing rubber products, originally mainly gloves and telegraph cables. The first factory operated from a modest building adjacent to the Pirelli family's home on Via Ponte Seveso, the site on which the Pirelli skyscraper stands today. At the time, the site was surrounded by agricultural land (A. Pirelli, 1946). Alberto Pirelli, Giovanni Batista's son, remembers how "I and my brother could hear the machines pulsing beyond the walls of our bedroom" (A. Pirelli, 1946, p. 7). The first factory employed forty blue-collar workers and five managers. From 1879 onwards, Pirelli's production expanded to telephone cables and bicycle and automobile tires, and over the decades that followed the company

26 CITY OF INDUSTRY

grew steadily through expanding its product range and with further
Italian capital investment ventures.

But Giovanni Battista Pirelli's ambition did not stop at local markets.
He was among the first European industrialists to launch an international
advertising campaign. Already in 1881, a budget for advertising appears
in the company's books: 5,000 lire out of a total budget of about 1 million
lire (Guizzi, 2015, p. 53). The promotion campaigns were so successful
that between 1892 and 1910 Pirelli displaced locally manufactured rubber products in countries as diverse as Austria, Argentina, Belgium,
France, and Great Britain (for an account of Pirelli's international activity,
see Colli, 2001). By the end of the nineteenth century, exports accounted
for 30 percent of Pirelli's income, and this figure rose to 40 percent in
1913 (Dalmasso, 1970; Bolocan Goldstein, 2003a; Colli, 2001).

MODERNIZATION WITHOUT CONFLICT?

Pirelli's success was not a singular phenomenon. At the end of the nineteenth century, Italy's industrial plants grew slowly but steadily in size,
productive capacity, and number of employees. Toward the end of the
nineteenth century, there was widespread optimism that Italian factories
could grow virtually without limits—and without class conflict. As companies grew, so did the involvement of Italy's industrialists in the country's
cultural, social, and political life. Pirelli's steady growth went hand in
glove with Giovanni Battista Pirelli's increasing involvement in politics.
In 1877, he was elected member of the City Council of Milan (1877–89),
in 1895 he became member of the board of directors of *Il Corriere della
Sera*, Italy's oldest and most popular newspaper, and in 1909 he was
elected life senator at the Senato del Regno d'Italia (Scotto di Luzio, 2001,
p. 358; Ciuffetti, 2004; Colli, 2001; Montenegro, 1985). Already from
those early days, the fates of the city of Milan and its industrial elites were
woven together in a tight and mutually supportive relationship.

Like many other Italian industrialists, Pirelli also engaged in extensive
philanthropic activities. Philanthropy became an important means for
entrepreneurs to improve their social standing, receive titles of nobility,
have their portraits displayed in benefactors' galleries, and pave their way

for a closer involvement in political life. After Italy's unification in 1861, philanthropy was also presented as a "moral and social obligation" toward constructing a socially coherent country (Conca Messina, 2017, p. 55). Industrialists funded schools, nurseries, and hospitals that directly or indirectly benefited the workers in their factories. Yet those philanthropic activities could by no means be construed as a form of welfare; as Conca Messina (2017, p. 57) documents, they comfortably coexisted with persistent and wide use of child labor in factories, long working hours, paltry wages, and the absence of any form of insurance or protection for workers.

Indeed, up until the 1880s there was complete absence of concern or dialogue around welfare provision in Italy. The workers' upheavals that had already forced welfare discussions to begin in England, France, and the United States had not reached Italy yet. This made Italian entrepreneurs optimistic that industrial capitalism could somehow evolve differently—more peacefully—in their country. They were convinced that the key reason behind the violent clash between capital and labor in other countries was the uncontrollable growth and intense spatial concentration of industrial activity (Conca Messina, 2017). For this reason, Italian industrialists declared early on their commitment to keeping industrial plants small in scale and to spreading manufacturing evenly across the country to avoid overconcentration. This way, industrialists believed, industrial activity would reflect in size and outlook "the peculiarities of Italian society," namely the importance of family and community values (Polese quoted in Rimoldi, 2017, p. 47). The young Giovanni Battista Pirelli fully endorsed this mode of thinking. He publicly expressed "disquiet about the degenerative effects that large factories could bring upon Italian family values" and defended "small-size enterprises [like his own] as the way forward" for a modernization without class conflict (quoted in Bigazzi, 1996, p. 41).

STRUGGLING TO TURN "FLEXIBLE" PEASANTRY INTO DISCIPLINED WORKERS

The commitment of Italian entrepreneurs to keeping enterprises small in scale to avoid class conflict seemed to work at first. Until the 1890s, workers' uprisings or strikes were scarce in Italian factories. However, this did not mean absence of class antagonism. As technological innovation intensified production rhythms, avoiding strikes was not the only concern. In order to make industrial plants functional, there was an urgent need to create a new work ethos, a new devoted and disciplined labor force that could guarantee the smooth functioning and expansion of industrial production and profit.

But those who were moving from the countryside to newly industrializing regions at the end of the nineteenth century in search of extra wages were men and women who had worked on the land all their lives. Their mothers, fathers, forefathers, and foremothers had also worked on the land all their lives. The men and women who were now plucked from agriculture to serve in the new industries constituted a low-cost labor force. But they were seasonal, unskilled, and "unreliable" (Conca Messina, 2017, p. 73). It was very common for unskilled female workers, who were employed in large numbers in the new textile industries, to flee back to the countryside after very short stints of work at the factories. Unskilled male workers also continuously moved back and forth between the countryside and the city, trying to supplement their meager factory salaries with part-time jobs in the agricultural sector—and vice versa (Conca Messina, 2017). Specialized workers were few and high in demand, so they also constituted an unstable and unreliable workforce as they moved freely from one factory to another in search of better wages and working conditions.

The "flexibility" and mobility of this early workforce created serious problems for industrial activity. The anthropological type of men and women that had been carved out of centuries of feudal relations of production and seasonal work on the land did not fit industrial production well at all. The new capitalist mode of production demanded the creation of a new anthropological type of worker: disciplined, place-loyal, fully committed to industrial labor, with a strong and able body that could sustain hard work and "guarantee a prolonged presence within the factory walls day or night" (Rossi quoted in Conca Messina, 2017, p. 74; Varini, 2012, 2023).

However, it was no easy task to turn peasantry into this new type of disciplined industrial labor that industrial capitalism demanded. Turning flexible peasantry into a stable means of production, an immobile fixed tangible asset (Conca Messina, 2017, p. 41), necessitated convincing men and women to shed their malleable work arrangements that oscillated between industrial work, domestic labor, and farming, to detach themselves from rural life, to abandon the habitual freedom of choice of work times and work types that they had "inherited from the old world of the worker-farmer," and to adapt to the new intensified rhythms that factory work demanded from their bodies and their lives (Varini, 2012, 2023; Conca Messina, 2017, p. 95).

Early entrepreneurs were becoming desperate over labor discipline. In a letter to a friend, Alessandro Rossi, a textile entrepreneur in Veneto, lamented that "creating this new generation of disciplined workforce" cost him "immense fatigue." The workers were continuously "trying to flee from being *enrégimenté.* . . . They don't know the discipline of organized factories; and their fathers did not know discipline, because in the old days they mostly worked at home, without fixed hours or fixed wages" (quoted in Conca Messina, 2017, pp. 73, 88). The same desperate tone was conveyed by the board of directors of the Cantoni cotton mills, near Milan: "It is necessary to educate populations raised under a regime of free and intermittent work in the fields, to make them fit the inflexible discipline demanded by large factories" (quoted in Conca Messina, 2017, p. 74).

"Educate" in this context meant convincing workers by coercion or conviction that their new life in the city had to be attuned to the demands and rhythms of factory work, to rotations of shifts and machine tempos. "Educating" workers also meant making them accept harsher working conditions and harder tasks, but also making them forsake the more creative or enjoyable aspects of work in favor of catching up with the rhythms of factory production. For example, conversation and singing were common among male and female workers in the early years of textile production, but the introduction of more efficient but much louder machinery made "conversation and singing impossible" (Benenati, 1998, p. 16). In factories, workers had to learn to work "following a [new] rhythm [of the machine], which, in the past had been achieved by singing" (Accornero, 2002, p. 36).

The rhythms and shifts of capitalist production affected not only talking and singing but also many other prime practices (sleeping, eating, socializing, procreating) that in the past had been attuned to the rhythms of the natural rotation of night and day and the succession of seasons. Many historical economists and sociologists have analyzed the prime importance of the capitalist construction of time in achieving discipline (Accornero, 2002; Cipolla, 1981; Gallino, 1978; Musso, 2023; Sombart, 1967; Thompson, 1981). Notably, Lewis Mumford (1934) argued that the most important machine of the industrial age was "the clock, not the steam-engine" (p. 14). Tuning the workers' bodies and voices to the rhythms and noises of the machine was key for forming discipline, as workers had to learn to accept management, hierarchies, and subordination. In Marxist terms, they had to become proletarianized.

Giovanni Battista Pirelli also encountered problems with labor discipline in his factory. But he devised early on strategies to avoid the "immense fatigue" that his peers experienced when trying to discipline their workforce. Pirelli deliberately sought out and employed soldiers who were freshly discharged from the Italian army. His conviction was that after their stint with the army, the young men were already fully trained to follow hierarchy and discipline. This would save him a lot of time, trouble, and money (Tranfaglia, 2008). In his report, written three years after the first Pirelli factory started production in 1875, Pirelli noted how crucial the workers' conduct was to the production process. Because different tasks required different skills, from delicate handling and precision to physical strength and hard work, it was necessary that at least part of the workforce be composed of "intelligent and robust men, but above all, disciplined men" (quoted in Tranfaglia, 2008, p. 678).

Giovanni Battista Pirelli's early insight into the importance of labor discipline is related to the educational trip he took to Germany just before he established his own factory. During his visit to the Krupp steel factory in 1871, Giovanni Battista reported back to his sponsors his admiration for Friedrich Krupp, who had managed to "regiment 1,500 workers with iron discipline" and transform his factory into what resembled "real military barracks" (Tranfaglia, 2008, p. 675).

THE 1898 BLOODY MILAN RIOTS: THE END OF HARMONIOUS LABOR-CAPITAL COEXISTENCE AND THE RISE OF PATERNALISM

At the end of the 1870s, industrial production in Italy grew rapidly and exponentially. Scrap iron imports increased from 1,657 tons to over 58,000 tons between 1862 and 1879, coal imports tripled, and raw cotton imports multiplied tenfold (Conca Messina, 2017, p. 70). The allure of quick growth and profit made Italian industrialists forget their early commitment to keeping industrial activity small in scale and evenly distributed across the country. Industrial plants expanded in size, and industrial activity concentrated in and around urban centers in search of economies of scale, ease of transport, and labor availability. Giovanni Battista Pirelli's earlier fervent support of small-scale enterprises was now cast aside as his own company grew rapidly.

With industrial production growing in intensity and output, the increased demands on workers' time, discipline, effort, and commitment did not come with better wages or benefits. As in other industries, Pirelli's workers were working overtime and overnight, but still receiving the same low wages: 20–30 cents per hour for male workers and 13–14 cents per hour for female workers (equivalent in today's purchasing power to 80 cents–1.20 Euros per hour for male workers and 52–56 cents per hour for female workers) (Tranfaglia, 2008, pp. 678–679). And as workers were concentrating in cities and living in rapidly deteriorating housing conditions, Italian industrialists became increasingly anxious about labor unrest.

Giovanni Battista Pirelli, who had skillfully capitalized on the training efforts of the Italian army to get a supply of ready-made disciplined workers, realized that the rhythm by which the army produced disciplined men could not keep up with the industry's growing appetite for disciplined labor. He now openly declared how anxious he had become about controlling this "chaotic crowd of workers whose 'deviant' behavior could become a risk for the smooth function of the production process" (G. B. Pirelli quoted in Galdo, 2007, p. 10).

Avoiding class conflict and forging a new disciplined work ethos became the most important concern. Italian entrepreneurs employed a variety of methods ranging from strict management regimes to punitive measures such as fines, penalties, wage reductions, and dismissals (Bigazzi, 1996). However, sanctions and strict management regimes proved ineffective to curb the burgeoning trade unionism in Italian factories. By the 1880s, Italian industries were plunged in widespread capital-labor conflict. The workers at the textile factories in Biella (the heart of Italy's industrial revolution near Turin) were the first to engage in organized industrial action. Prolonged strikes and protests prevailed throughout the 1880s and 1890s, with workers demanding in the first instance mainly better salaries. But welfare demands soon came to the fore as well for the first time: healthcare, workplace safety, housing. In 1891, two thousand manual labor workers from various factories in and around Milan went on strike for fourteen days. A growing number of men and women working in factories joined the movement, threatening a general strike across the city. In 1891, Pirelli's factory in Milan experienced its first strike action. Giovanni Battista Pirelli was apprehensive: he saw the strikes as the direct result of the penetration of Socialist politics into his factories and declared his determination to "keep socialism outside the company's gates" and to clamp down on any "attempt from . . . foreign elements to provoke his workers into protests and strikes" (Bellavite Pellegrini, 2017, pp. 14–15). Later, during the 1896 national electoral campaign, he sent a letter to his workers criticizing Socialist ideas and directly inviting them to vote for the liberal candidate (Tranfaglia, 2008). The workers' upheaval, which was supported by the increasingly popular Socialist movement, was instilling fear in the industrial elites (Conca Messina, 2017, p. 69). Italy's political and entrepreneurial elites became seriously concerned about "the evil [i.e., strikes] that until that point had been absent from Italian factories" (Benenati, 1999, p. 52).

The strikes continued for several years, while industrialists tried to clamp down on labor with punitive measures. Eventually, the police and army forces were called in to "help." In May 1898, the workers' movement was brutally attacked in one of the harshest historical clashes between workers and the police, which "lasted several hours and ended . . . with 80 dead and 450 wounded" (Tranfaglia, 2008, p. 703; Rimoldi, 2017). This violent clash became known as the "bloody Milan riots of May 1898" (Bellavite Pellegrini, 2017, p. 14). It was a clear wake-up call for all those who had believed that a harmonious coevolution and symbiosis between capital and labor was possible. After that moment, controlling the growing numbers of workers became the major concern of industrial and political elites, and entrepreneurs entered, for the first time, into discussions with workers around welfare provision.

It was at this time that Giovanni Battista Pirelli took on his role as the benevolent capitalist. He noted that for workers to become disciplined, they first had to become loyal to the company. And for this to happen, he argued, they should be offered "some excitement" in the form of participation and a sense of belonging to the company (G. B. Pirelli quoted in Varini, 2012, p. 118). This sense of belonging, according to Pirelli, would create a sense of accountability that would deliver results beyond official productivity and performance targets. Work discipline could be best achieved, not through strict management regimes, but through forging a sense of belonging to a corporate community for working men and women (Varini, 2012, 2023). It was this reasoning that drove Giovanni Battista Pirelli to finance the creation of a mutual aid and social security fund for his workers and, after lengthy and intense negotiations, to cosign with his workers, on May 3, 1902, one of the first collective labor agreements, the Workers' Concordat. The pioneering agreement included the creation of a workers' commission that could "negotiate directly with the company's management on all matters concerning rights, duties, and economic and living standards for the workforce" (Tranfaglia, 2008, p. 705). During the same period, other industrialists also started listening to workers on matters of welfare provision but still refused to sign collective labor agreements (Conca Messina, 2017, p. 85).

The Workers' Concordat was a unique success for Pirelli's workers, but it was an equal success for Pirelli's management. As Italian sociologist Aris Accornero (2002) notes: "Cooperation between workers and entrepreneurs was essential for the survival of capitalism . . . [since] . . . the key novelty of industrial capitalism lay [not with technological and scientific innovation] but with the new type of social relations it established" (p. 15). Industrial production instituted intense antagonism between capital and labor but also a strong interdependence between these two "factors of production," as they were both "indispensable building blocks for an industrial capitalist society" (Accornero, 2002, 15).

MOBILIZING LAND: GROWTH, EXPANSION, AND INTERVENTIONS IN CITY PLANNING

The importance for the survival of capitalism of maintaining a working relationship between these two essential factors of production (capital and labor) can explain the efforts on the part of capital to mitigate conflict and maintain the strongest possible levels of collaboration, particularly in the early stages of industrialism. But as this book is set to show, this important mitigation was achieved by using as a lever a third factor of production: land. The production of new imaginary roles and material uses of industrial land through the production of social spaces in and around factories were essential components for mitigating labor/capital conflict and for the survival of capitalism, not only in those early years, but continuously, as we shall see while the story in this book unfolds.

After the 1898 bloody Milan riots, Italian entrepreneurs started paying closer attention to international examples of industrial paternalism. The family-type arrangement of industrial relations that paternalism evoked was seen as a good fit for the perceived "peculiarities" of Italian society with its strong family and community ties (Bigazzi, 1996, p. 38). Hoping to capture some of the secrets of industrial paternalism in disciplining labor, Italian industrialists started visiting factories abroad. Noisiel and Mulhouse in France, the workers' districts built by Krupp in Essen, Germany, and the workers' villages of Bournville and Saltaire in England were particularly favored destinations (Conca Messina, 2017). As noted earlier, Giovanni Battista Pirelli had already visited the Krupp plant in Essen early on and had recorded how impressed he was by the welfare regime that Krupp had established there, which included housing, schools, kindergartens, a labor accident fund, an elderly workers' fund, and even an agreement for limited profit-sharing with workers (Tranfaglia, 2008, p. 676).

Inspired by industrial paternalism abroad, Italian entrepreneurs started experimenting. The first decades of the twentieth century saw industrial and agricultural land at urban peripheries across Italy transformed into new working/living spaces, resembling what Lewis (2004) termed *manufacturing suburbs*. Expanding industrial activity under conditions that could mitigate labor/capital conflict and secure a continuous

CLASS MEETS LAND　　35

supply of a place-bound workforce proliferated and soon became the norm for peri-urban development.

But as in the rest of the industrialized world—from Manchester, London, and Paris (Cherry, 1996; Dewhirst, 1960; Daumas & Payen, 1976; Stovall, 1990), to Montreal (Lewis, 2001, 2004), San Francisco (Walker, 2001), Pittsburgh (Muller, 2001), and Los Angeles (Hise, 2001)—the introduction of industrial paternalism was coupled with the introduction of new methods of "scientific" personnel management. Hand in glove, industrial paternalism and Taylorism would secure the labor discipline necessary for achieving improved efficiency and effective risk management (Benenati, 1999).

Paternalistic practices demanded extensive control and/or ownership over land on the part of industrialists. But as industrial paternalism proliferated in Italy, Pirelli found itself restricted by its spatial arrangements, as it was "landlocked" in its original factory location, a small parcel of land in Milan's city center. This original Pirelli plant became so overcrowded and polluted that it acquired the nickname *La Brusada* (the Burnt House), which invoked the gloomy, smoky, and insalubrious atmosphere that characterized production and work there. The toxic work conditions intensified labor unrest. In response, Giovanni Battista Pirelli first tried to acquire adjacent land and buildings. But these were not even sufficient to expand his industrial production, let alone start on a spatially demanding program of welfare provision. Structural barriers, planning restrictions, and the relatively high cost of acquiring new land in Milan's city center made further expansion on Pirelli's original site impossible.

But all this changed in 1906, when Giovanni Battista Pirelli, with the help of the Banca Feltrinelli, purchased 1,280,870 square meters of agricultural land northeast of Milan, comprising the "Bicocca Contessa Sormani" estate of 1,151,440 square meters; the "Sala Serafino" estate of 25,680 square meters; and the "Girola Giuseppe" estate of 103,750 square meters (Pavese, 1997; G. B. Pirelli, 1907). The area took its name from a manor house (Bicocca) that had been built there in the fifteenth century by the Arcimboldi family (Pirelli, 1984). In 1907, Pirelli started constructing his new factory on part of the Bicocca estate, and the Arcimboldi manor house first became a display shop for the company's products and later (in

1922) was repurposed into a school for the children of Pirelli's workers (A. Pirelli, 1946).

Of the total 1,280,870 square meters of agricultural land that came under the ownership of Pirelli and Banca Feltrinelli, 120,000 square meters were allocated immediately for Pirelli's new industrial functions. In the meanwhile, another 1,320,000 square meters of neighboring agricultural land were acquired by Breda, Banca Commerciale Italiana, Banca Pisa, and Strade Ferrate Meridionali (Bigatti, 2018; Pavese, 1997; G. B. Pirelli, 1907). On January 4, 1907, the new land owners around Bicocca (Pirelli, Banca Feltrinelli, Breda, Banca Commerciale Italiana, Banca Pisa, and Strade Ferrate Meridionali) formed the Società Anonima Quartiere Industriale Nord Milano (SAQINM), to which they transferred a total of 2,480,870 square meters of their land holdings (the remaining 1,160,870 square meters from Pirelli's Bicocca plus 1,320,000 square meters from the other consortia). The aim of the formation of the SAQINM was to propose a plan for developing this agricultural land northeast of Milan into a new industrial district (Pavese, 1997, p. 134). The proposal received wide and favorable publicity for its "innovative character and ambitious scope," notably in the pages of *Le Case Popolari e le Città Giardino*, a magazine on social housing (Nurra, 1910).

By 1913, just before World War I erupted, Pirelli's plant at Bicocca already employed 3,725 workers. The plant became a reference landmark in Milan's periphery and produced a buzz around it. Soon, as more factories located near Pirelli, Bicocca morphed into the dense industrial district that was nicknamed "the City of Factories" (Irace, 1997), and whose construction was captured in Boccioni's painting (figure 1).

The rapid industrialization northeast of Milan that started with Pirelli's plants at Bicocca had wider implications for city making. Up until that point, the city of Milan had grown mainly through ad hoc and adaptive spatial expansion practices (Bolocan Goldstein, 2003b). Now, as the new class of industrialists took on increasingly crucial roles as funders and producers not only of factory space but also of services and social spaces for workers, Italian entrepreneurs became increasingly involved in decisions regarding city making and city planning. Many among them established private research and planning institutes to provide the scientific basis for persuading local administrators to facilitate the spatial expansion of their private industrial activity with the provision of publicly funded social services and transport connections (Bolchini, 1967; Irace, 1997). A mutually beneficial relationship developed between the city's industrialists and the city's authorities that would last for many decades to come. On the one hand, Milan's local government was keen to explore the more comprehensive planning proposals for urban expansion that were suggested by the research institutes of private companies. On the other hand, industrialists could not fully finance and implement the expansion of their production without a close collaboration with local and regional governments.

The Società Anonima Quartiere Industriale Nord Milano exercised strong influence on planning and urban development decisions and played a key role in the "spatial revolution" of Milan. Soon after the acquisition of Bicocca, the City Council of Milan was persuaded to build a new tram line, the "Bicocca line," to facilitate the commuting of workers to the factory (Galdo, 2007). Aware of their strong contribution to the occupational, technological, and economic development of Milan, the consortium of industrialists also proposed the construction of a large boulevard that would run from the center of Milan through Bicocca to the direction of Sesto San Giovanni. The boulevard had designated lanes for the circulation of old and new means of transport—tram, omnibus, bicycles, and automobiles—and three adjacent rows of housing, blocks of flats, and workshops. The plan was inspired by the radical visions for a rational, well-ordered modern city that circulated at the time across Europe and the Western world, most notably Arturo Soria y Mata's Linear City (Ciudad Lineal) in Madrid. The development axis ran parallel to the properties owned by the consortium of entrepreneurs who proposed it, and the transport and housing development it envisioned would help propagate Breda and Pirelli's fortunes, not least because almost half of Pirelli's income in Milan at the time came from the sales of bicycle and automobile tires (Bolocan Goldstein, 2003b). Giovanni Nassi, who worked for Pirelli in management roles starting in the 1970s and during the last years of his life acted as vice president of the real estate division of Pirelli (Pirelli RE), notes: "It has always been like this. Pirelli would develop transport plans, which would then be put in place by the municipality as a favor to Pirelli, but also as a service to the workers who had to get to the factory" (Nassi, interview, February 22, 2007).

THE AESTHETICIZATION OF SPACES OF PRODUCTION AS THE MEANS TO FORGE A NEW ANTHROPOLOGICAL TYPE OF WORKER

Moving toward the early twentieth century, industrial paternalism gained momentum across Italy with extensive provision of workers' housing and welfare schemes. Franco Tosi's engineering plant in Legnano, Lombardy, was among the first to offer "a health insurance plan, schools, a company shop, a café-restaurant for evenings and weekends, and some housing for workers, as well as two thousand square meters of land for leisure activities" (Bigazzi, 1996, p. 46; see also Macchione, 1987). Also in Lombardy, the textile entrepreneur Cristoforo Crespi was so impressed by his 1889 visit to Saltaire in England that upon his return he transformed the land surrounding his cotton mills into a workers' village with "self-contained cottages, a nursery, an elementary school, a grocery store, a hospital, and a church" (Conca Messina, 2017, p. 89). In the Veneto region Gaetano Marzotto used part of his industrial land to plant fruit orchards for his workers and to build "a cooperative shop and houses equipped with laundry facilities and efficient kitchens" (Benenati, 1999, p. 55). There were even radical experiments with anarchist utopian ideas: in northern Italy, Alessandro Rossi developed the "new Schio" around his wood mills, a garden city that aimed to fulfill "the 'social' needs of workers . . . inspired by the ideal of a classless society, and sustained by . . . institutions that can support all generations of workers and their families with kindergartens, elementary schools, and spaces for theater events, singing classes, poetry recitals, evening classes, public baths, houses for pensioners, a public library" (Bigazzi, 1996, p. 44).

These extensive paternalistic practices were strongly rooted in the belief that the mobilization of industrial land to host social services would act as a stabilizing force, reduce the cost of social conflict, and secure smooth growth of production output and profit. Many Italian industrialists extended their spatial interventions beyond the land around their factories and funded public gardens as well as sports and cultural facilities in other areas. These new spaces were meant to forge character, inspire positive social values, and occupy workers after factory labor with pleasant but politically benign activities that would keep them at arm's length from "the two big evils": drinking and political activism.

The construction of Pirelli's new factory at Bicocca became an opportunity to embrace both industrial paternalism and Taylorism in one stroke. The new plant combined a pleasant working environment with industrial efficiency. The design was equally inspired by the paternalistic principles found in small-scale factories in England—particularly Saltaire and Bournville—and by the strict scientific management regimes of larger-scale industrial plants in America and Canada, notably the tire production plants of Goodrich, Goodyear, and Firestone in Akron, Ohio (Lewis, 2000, 2001, 2004; Walker, 2001; Walker & Lewis, 2001).

The visit that Alberto Pirelli, Giovanni Battista's son, had paid in 1905 to the plants at Akron, just before the construction of Pirelli's factories at Bicocca, contributed greatly to promoting these ideas back home. Alberto Pirelli wrote to his father: "Dear father, visiting these factories in America has made me dream of renovating ours; of building wide beautiful halls and not holes, [that would help] reach the beautiful production figures they achieve here. This trip is a real revelation, . . . a mind opener. I have lots of projects in mind and cannot wait to discuss them with you" (Documenti per la storia delle industrie Pirelli, no. 668 ASIP, Archivio Storico Fondazione Pirelli, quoted in Galdo, 2007, p. 7).

Piero Pirelli (Alberto's brother) echoed his brother's ideas and praised the benefits of scientific management at Bicocca's factories during a lecture he gave to Italian industrialists: "The preparation of the rubber mixture was originally carried out in small units of single workers that could process only a few tens of kilos at any given time. . . . Now we use a mechanical mixer called 'the Bambury' and the workers' task is limited to feeding and watching this machine, which has the capacity to process several hundreds of kilos of rubber and other ingredients at a time" (P. Pirelli, 1930, p. 42).

But the new Pirelli plant at Bicocca did not only showcase up-to-date industrial infrastructure. It became an emblematic site for showcasing that efficient capitalism could also be socially benevolent. The new infrastructure at Bicocca was the exact opposite of Pirelli's first crowded, dark, and gloomy *Brusada* factory in Milan's city center. A "well-ordered hierarchy of buildings, aligned along a rational grid, replaced the old maze of alleyways" (Pirelli, 1986, p. 15). Bicocca featured low-density, well-designed two- or three-story manufacturing plants, warehouses, and con-

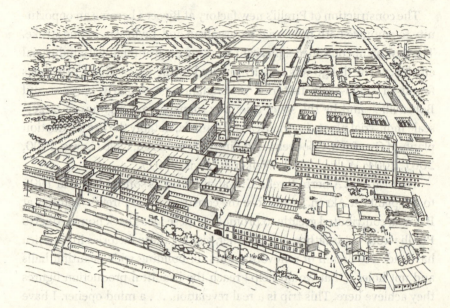

Figure 2. The Bicocca factory and the workers' village (top left background). Artist's impression of archival photographic material. Drawn by Chiara Ricci.

necting walkways made of brick, glass, concrete and steel (Irace, 1997, p. 146). The brand-new buildings offered ample space for workers and production functions (figure 2). The original Pirelli plant in the city center had been "a functional structure for production.... It belonged to the reign of useful things associated with a modernizing ideal that [focused on] ... the perfect efficiency of the rubber production machines" (Irace, 1997, p. 139). By contrast, the new plants at Bicocca invoked a new modernizing ideal that went beyond efficiency. They aspired to become architectural landmarks and to be didactic about how an industrial plant should look and operate. With its distinguished brick and glass designs, the new Bicocca plant made a statement not only about production efficiency but also about factory aesthetics (Irace, 1997, p. 139).

The aestheticization of factory production was not limited to buildings and materials. It extended to the attire and manners of Pirelli's workers. At Bicocca, men and women doing blue-collar work were required to wear clean uniforms at all times. The ones assigned to the dirtiest jobs had to wear white uniforms and change them regularly.

Originally associated with images of dark, bleak, dirty sites, industrial sites were now redesigned to become clean, bright, and pleasant spaces, that would unify production with reproduction activity for workers. The peasantry that was morphing into an industrial proletariat found alienating the new relations of production, waged labor, and new architectural forms, rhythms, and spatial organization that factory production imposed on their bodies and their lives. The separation of workspaces from living spaces was also alienating. But the unified working and living spaces that industrial paternalism was now creating, resonated with the traditional blurring of working and living environments in peasant life and gave industrial workers spaces that they could—and would—call their own. Work, and life, schools, crèches, housing, recreation grounds, all became part of a unified experience of factory life. Industrial landscapes soon became something more akin to lively workers' villages. Still heavily polluted, but now in good order and embellished with workers' homes, schools, and social activities, the new industrial landscapes acted as "emblematic signs of the [positive] impact that industrialization could have" on both society and space (Colli, 2001, p. 495).

The production and proliferation of this entirely new typology of spaces that were both working and living environments became instrumental for forging the new anthropological type of working men and women that industrial capitalism needed: workers loyal to the spaces in and around the factory, human beings whose bodies and lives were bound to production spaces and who were willing to be part of a "solidarity network" between capital and labor that was grounded on very specific spatial configurations (Benenati, 1999, p. 48).

"CORRUPTING" CLASS CONSCIOUSNESS: THE FAILURE OF CRITICAL SCHOLARSHIP TO ACCOUNT FOR THE IMPORTANCE OF CLASS STRUGGLE OVER SPACE

Paternalistic practices were so successful in producing a new anthropological type of worker that both the labor movement and critical scholars in Italy blamed company welfare practices for "corrupting" class consciousness, arguing that the "solidarity network" between entrepreneurs

42   CITY OF INDUSTRY

and labor that paternalism promoted prevented workers from building solidarity networks around class or ethnicity (Benenati, 1999). Many scholars describe paternalism as a "successful ideological legitimation of bourgeois class domination" (Conca Messina, 2017, p. 41), a class project aiming to create the illusion of a mutually beneficial growth practice that would repress legitimate and necessary class antagonism (Merli, 1972; Guiotto, 1979). Workers who subscribed to paternalism were seen as betraying their class consciousness, since they could not be at the same time loyal members of both the labor movement and industrial residential communities. Most workers' unions condemned paternalistic practices as "controlling and corrupting the worker" and accused workers who supported paternalism of betraying their class in return for receiving material privileges (Benenati, 1998, p. 6).

The strongly held view that paternalism was "corrupting" class consciousness is also the key reason why many critical scholars treated the history of industrial paternalism in Italy as a history separate from that of the labor movement; they depicted paternalism to be "a residue" of feudalism and thus considered workers laboring under paternalistic relations to be incapable of developing working-class consciousness (Bigazzi, 1996). Early industrial social relations—paternalistic or not—comprised "residual" or "neofeudal" elements not only in Italy but also in all other parts of the world, notably in the European and the Global South (see Vergopoulos, 1975; Tsoukalas, 1981). But in Italy, the persistence of paternalism was seen as proof of the "backwardness of the Italian industrial world" (Benenati, 1998, p. 6) that resulted in an "oxymoronic coexistence between modern technological-managerial practices and pre-modern industrial social relations" (Guiotto quoted in Benenati, 1998, p. 22; see also Bigazzi, 1996).

The persistent dismissal by key scholars of industrial paternalism as a "feudal residue" has three serious implications that still haunt political economy and socio-spatial scholarship today. First, by seeing paternalism as an unimportant stage before "real" capitalism settled in, much of critical scholarship refused to see capitalism for what it always has been and still is: a less-than-perfect system that never fully breaks with the past but continuously absorbs components of the previous mode of production in the way it develops and functions.

Second, by dismissing industrial paternalism's spatial practices as a residue of feudalism, critical scholarship failed to examine the important role that the production of space played in the transition from feudalism to capitalism right from the start. Industrial paternalism practices were the first instances when industrial capital discovered and explicitly used the production of space to its advantage.

The third implication for socio-spatial scholarship of the dismissal of industrial paternalism as a "feudal residue" is that, by treating the history of industrial paternalism as a history separate from that of the labor movement (and paternalism as unworthy of full class analysis), critical scholarship failed to see the important link between the history of class struggle and the history of land and of the production of space. By failing to examine the link between the production of industrial land and the reproduction of social relations embedded within it, critical scholarship did not examine the full range of the ways in which land acted not only as a force of industrial production but also as a force of (re)production of new types of industrial relations.

Marx's early analysis (eagerly taken up by critical scholars) of industrial land as an unproductive asset greatly contributed to the three failures outlined above, as it held critical scholarship locked into the notion of land's unproductiveness for many decades (Harvey, 1982a, 1982b). This book's examination of the history of class and land side by side is the first historically geographically grounded analysis that aims to overturn this tradition. By examining the history of industrial land in conjunction with the history of class struggle, we show that the attention to, and investment in, the production of land and space in and around factories was no feudal residue and was not serendipitous either. Right from the start, the production of space became a key component for launching industrial capitalism into expansive practices. Our historical and contemporary analysis shows that land has never been an unproductive asset; it was an essential element of production right from the beginning of industrial capitalism, essential for mediating capital/labor relations and vital for securing the steady growth of profits.

By inserting the production of space and the assetization of industrial land into the analysis of class struggle right from the beginning of industrial capitalism, we show that land assetization (and financialization) is

CITY OF INDUSTRY

not a twentieth-century phenomenon; industrialists discovered and capitalized on the full spectrum of the possibilities for profit making through land early on. By engaging in the provision of social spaces and services for their workers, Italian entrepreneurs soon became aware that the land they owned or could acquire around the factories could be replanned, redesigned, and reorganized to become much more than the "unproductive asset" that Marx had depicted it to be. It could become a valuable asset, generative of the new social relations of labor that they wanted to promote.

In those early stages of industrial capitalism, land did indeed become a strong ally for forging the loyalty of the workforce and for producing the new anthropological type that factory production desired and demanded. However, land also became right from the beginning *generative* of class consciousness for both workers and labor. As we shall see in the next chapters, in a beautiful stroke of irony, the very same spaces that were meant to control, stabilize, and anesthetize what G. B. Pirelli called "the insubordinate spirit of the workforce" soon acted as powerful catalysts for the development of resistance against Fascism (chapter 3) and of radical ideas and practices for class struggle (chapters 4 and 5).

2 Land as Catalyst for Forging Class Consciousness (1922–1939)

The success of factory-based solidarity networks in forging disciplined and loyal workers was such that many generations of critical scholars blamed factory welfare for "corrupting" class consciousness. In this chapter, we turn this argument on its head. The original material and analysis we present here show that, contrary to "corrupting" class consciousness, the significant symbolic and material roles that industrial land acquired under paternalism became a strong ally in *forging* class consciousness for both labor and capital. This chapter documents how class identity formation was deeply intertwined for both labor and capital with the material production of industrial land as social space; and for labor in particular, with the imaginary of a collective ownership of industrial land under paternalism.

Industrial paternalism was already strong in Italy when Mussolini came to power in 1922. However, under Fascism, it acquired a heightened sociopolitical role. This chapter chronicles how, under the Fascist ideology of *Corporativismo,* which demanded welfare provision at the factories as proof of loyalty to the regime, factory towns proliferated across Italy. Now spatial arrangements managed not only the workers' bodies on the shop floor but also their families' bodies during schooling, shopping, and recreation. Adding housing, sports grounds, and schools to Bicocca, Pirelli created the Borgo Pirelli, a workers' village conceived as a homage to Pirelli's legacy and growing power. Workers, however, perceived and lived the same village as their very own social space. As population density and class homogeneity increased in factories, workers started acquiring a spatially engrained class consciousness that was deepening as company welfare provision expanded. This chapter argues that workers formed a *multiplicity* of loyalties to the new sociospatial arrangements that facilitated production, but also hosted, their communities, unions, homes, healthcare, schools, and social life. Importantly, this chapter argues, these intermingled loyalties had a clear *hierarchy* that would be starkly revealed only in the decades that followed, when Bicocca's land became the launching pad for radical forms of class struggle.

INTERWAR YEARS: SPATIALLY SPREADING THE RISK OF LABOR UNREST THROUGH COLONIAL RELATIONS

The strong presence of paternalistic policies in Italy did not stop workers from entering the *biennio rosso,* two revolutionary years (1919–20) after the end of the First World War (Bertrand, 1982). The workers' villages that were originally produced to subordinate the workers' spirit became instead the fulcrum of a strong working-class movement when working men and women started appropriating industrial land—first symbolically, and then also materially—as a place for free social and political expression. The prolonged strike action and factory occupations during the *biennio rosso* demanded wage increases, improvements in working conditions, and reduction of weekly working hours. Density and class homogenization in workers' villages played a key role in these movements. The multiple loyalties that workers held to the spaces that hosted both relations of production and their own social life and reproduction also played a key role. These loyalties turned out to be neither uncritical nor free of hierarchy. Loyalty to class proved to be at the top of this hierarchy as working-class consciousness prevailed over factory loyalty during the intense disputes over industrial relations. Workers' loyalty to paternalistic spaces was instrumental rather than blind. Perceiving the factories as social spaces that belonged to workers increased the momentum and self-righteousness of the labor movement as it facilitated extensive strikes and factory occupations.

Among other things, workers demanded state intervention and institutionalization of their rights and welfare practices. Capital was horrified by the strength and momentum of the working-class movement. Faced with the "specter of Bolshevism," industrialists did not hesitate to use raw violence against workers' insurrections, and on many occasions this violence was "contracted out" to the gradually forming paramilitary Fascist squads (*Fasci italiani di combattimento*) (Di Paola, 2009, p. 1; Detti, 1978). The persistent lack of state intervention in industrial relations that paternalism had demanded now created space for Fascism to grow stronger. This is why many scholars link the failure to institutionalize the demands of Italian workers during the interwar period to the rise of Fascism. This failure was crucial for the failure to form a liberal state in Italy, which, in turn, could have prohibited the rise of Mussolini to power in 1922 (Di Paola, 2009; Detti, 1978). As Walter Benjamin perceptively noted, the rise of Fascism was but a symptom of the failure of Socialism.

Workers at the old and new Pirelli factories took a central part in the upheavals and prolonged factory occupations. They formed a Workers' Commission (*Commissione operaia*) and invited Alberto Pirelli to work with them and forge a new vision for the "social" management of Pirelli's factories (A. Pirelli, 1946; Rimoldi, 2017). Alberto Pirelli (the son of Giovanni Battista) was by that time running the business together with his father and his brother, Piero Pirelli. In his memoirs, Alberto Pirelli highlights the company's success in opening a dialogue between the workers and the management during the interwar period. But this dialogue was established in the first place through workers' militant demands. Despite opening a dialogue with its workers, the corporation remained affected by increasing labor unrest, at a moment when it was also heavily bruised by the instability and profit loss that the First World War brought to industrial production and international trade.

48   CITY OF INDUSTRY

However, while the interwar period found Pirelli negatively affected by labor unrest at home, new opportunities were rising globally. Between 1910 and 1930 the global annual demand and production of rubber grew from fifty thousand tons to three hundred thousand tons, and this figure reached over one million tons in 1938 (A. Pirelli 1946, p. 33). This large profit potential galvanized Pirelli's leadership to follow a strategy that would spread geographically the risk of labor unrest, production costs, and trade and marketing fluctuations. In a report that accompanied Pirelli's 1920 financial statement, Giovanni Battista Pirelli strongly advocated an international expansion of production and marketing that would offer the company a geographically broader and more stable base: "Through establishing connected, yet geographically dispersed production and trading locations, production will never have to come to a halt again. Even at times when there is a crisis in one location, production, trading, and marketing can continue in all other locations" (Giovanni Battista Pirelli quoted in Montenegro, 1985, p. 25).

And so it happened. Pirelli launched an international development strategy during the interwar period that aimed to circumvent possible future local crises in Italy. This strategy featured several characteristics of multinational capitalism, as it aspired to take advantage of favorable raw material costs and socioeconomic and labor conditions in different locations, spread geographically the company's market base, and—not least—spread the risk of sourcing raw material by pursuing overseas environmental and labor exploitation practices.

Pirelli expanded production to the United Kingdom, Spain, and Argentina. It also acquired two rubber plantations in the Far East: in Ulu Tiram, on the Malaysian peninsula, a few kilometers away from Singapore; and in Boenisari Lendra on the island of Java (Bellavite Pellegrini, 2017; Montenegro, 1985). Alberto Pirelli (1946) dedicates a full chapter of his personal memoirs to Pirelli's "raw materials and rubber plantations," where he explains what, for him, were the two key drivers for the acquisition of the plantations: first, the need to overcome the volatility, price fluctuations, and speculation in the natural rubber markets, and second, the need to experiment with grafting and other sophisticated cultivation techniques in order to improve the quality of rubber and in turn improve tire performance. By that time, all of Pirelli's major competitors (Michelin, Dunlop, Goodyear, Goodrich, and Firestone) had already acquired their own plantations in the Far East, and global competition in the tire industry revolved mainly around performance enhancement through continuous quality improvement of "ingredients" and product characteristics (Montenegro, 1985).

When Alberto Pirelli visited Pirelli's plantations in Malaysia in the beginning of the 1920s, he reported how astonished he was by the extent and intensity of human labor that was mobilized to produce the amount of rubber that Pirelli needed. He also noted the extreme poverty under which plantation workers had to live. His narrative demonstrates understanding and a certain apprehension of the colonial exploitation dynamics upon which the prosperity of Pirelli and the Global North as a whole was predicated. But at the same time, his narrative (like almost all Western narratives of the time about colonial practices) depicts this exploitation as "inevitable" because of the "dramatic interdependence between social and economic problems." He notes that "it is impossible for Pirelli alone to improve the living conditions of plantation workers. . . . To anyone with a sense of humanity it would appear just and necessary to improve the [working and living] conditions of plantation workers. . . . However, if such improvements are not compensated by increase in productivity, or reduction of other costs, these [improvements] will certainly jeopardize the ability of plantation-derived rubber to compete with synthetic rubber. If that were to happen, it would bring a serious crisis to the plantations" (A. Pirelli, 1946, pp. 102–103).

The colonial-type interdependence of production and trade relations between Europe and the Far East that rubber plantations established also meant that a large chunk of the jungle was destroyed to make space for the plantations that were feeding the growth of the economies of the Global North. In fact, this practice was recognized and mentioned during the grand ceremony organized by the local population to welcome the "European chief" Alberto Pirelli. During the ceremony, the local boss at the Malaysian plantations declared without critical edge but with a good dose of irony that "here we once had tigers and snakes; now, we have the Pirelli" (A. Pirelli, 1946, p. 103).

ITALY'S FIRST MULTINATIONAL COMPANY: INTERNATIONAL EXPANSION IN THE MIDST OF GLOBAL RECESSION

As Pirelli's international operations grew from plantations and factories to commercial enterprises, Pirelli also changed its governance structure to mitigate risk (see figure 3). All the production plants in Italy were grouped in one entity, the Società italiana Pirelli (SIP), while international activities, including the plantations, were transferred to a new company, the Compagnie Internationale Pirelli (CIP), which was registered in Brussels in 1920 (Montenegro, 1985, p. 26). The CIP's financial activities were channeled through Pirelli's office in Switzerland (Montenegro, 1985). Between 1920 and 1924, the company significantly increased its share of the global tire market from 7.1 to 13.3 percent and grew steadily until 1925. Like most family-owned companies, Pirelli was interested in long-term investment ventures but was averse to risk exposure through external borrowing that might result in nonfamily members (let alone international actors) intervening in the company's management practices (Colli, 2001).

However, Pirelli's expansion and growth eventually demanded an increase in short-term debts and led to a liquidity crisis that could not be absorbed by the Italian bond markets alone (Bellavite Pellegrini, 2017, p. 36). To resolve this crisis, Pirelli decided for the first time to extend its capital base beyond Italian capital markets. In 1925, Alberto Pirelli convinced his father to pursue the company's first long-term loan. Between 1925 and 1927, the SIP, which was running the production plants in Italy, negotiated with a team of New York banks led by J. P. Morgan a US$4 million loan in the form of twenty-five-year bonds. Giovanni Battista Pirelli took careful measures to secure that control of the company would remain within the family. To prevent foreign banks from interfering in management, he restructured Pirelli by splitting responsibilities and liabilities between three companies (see figure 3). The first, Pirelli & C., became the holding company and acted as the "family's strongbox" (*cassaforte di famiglia*) that would "oversee the Group's general strategy, management and coordination, with particular focus on financial and funding operations" (Bellavite Pellegrini, 2017, p. 30).

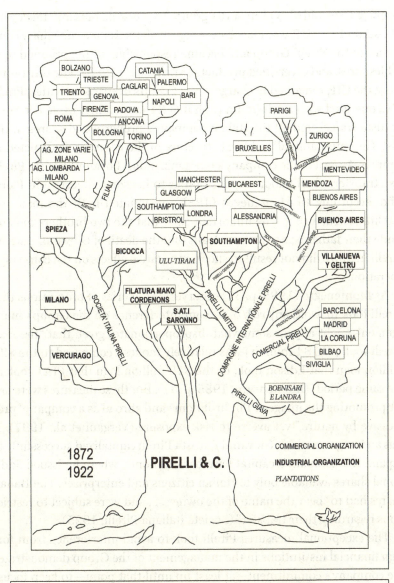

Figure 3. The Pirelli Company in 1922. Artist's impression of archival images from the online Archivio Storico Fondazione Pirelli. Drawn by Fernando Schrupp Rivero.

Pirelli & C. would also protect the group from hostile bids and takeovers. The second, the SIP, was placed in charge of all the Italian subsidiary companies of the Pirelli Group and became responsible for the production of cables, tires, and diversified products (Anelli et al., 1985). The third company, the CIP, remained in charge of the Group's overseas activities. Pirelli & C. operated with a minimum capital of 24 million lire, while Giovanni Battista transferred all the Italian company's property and shares to the SIP. The international and local structure of the company is depicted in figure 3. As part of the company's reorganization, Giovanni Battista Pirelli also transferred all major responsibilities to his sons, Alberto and Piero, who, according to Montenegro (1985), negotiated both the loan and Pirelli's restructuring. The important roles that the two brothers took on while their father was still alive meant that the death of Giovanni Battista Pirelli in 1932 did not result in shock or negative effects on the company's operations.

As Montenegro (1985, p. 37) observes, "The series of precautions that Pirelli took to avoid any risk of foreign interference on the Group's management might appear somewhat disproportionate" given that "the loan Pirelli took [US $4 million] was relatively modest, compared to the $20 million loan that Edison took, or the $10 million loan that FIAT took at the same period" (Montenegro, 1985, p. 37). But these measures were key for promoting the image of Pirelli at home and abroad as a company "progressive by nature," yet averse to risk exposure (Vergani et al., 1997). It was an image on which Giovanni Battista Pirelli capitalized successfully to expand the company's capital base back at home, where he issued additional shares available only to Italian citizens and enterprises. The Italian shares had to "bear the name of the owner . . . and were subject to restrictions regarding their transfer" (Società italiana Pirelli, 1925).

The exceptional measures Pirelli took to avoid interference from foreign financial institutions in the management of the Group demonstrates the company's commitment—at least up until that point—to keep focusing on the expansion of Pirelli's core business, industrial production, and not to yield to the temptation to enter a financial logic. Before that point, Pirelli had mobilized financial instruments only when necessary to boost the company's core business of industrial production. The loan operation was a great success and culminated with Pirelli becoming the first Italian company to be listed on the New York Stock Exchange on May 13, 1929, which further enhanced the company's image (Bellavite Pellegrini, 2017, p. 36).

By 1929 Pirelli and its French competitor, Michelin, covered half of the entire world's tire market (Montenegro, 1985, p. 44); the other half was covered by US and Canadian companies. In 1929, in the midst of the global recession crisis, Pirelli managed to sustain considerable growth.

THE RISE OF MUSSOLINI TO POWER: LABOR SUBORDINATION AND THE "UNFORGIVABLE SILENCE" OF CAPITAL

Pirelli's success during the interwar period was due to several reasons. First, the liquidity that the US loan offered enabled a timely investment in production expansion right at the moment when demand was increasing (Bellavite Pellegrini, 2017). Second, in 1929, in the midst of global recession, Pirelli could mitigate risk, as it had already built "a dense and highly efficient international network of dealers extending from large cities to the tiniest countryside locations" (Montenegro, 1985, p. 45). Third, Pirelli was one of the first European companies to acknowledge the importance of advertising and launched international campaigns to strengthen the brand's name and popularity; one of these, from the 1910s, illustrates the front cover of this book. Moreover, as Chiara Guizzi (2003, p. 28; see also Guizzi, 2012) notes, Pirelli was one of the first companies to pay particular attention to the preservation of its own history, legacy, and *res gestae*. Early on, the company started to archive documents and visual material related to its industrial history and even created the very first industrial museum in Italy, the Museo delle Industrie Pirelli, which was inaugurated on June 25, 1922.

But Pirelli's ability to thrive in the midst of a global crisis was also related to an external factor: the rise of Fascism. It was only after Fascism rose to power that the whole of the Italian industrial world (and Pirelli too) could finally see the scales of class struggle tilt in favor of capital. Despite its international expansion, Pirelli's strong protectionism of its home base meant that Milan's Bicocca remained the most important production plant for the Group (and would continue being so until the 1970s). During the interwar period, Bicocca hosted three large production units (tires, cables, and diversified rubber products) as well as the company's Research and Development unit, which occupied in total almost 50 percent of the entire Pirelli Group's workforce (Rimoldi, 2017, p. 79). And although international expansion and colonial relations allowed Pirelli to exploit favorable prices for raw materials and labor contracts in other countries, labor relations at home remained explosive, as we saw in the beginning of this chapter.

But when Benito Mussolini rose to power (on October 31, 1922), he became a great ally of industrial capitalism by abolishing both the right to strike and the right to hold workers' meetings. Fascism declared strikes and workers' meetings not only illegal but also "unnecessary" since, according to the Fascist ideology of *Corporativismo*, class conflict simply did not exist (Montenegro, 1985, p. 35). The authoritarian suppression of workers' rights was a direct gift to all Italian entrepreneurs, as it assisted with disciplining the unruly workforce and helped suppress salaries and manage labor costs (Benenati, 1999). According to Montenegro (1985, p. 46) the "unscrupulous use" of the "total subordination to which the working class was subjected under the iron rule of Fascism" helped industries to systematically reduce salaries and intensify production without strong objections from the labor force. This was crucial in sustaining Italian industries' competitive edge in international markets under strained conditions (Rimoldi, 2017).

The entirety of the Italian industrial world benefited from the social "tranquility" imposed when Fascism imprisoned or confined the leaders of the working-class movement and forced workers to join the new Fascist "trade unions" (Montenegro, 1985; Bigatti, 2015; Melograni, 1980). Bigatti (2015) notes that "although Italian industrialists expressed discomfort about the more violent aspects of the regime, in one way or another they all gave their support to Mussolini" (p. 31). In a renowned article that appeared on August 6, 1924, on the front page of the national newspaper *Il Corriere della Sera*, the senator Luigi Einaudi, a liberal politician who was elected president of the Italian Republic on May 12, 1948, described "the unforgivable silence of industrialists" when faced with the violence and suppression of democratic freedoms as a "deliberate choice" and directly accused industrialists of not standing up against the brutality of the regime, as other professions had done (journalists, lawyers, politicians):

> Italian industrialists insist on the necessity for a strong government; they consider social tranquility, absence of strikes, intensification of work, and balanced budgets to be tangible and effective goods far superior to . . . political freedom. . . . They maintain that the choice Italy has is between the present regime (with all its restrictions on political freedom) and Bolshevism. To them, the choice between the two is a no-brainer; it is worth paying a small tribute of money and freedom to save themselves from the danger of Bolshevism. (Einaudi, 1924, p. 1, quoted in Bigatti, 2015, p. 31)

Einaudi continues, supporting the choice of "industrial democracy":

> This way of reasoning, which is widespread among the Italian industrial classes, proves that the great technical progress that occurred in Italy is not matched by equal progress in political education [of industrialists]. For if we had forward-looking industrialists, they would be able to enter negotiations and prevent or contain strikes, while at the same time pursuing the growth of their enterprise. . . . Industry today needs not only skilled technicians and shrewd tradesmen; it needs also leaders of men. One does not work only to produce textiles, rails, or wheat but also to create better living conditions for all those who participate in the production process, from bosses to workers. (Einaudi, 1924, p. 1, quoted in Bigatti, 2015, p. 31)

The publication of the article cited above provoked strong reactions. The editor and co-owner of the newspaper, Luigi Albertini, was forced to resign and sell his shares of the newspaper (Bigatti, 2015). The Milanese entrepreneur Giovanni Silvestri replied through the pages of the same newspaper (*Il Corriere della Sera*) that violence and loss of freedom were lesser evils compared to the great evil called Bolshevism.

However, according to Bigatti (2015), Italian industrialists did not exactly "rush to get the Fascist party membership card" (p. 33), and many, including Alberto Pirelli, Giovanni Agnelli (patron of FIAT), and Ettore Conti (electrical entrepreneur), complied only when it became "too difficult to refuse." Bigatti (1985) describes the industrial world under Fascism as "a feudal system led by a handful of powerful industrial groups headed by charismatic figures, who were fully concentrated on their industrial activity and economic affairs and remained indifferent to what was going on in the rest of the society" (p. 33). Entrepreneurs themselves made no secret of, and no excuses about, their position; Giovanni Silvestri declared openly that "entrepreneurs *had* to stay away from politics to concentrate their attention on their business" (quoted in Bigatti, 2015, p. 33).

Alberto Pirelli described himself as an "independent technician" who did not want to get involved in politics (Montenegro, 1985, p. 61). Yet "Mussolini held a high regard for Alberto Pirelli the man, as well as for Alberto Pirelli 'the technical expert'" (Anelli et al., 1985, p. 59) and offered him the position of economy minister. Alberto Pirelli declined. According to Montenegro (1985, pp. 63–64), Alberto Pirelli played an important role during the "war of the Duce" in Ethiopia (1935–36) when, thanks to his diplomatic experience and connections in both Italian and British ministries, he was involved in developing solutions to avoid a clash between Italy and Great Britain after the latter strongly opposed the incorporation of Ethiopia into Italy just before the Second World War.

According to Bellavite Pellegrini (2017) and also Montenegro (1985), the war in Ethiopia helped many Italian industries to reverse the negative effects of the global crisis, mainly thanks to large orders placed by the Fascist army during this period. Pirelli increased its total sales figures from 279 million lire in 1935 to 484 million lire in 1936. During the second half of the 1930s, Fascism's *autarchy* period characterized by import substitution and self-sufficiency policies also favored Italian industries. For the rubber industry in particular, the difficulties with natural rubber imports during this period led to a joint venture between Pirelli and the National Institute for Industrial Reconstruction (IRI) for the institution of SAIGIS (Società Italiana per la Gomma Sintetica), a company established specifically for the development and production of synthetic rubber (Bellavite Pellegrini, 2017). When the Second World War broke out, Pirelli manufactured 5.3 percent of the rubber products exports to Italian Oriental Africa, which accounted for 20 percent of the company's national production between 1935 and 1943 (Montenegro, 1985, p. 66).

MONUMENTALIZING PATERNALISM: *CORPORATIVISMO* AND "FORCED" WELFARE

Despite the benefits it offered to Italian industrialists, Fascism's *Corporativismo* dogma was Janus-faced. While this ideology denied the existence of class conflict, at the same time it made cooperation between labor and capital mandatory, and declared workers' welfare to be the sole responsibility of industrialists—an essential prerequisite for the construction of the ideal Fascist Italy (Benenati, 1998, p. 8). Within the ideology of *Corporativismo*, Fascism *demanded* from industrialists welfare provision for workers as a proof of their loyalty to the regime (Benenati, 1999). Mussolini famously said that "intelligent capitalists take care not only of their workers' salaries but also of their workers' houses, schools, hospitals, and sports grounds" (quoted in Benenati, 1999, p. 72).

To "persuade" companies to provide social welfare to workers, Mussolini instituted the Opera Nazionale Dopolavoro (OND; Italian Fascist leisure and recreational organization) (Agnelli, 1930, p. 277; De Grazia, 1981; Caprotti, 2007; Caprotti & Kaika, 2008). As the Fascist regime directed resources to military operations, the OND was a policy instrument working toward compensating for the lowering living standards of Italian workers due to deflation, global economic recession, and austerity. But the OND also aimed to "fill the gap created by the suppression of both Catholic and socialist organizations which, prior to Fascism, had instituted a large welfare and support network for workers across the country" (Bigazzi, 1996, p. 49; see also De Grazia 1981; Caprotti 2007).

Fascism's campaign to make industrialists responsible for welfare provision was successful. Between 1929 and 1931, the number of companies that provided new leisure and recreational facilities for their workers almost doubled (from 1660 to 2938; see De Grazia, 1981, p. 81; Benenati, 1998, p. 5). Fascism's power of "persuasion" extended from small and medium to large and powerful enterprises like FIAT and Pirelli. During a lecture at the School of Engineering in Pisa organized in 1930 by the Fascist Industrial Confederation, Edoardo Agnelli, vice president of FIAT, underlined the role played by "welfare provision for workers and their families in creating the fortunes of the automobile factory" (Agnelli, 1930, p. 277).

Figure 4. Contemporary view of one of Borgo Pirelli's homes for workers. Photo by Luca Ruggiero.

Fascism's push for industrial welfare provision made the spatial interventions of Italian entrepreneurs broader in scope, more permanent in character, and at times even monumental in scale (Bigazzi, 1996). While Pirelli's new Bicocca plant was functional but still expanding, Pirelli made an agreement with the Istituto Autonomo per le Case Popolari (Institute for Social Housing) for the construction of a full village—the Borgo Pirelli—with houses and apartments for workers (one of these houses in its current condition is shown in figure 4). According to Giovanni Nassi, who was CEO of Progetto Bicocca SpA in the 1980s, Pirelli undertook the construction costs, but the subsequent management and maintenance costs were met by the Instituto Autonomo per le Case Popolari (Nassi, interview, 2007; see also Pirelli, 1986; Galdo, 2007). In 1923, Pirelli added to Bicocca's industrial land a sports stadium, a gym, tennis courts, and ball game courts (*campi da bocce*). As Benenati (1999) notes, "The desire for the grandiose that characterized many corporate social initia-

LAND AS CATALYST FOR CLASS CONSCIOUSNESS 59

tives [at the time] ... helped the prestige of the corporate brand; on the other hand, it underlined the power of the industrial world, not only in [managing] resources and production, but also in [managing] its own social model, its community life, and the living standards of its workers" (p. 49).

The workers' village at Bicocca, the Borgo Pirelli, soon became Pirelli's own signature miniature village. With its construction Pirelli made two clear statements. The first was about his commitment to providing services to workers, which he also believed would avoid a Socialist revolution. The second was about the importance of architectural order, spatial organization, design, hierarchy, and discipline as strong allies to capitalism's "civilizing" mission. In short, a well-ordered space could help capitalism thrive. The plan and architectural forms of the new Bicocca indeed established spatial order and hierarchy over the anarchic maze of the old streets; it was expected that social order would follow suit.

Borgo Pirelli was acclaimed as an "example of a working-class architecture that did not succumb to the tendency to build high-rise, low-cost, ugly barrack-like buildings" (Einaudi quoted in Galdo, 2007, p. 11). But while tradition characterized the architectural forms of Borgo Pirelli, modernization characterized the function not only for production but also for the workers' dwellings, which featured the latest technological innovations and the luxury of fitted private bathrooms. The new Bicocca established the factory as a totalizing modern experience for the worker and his or her family. The modernization in managing workers' bodies and behavior inside the factory now extended to the management of workers' lives and activities in their homes and in schools, shops, hospitals, recreation grounds, and public spaces (Bigazzi, 1996).

The construction of the workers' village granted Pirelli the status of both industrial innovator and social benefactor not only for the workers' community but also for the city of Milan as a whole. Bicocca became to Pirelli's workers not just a place of production and control but also a basis for reproduction, communal life, a space for creative and political expression, for socializing, leisure, and congregation. As other enterprises located in the northeastern suburbs of Milan followed similar practices, the area around Bicocca acquired both population density and class homogeneity.

60   CITY OF INDUSTRY

Later on, company welfare provision at Pirelli extended from "cradle to grave," and included crèches and schools housed in palatial historical buildings, training schools for future workers, and the famous "suggestion box," placed in a discreet location, where workers could make direct but anonymous comments and recommendations to their managers without the fear of being seen (Soldini, 1952). The provision of social spaces for workers even extended beyond factory location, giving workers access to seaside holiday resorts and a company-run lakeside retirement home. A striking example of the deep sense of appropriation of space by this generation of workers at Bicocca is described in an article published in *Rivista Pirelli* in 1952 (issue 5, October 1952): "There are only two places [in La Bicocca] where one is not allowed to go without permission: the chicken farm, run by Alieri, a seventy-two-year-old Pirelli retiree; and a small allotment, cultivated by Pollastri, a sixty-eight-year-old Pirelli retiree. . . . Ever since they were granted these privileges the two ex-workers have treated these places as their own private property" (Soldini, 1952, p. 38).

The company also supported the symbolic construction of factory space as the workers' own through linguistic symbolism, making references to workers as "the barons in overalls" and to workers' families as "the Pirelli dynasties." The very first article of the *Rivista Pirelli* magazine, authored by Alberto Pirelli himself (1948, p. 8), was titled "This Is *Our* Magazine" and made repeated references to "our" company. In the same magazine, the frequent references to the legacy of the Pirelli family were mirrored by references to the legacy of the Pirelli workers' families. An article by Alberto Cavallari titled "Bicocca's Worker Dynasties" identifies six "dynasties" of "barons in overalls," that is, Pirelli workers. Anna Somalvico is identified as a member of "the fourth dynasty." She is featured on her bicycle, in a photograph taken at the gates of the factory in 1928, the year she started working there. She did not have children of her own but brought her sister and brother-in-law to work at Pirelli; her niece, nephews, cousins, all their husbands and all their wives, as well as all their mothers, fathers, sisters, and brothers-in-law also worked for Pirelli. The full list, a "litany" of names and jobs, is presented in a ceremonial manner, and the article concludes: "I challenge anyone to find something as close to the Old Testament as this epic . . . list of [people] and jobs" (Cavallari 1952); see also Pirola & Magistroni, 2008, p. 212).

LAND AS CATALYST FOR FORGING CLASS CONSCIOUSNESS: THE IMPACT OF THE *LONGUE DURÉE* OF INDUSTRIAL PATERNALISM

There is no singular or simple explanation for the importance and scale that paternalism acquired in Italian industrialization. Already in the first decades of the twentieth century, the Italian state had been actively promoting paternalism as a convenient private solution to welfare provision (Benenati, 1998; Bolchini, 1967). In 1919, before Fascism came to power, the Italian state instituted, during the Francesco Saverio Nitti government, a special bureau for the promotion of corporate welfare systems, which actively encouraged Italy's largest enterprises to invest significant resources in social programs and services for their workers (De Grazia, 1981). So when Fascism triumphed, it only intensified and prolonged what was already there.

But a multiplicity of other cultural, social, economic, and political factors also contributed to the *longue durée* of industrial paternalism in Italy. Industrialists themselves often presented paternalism as part of the traditional practice of *bonum facere* within which entrepreneurs should always be well disposed toward workers (Lanaro, 1988, p. 43). This practice was, in turn, strongly rooted in the Catholic Church's official nineteenth-century *Rerum Novarum* dogma, in which the pope himself declared the imperative for interclass cooperation instead of conflict, based around the imaginary of a benevolent capitalist who would take care of the social needs of his workers (Benenati, 1999). Alessandro Rossi, one of Italy's most prominent industrialists, declared state regulation a "personal offense," given the extensive welfare-related services he provided to his workers, never mind that many of them were minors or underaged. The fear of Socialism that followed the Russian Revolution was another key reason behind the duration and scale that industrial paternalism took in Italy (Benenati, 1999; Bolchini, 1967). Finally, many scholars also insist that paternalism offered additional profits to industrialists, by turning workers' housing into a new profit-making machine through rent collection (Conca Messina, 2017).

Whatever the underlying reasons, the fact is that the prolongation of industrial paternalism in Italy had a number of serious and far-reaching consequences. First, it kept at bay state intervention in labor-capital

62   CITY OF INDUSTRY

relations and delayed for several decades centralized institutionalization of regulations around workers' rights, safety, length of working day, wages, overtime, night work, and child labor (Conca Messina, 2017; Guiotto, 1979; Merli, 1972). Many scholars argue that this is the key reason behind Italy's "industrialization without modernization"; the fact that Italy managed to achieve an industrial development comparable to other leading industrialized nations without a parallel development of state- or civil society–driven political, social, and cultural institutions that could manage labor/capital relations and accommodate further capital accumulation (Bigazzi, 1996, p. 61; see also Buntrock, 1996).

A second serious consequence of Italy's prolonged industrial paternalism, according to Bigazzi (1996), was the belated "development of impersonal labor relations that would rely on contracts, rather than on the benevolence of the entrepreneur" (p. 61). The promotion of the image and practice of the entrepreneur as a father figure who exuded authority but also responsibility for workers, and the metaphor of the company as an extended family, demanded the workers' dedication and hard work.

Third, according to Cafagna (1990, p. 396), the extensive and forced presence of industrial paternalism in Italy accounts for Italy's smooth and "gradual industrial evolution," characterized by the absence of strong shocks and conflict (see also Bonelli, 1978; Bigazzi, 1996; Amin et al., 2002; Hunecke, 1978).

Fourth, many scholars see the persistence of paternalistic industrial relations as the key reason behind setbacks in Italian technological and managerial innovation (Bigazzi, 1996; Guiotto, 1979). The loss of the workforce's bargaining power due to paternalism (and Fascism) made labor intensification, wage reductions, and redundancies easier and more cost-efficient ways to increase competitiveness than investing in technological and managerial innovation (Montenegro, 1985).

The above four lines of analysis of the consequences of the *longue durée* of paternalism in Italy give us significant insight. However, the importance of land development and the production of space under industrial paternalism does not feature as a factor worthy of analysis in any of them, since the key focus is placed on economic and industrial relations. We argue that this lack of engagement with the importance of the production of space explains why this body of scholarship, important as it is, actually has failed

LAND AS CATALYST FOR CLASS CONSCIOUSNESS   63

to account for a very significant historical fact: the fact that those working men and women who were supposedly unable to develop class consciousness under paternalism (like Bicocca's workers) were *precisely* the ones who ended up leading not only the workers' anti-Fascist movement during the Second World War but also the workers' revolutionary class struggles after the end of the Second World War (Benenati, 1999; Bigazzi, 1996). Bicocca's Borgo Pirelli is an emblematic case. Although it was conceived and constructed as a means to pacify and subordinate the workforce, it became the stronghold of workers' power and hosted continuous class struggle and increasing radicalization of the workers' demands.

It is true that working men and women were becoming loyal under paternalism—but not to capital or management, as several scholars before us have claimed. Their loyalty lay with the new socio-spatial arrangements around production, which were inscribed onto a piece of industrial land that they came to call their own. We argue that workers developed a *multiplicity* of loyalties: to spaces of production; to spaces hosting their homes, families, and reproduction activities; to workers' communities and unions; and to a collective social life that was strongly geared to debating and demanding class rights (Benenati, 1998; Bertucelli, 1999). Importantly, the workers' multiple—and at times contradictory—loyalties had a *hierarchy* that would become clear, first, right after the end of the First World War, when factory villages became strongholds of industrial action; then during the Second World War, when many Italian factory towns became hubs for anti-Fascist resistance (chapter 3); again immediately after the end of the Second World War, when, for a brief time, Bicocca's workers actually took over the means of production and the management of the factories (chapter 3); and later (1960s–1970s), when the same industrial social spaces became hosts of Italy's *Operaismo* movement and of radical forms of workers' uprising (chapters 4 and 5). The history told in this book demonstrates that the material and symbolic production and mobilization of industrial land as workers' own spaces can actually *explain* how the multiple and often contradictory loyalties that workers developed were held together in ways that both supported and undermined capitalism.

In the timeful analysis that we offer in the following chapters, we focus on class struggle as a force for the production of space to reveal the fallacy

64   CITY OF INDUSTRY

of the argument that industrial paternalism led to betrayal or "corruption" of working-class consciousness, and we instead turn this argument on its head. Our intertwined and timeful analysis of the history of industrial land and class struggle demonstrates that the social spaces in and around industrial land that paternalism produced were in fact *generative* of working-class consciousness. And this is why the same spaces ended up hosting the most radical forms of class struggle in the decades that followed.

With the deepening inscription of workers' lives onto factory spaces, working-class identity formation became inseparably intertwined with the imaginary of a collective ownership of industrial land and of the socio-spatial practices that guaranteed workers' active participation in and decision-making around factory production. Importantly, as we shall show in the following chapters, this imaginary of collective ownership of industrial land (and the means of production) was not the phantom of a deceived proletariat or a "corrupted" class consciousness. By contrast, it became the lever for increasingly stronger class demands, and in the case of Bicocca for the iconic takeover of the means of production by workers, for a brief time, right after the end of the Second World War, as we shall see in the next chapter.

PART II City of Workers

LAND AS SPACE FOR COMMONING
AND RADICAL POLITICAL ACTION
(1939–EARLY 1970S)

3 Land as Citadel of Workers' Anti-Fascist Resistance (1939–1945)

During the dark World War II years, and under Fascism's full reign, industrial land in Italy took on an unexpected social and political role, when socialized spaces in some workers' villages became safe havens for the circulation of anti-Fascist ideas. Bicocca was an exemplary case. This chapter documents how the spaces that had been designed to control and anesthetize "the insubordinate spirit of the workforce" acted as powerful catalysts for nurturing radical ideas and praxis when, during the years of the Great War, Bicocca became the stronghold of the Comitato di Liberazione Nazionale, an outlawed anti-Fascist resistance group.

The sense of belonging and emancipation that was forged in Bicocca during these years was such that, when the war ended and Pirelli's managers relocated to Switzerland for a short period, Pirelli's workers resolved to run and manage the factories by themselves. This chapter will unfold how the workers' claims to ownership of the means of production expanded from land and social spaces to the factory shop floor, machinery, and management. We assert how the radical imaginary that land belonged to workers, which had been cultivated in previous decades, was very important for this change.

68 CITY OF WORKERS

When Pirelli's management returned, they took back the means of production but for a brief period allowed workers to continue being heavily involved in decision-making and factory management. The material and analysis that will be presented in this chapter is important for understanding why later, after the end of the war, when Italian society and state politics became increasingly conservative, Bicocca remained an important forum for debate between workers, management, and the Italian progressive intelligentsia.

BICOCCA DURING WORLD WAR II: SPACES OF PRODUCTION AS SPACES OF ANTI-FASCIST RESISTANCE

During the Second World War, Pirelli considerably expanded its production and marketing base in Italy and abroad with factories and commercial enterprises in Spain, Argentina, the United Kingdom, France, Belgium, and Egypt (Bellavite Pellegrini, 2017). The company's expansion was due to the increased international demand for rubber products to feed the rapid expansion of motorization but also to serve the expanding industrial sector and telecommunications networks (Guizzi, 2012). But the success was also due to the fact that Pirelli's multinational organization, with multiple production and distribution locations, allowed the company to reap benefits from both sides during warfare. It could circumvent US and European sanctions against Italian commodities by exporting its products from locations outside Italy; at the same time, it could benefit from the Italian countersanctions against European and US commodities and grow its share within Italian markets. Pirelli's most important European competitor, the French company Michelin, had its Italian-based plants confiscated by Mussolini in 1940, immediately after the war against France was declared. Furthermore, Pirelli won lucrative military contracts between 1936 and 1939, when Mussolini decided to support Franco's nationalist fraction during the Spanish Civil War (Montenegro, 1985). To prevent the anticipated negative economic effects that war would have on the company, Pirelli dissolved the relationship between its two holding companies (one in Italy, which controlled Italian operations, and one in Belgium, which controlled international operations), and "moved the registered command and control center of its overseas activities from Belgium to neutral Switzerland" (Bellavite Pellegrini, 2017, pp. 43–44). This move, combined with the political neutrality and good relationship Alberto Pirelli had established and sustained with US and British business and political elites, "allowed the exclusion of Pirelli's Swiss holdings from the Allied Forces' blacklist of companies operating in hostile countries" (Bellavite Pellegrini, 2017, p. 44).

Still, the fact that during the Second World War Pirelli's industrial plants at Bicocca were strategic for supplying the Italian army made Bicocca the target of the Allied forces' air raids (Rimoldi, 2017). However, as we saw in chapter 2, by that time Bicocca was no longer just a location for industrial production. It had become a place with housing, schools, and social services for thousands of working men and women. During the war, the close-knit workers' community that was woven around the social and spatial qualities of workers' villages at Bicocca and neighboring industrial plants, like Breda, Falk, and Innocenti, contributed to turning several workers' villages and factories into hubs of resistance against Fascism (Benenati, 1999). Between September 1943 and April 1945, the factories and workers' village at Bicocca became the stronghold of the militant anti-Fascist CLN. According to Secchia and Frassati (1965, p. 1011),

> The factories became the fulcrum of anti-Fascist struggle . . . and played a more important role [in overthrowing Fascism] than the military activities of the Resistenza [the partisan army against Fascism]. Here [at the factories] was where the workers' strength was concentrated; here, artillery for anti-Fascist resistance was hidden in workshops. Pirelli, Breda, Falk, and Innocenti became the launching grounds for the "Gappisti"[1] and the "Sappisti,"[2] the partisan guerrilla groups who systematically assaulted Fascist barracks and roadblocks.

It is well documented that Pirelli's middle management supported the partisan movement by allowing or even participating in secret meetings with clandestine organizations inside the factories. In fact, the workers'

70 CITY OF WORKERS

welfare office that was set up between March and April 1944 became a cover for helping those who were politically persecuted (Luciani, 1976). Pirelli's archives hold extensive material on the workers' anti-Fascist struggle, documenting how in Bicocca "a new fighting spirit, a new friendship developed, based on solidarity and trust between people who belonged to different political parties, people from different ranks, workers, technicians, and managers. Several workers were saved from deportation this way, several women and children were supported" (Pajetta, 1945, p. 1). *L'Unita*, the newspaper founded by Antonio Gramsci, described the Bicocca as a "citadel of workers' resistance against Fascism":

> The Fascist police never managed to crush [La Bicocca's] Communist cell. ... Workers, men and women, were always present, and stood up against the enemy time after time again. They turned the machines off during anti-Fascist protest strikes, they sabotaged the production that served the Fascist war, they organized clandestine support work for the Communist Party, for the trade unions, for the young and the women in every department, every rank. When the Fascist terror became more ferocious, Bicocca's workers saw their people fall dead but continued the struggle. (Pajetta, 1945, p. 1)

The article in *l'Unità* is written in fiery language, but the facts are not exaggerated. The partisan struggles in which Pirelli's workers engaged counted many victims. Hundreds of militants fled, others got arrested or killed. In November 1944, during an anti-Fascist protest strike, 186 Pirelli workers were arrested, of whom 171 were sent to Germany, and onwards to concentration camps at Flossenburg and Mauthausen. Several died there (Valota, 2008).

The special place that women and men working in factories held in anti-Fascist resistance and the tragic loss of life it entailed represented a decisive moment in strengthening the workers' movement across Italy. The anti-Fascist struggle catalyzed stronger solidarity among workers, particularly in workers' villages, where spatial arrangements enabled men and women to build stronger class and political consciousness. During the anti-Fascist resistance, workers accumulated experience both in forming and enacting effective industrial action and in articulating clear demands (Bolchini, 1967; Dell'Agnese, 2005). So when the war ended, "a new life began, in which workers did not want to forget the past, did not want that precious experience to be lost" (Pajetta, 1945, p. 1).

The anti-Fascist struggle at Bicocca also exercised strong influence on Pirelli's owners and management, notably on Giovanni Pirelli, who was supposed to succeed his father Alberto and uncle Piero as head of Pirelli but decided not to take on this role (Scotti, 2018, p. 19). For all his life, Giovanni Pirelli had been groomed, trained, and educated to become the perfect businessman. He studied foreign languages, attended the Commercial University Luigi Bocconi in Milan, and did internships at the Pirelli plant in Southampton, UK (Tranfaglia, 1990). When he was thirteen, his father, Alberto, wrote to him from Detroit describing the city as "ugly and provincial for those without industrial interests" but as "an important center to visit if you are motivated and have the aptitude to become an industrialist. I hope this is the case with you" (Alberto Pirelli quoted in B. Pirelli, 2002, p. 15).

However, in his twenties, Giovanni Pirelli served as an officer in the Italian army and was sent to the war front, first to France (1940), and then to Greece (1940) and Montenegro (1941), where he was shocked by the absurdity and violence of "killing without mercy those who fight for a faith which is holy to them, even though it is different from ours" (Giovanni Pirelli, quoted in Tranfaglia, 1990, p. 30; see also Scotti, 2018). In January 1942, Giovanni Pirelli was transferred to Berlin for five months; from there he wrote extensively about the things he witnessed, including "the revolting acts against Jews" (G. Pirelli, 1990, p. 206) and the way in which Italian workers were treated, like "animals," in German factories (G. Pirelli, 1990, p. 184). After Germany, Giovanni Pirelli had further traumatic war experiences in Russia and France. When he finally returned to Milan, he—like millions of other soldiers—was an altogether different man; he had become radicalized. He got in touch with Bicocca's anti-Fascist and anti-Nazi groups, and despite the intense suggestions of his father to remain neutral, he joined the partisan struggle in 1944 (Scotti, 2018). From the letters he wrote to his family from abroad, collected in a volume edited by Tranfaglia (1990), it is evident that Giovanni Pirelli had grown uncomfortable with the privileges of his class and had become eager to explore the world beyond bourgeois privilege. In a letter from Berlin to his younger brother, Leopoldo, on February 4, 1942, he wrote:

72   CITY OF WORKERS

> I detest conformist wealthy people . . . who have had it too easy in life and therefore have a teeny, weeny mind. . . . These people live enclosed in their towers of elegance and light, indifferent to the problems of humankind. . . .
> It is in humble people that I found the greatest pride of spirit, and it is among the humble that I feel life's problems palpitate, naked, and raw, without the affable mask of the affluent classes. (Giovanni Pirelli quoted in Tranfaglia, 1990, p. 196)

Many historians have studied how Giovanni Pirelli's war experience, combined with the close contact he developed with revolutionary groups inside the factory, contributed to his decision to refuse to lead one of the most important Italian companies of his time and to become a writer instead (Scotti, 2018; Tranfaglia, 1990). When in 1946 Giovanni Pirelli informed his father Alberto that he would join the Italian Socialist Party of Proletarian Unity (Partito Socialista Italiano di Unità Proletaria, PSIUP), his father Alberto tried desperately to take him away from Bicocca's "subversive" circles by offering him an important managerial role at the Pirelli plants in Turin, but Giovanni Pirelli did not accept (Scotti, 2018).

END OF WORLD WAR II: FROM COLLABORATIVE MANAGEMENT TO THE RESTORATION OF CORPORATE POWER

As outlined above, Pirelli thrived during the war years mainly thanks to the elimination of its European competition, the "social tranquility" promoted by Fascist authoritarianism, and the increasing demand for Pirelli's products for military operations and for the expansion of telecommunication networks worldwide. But things changed dramatically after the end of the Second World War. Pirelli lost the privileged monopoly status it had enjoyed during the war and had to come to terms with real market conditions and increasing global competition. Piero and Alberto Pirelli relocated to Switzerland for a brief period after the war (1945–46), while the company's plants in Italy were placed under administration (Bellavite Pellegrini, 2017, p. 47). From Switzerland, the Pirellis continued to manage and exert important influence in decisions regarding international operations. Back home, however, Bicocca's workers resolved to run the factory on their own. The CLN stepped in and played a key role in management. Some of its members suggested then that Giovanni Pirelli, who remained in Italy, should take over the leadership. However, Alberto Pirelli vetoed his son's involvement, deeming his political "passions" incompatible with managing a large industrial enterprise (Scotti, 2018).

In the brief period when the Pirellis were abroad, workers in effect took over the means of production and instituted a collaborative form of factory governance by bringing into the company's management representatives from progressive political parties and trade unions who had participated in the anti-Fascist liberation movement: the Communists, the Socialists, the Christian Democrats, and the Republicans (Anelli & Bonvini, 1985). These practices, which also occurred—though not so extensively—in other Italian industries, complexified the relationship between workers and factory spaces, multiplying further the workers' conflicting loyalties.

> In the postwar years [after World War II], ... it was not uncommon for workers to hold simultaneously opposing identities and beliefs. ... Anticapitalist feelings co-existed with the commitment to increasing factory productivity (*produttivismo*) and with accommodating small requests by the management [in the name of keeping production running smoothly]. This situation was particularly widespread in the factories of northern Italy, where workers had become accustomed to defending and running the factories during the anti-fascist Resistance. After the Liberation, they kept going, supported by left-wing parties and a unified national labor union. (Benenati, 1998, p. 21)

The coexistence of progressive political ideas with the commitment to increasing industrial output was particularly strong at Bicocca. It was part of the workers' widespread sentiment that through strengthening industrial production they were together rebuilding a strong economy for a democratic Italy. It was the "right" thing to do: to build the nation's economy after having fought hard to overthrow Fascism (Benenati, 1998).

Although Italian society as a whole was gradually shifting toward more conservative political positions after the war, the Bicocca remained a stronghold of progressive forces. The political parties' and trade unions' strong representation that had been established during the absence of Alberto and Piero Pirelli gained significant contractual power (Anelli & Bonvini, 1985). For example, Bicocca's "Recruitment Control Commission," which was established while the Pirelli brothers were absent, now played a strong role. Between March 1946 and August 1947 the commission launched a large recruitment campaign to hire 5,500 new workers. It had also unilaterally decided to honor the workers' historic demand for a forty-hour workweek (Anelli & Bovini, 1985, p. 95). The renewal of social relations necessary to reconstruct the country after the war started inside the factories (Anelli & Bonvini, 1985, p. 95), and the material and imaginary appropriation of space by workers at Bicocca became central in mobilizing and implementing a process of "collaborative management" that could become a "first step toward a new organization of production in which the empowerment and participation of the workforce would guarantee . . . the delivery of concrete production goals" (Anelli & Bonvini, 1985, p. 95).

However, the materialization of the fantasy of ownership of the means of production by workers, and the collaborative management experiments that aspired to build democratic economic growth for the company, and for the country as a whole, were short-lived. When Piero and Alberto Pirelli returned to Italy on May 7, 1946, they resumed full control and management of the factories and exerted pressure on workers' representatives to regain the ground they had lost. Their first success was to revert the workweek back to forty-eight hours. Further losses for the workers' movement followed suit, and another round of intense class struggle became inevitable. In May 1949, Pirelli's workers went on strike for seventy-nine days in a row, demanding the introduction of a production bonus. Pirelli retaliated by imposing total lockdowns of factories. When the workers showed the first signs of physical and economic fatigue, Pirelli took the opportunity to actively oppose the collaborative management practices. According to Francesco Tadini, a member of the Milanese Communist workers' federation at the time, Pirelli's management launched a "violent attack" that involved: abolishing pay and time compensations for political party and trade union representatives; restricting the right to hold meetings during working hours; and forbidding the distribution of political propaganda material in and around the factories (Tadini, quoted in Anelli & Bonvini, 1985, pp. 97–98). By the first half of the 1950s, Pirelli's corporate power was fully restored with the abolition of the Consiglio di Gestione (CDG) and the revocation of the right of workers to participate in the company's management.

According to Pirelli workers' militant groups, the deterioration of the relations between workers and the company's directors during that period should also be attributed to Giovanni Pirelli's decision to sever all links with Bicocca and its workers (Scotti, 2018). During the time he spent among Bicocca's workers after the Second World War, Giovanni Pirelli had played a strong role as mediator between workers and directors and as guarantor of experiments in collaborative management. After his departure, Pirelli's management reasserted its power at Bicocca. Several workers wrote to Giovanni Pirelli, expressing their regret for his departure, and describing as "humiliation" the way they were treated when they tried to negotiate with management:

> The situation is getting worse by the day; we are now helpless, witnessing the persecution of trade unionists and politicians. [Pirelli's management] retracted everything that had been agreed upon in the past. . . . In many respects the workers' life has returned to what it was back in 1938. . . . You can't believe how much pain this causes me and how worried I am about all those who worked so hard, for so long, and in good faith for a just purpose. (Mazzacurati, quoted in Scotti, 2018, p. 44)

Another worker's letter addressed to Giovanni Pirelli notes:

> Forgive me for taking the liberty to write to you again. I wanted to tell you that your words gave me some courage when my spirits were really down. Here they chastised a worker who has five children, . . . just because he was caught smoking. . . . If you had been here, this would not have happened. . . . These gentlemen subject us to so much humiliation; they make us pay dearly for our poverty. . . . Many men and women in the factory are asking after you and want to have news from you. (Stucchi, quoted in Scotti, 2018, p. 44)

INDUSTRIAL LAND AS CULTURAL SPACE: A NEW MEANS OF REBUILDING REPUTATION

While Piero and Alberto Pirelli were engaged in class struggle to gain back control of the factories' land and operations, they nevertheless wanted to

76 · CITY OF WORKERS

avoid tarnishing Pirelli's legacy as a socially caring and benevolent company. Alberto Pirelli published a book (A. Pirelli, 1946), entitled *Pirelli: Vita di una azienda industriale* (Pirelli: The life of an industrial company). There he praises the fact that the company maintained its distance from Fascism but also emphasizes the important contributions that Pirelli made to Italian society for many decades before the war. He pays particular attention to the role that the social production of space and welfare provision played in establishing Pirelli's legacy as a socially caring company (Rimoldi, 2017; Bellavite Pellegrini, 2017):

> All *Pirelliani* [workers and managers depicted as a big family] know that the company remained at the top of social welfare provision even during Fascism. All of them have borne witness to the company's independence from Fascist political interference—to the fact that the company did not privilege the workers affiliated with the Fascist Party but that it did not damage the careers of anti-Fascist workers either. Everyone knows how the jobs of Jewish staff were defended even when the Fascist law dictated they should be fired. (A. Pirelli, 1946, p. 72)

As part of the efforts to reestablish Pirelli's public image as a socially caring company in the midst of a new round of class struggle, Piero and Alberto Pirelli once again turned to land. Producing space once again became a means to pacify social unrest. To this end, they commissioned Pirelli's first iconic building, the Pirelli skyscraper (Grattacielo Pirelli) (see figure 5). The thirty-one-story-high skyscraper, which was nicknamed *Pirellone* (Big Pirelli), was designed by Giò Ponti, Pier Luigi Nervi, and Arturo Danusso, who ranked among Italy's leading modernist architects and engineers at the time (Irace, 1997). Ponti and Nervi pioneered innovative construction engineering solutions; because the cranes available at the time in Italy could not reach the desired construction height of the Pirelli Tower (127 meters), a system of two tower cranes, one on top of the other, was devised to reach the required height (Fondazione Pirelli, 2020). Upon its official opening in 1960, the *Pirellone* was the tallest building in Italy and one of Italy's first "corporate cathedrals." The building aimed to become a symbol of the central role that Pirelli had played in the recovery of the Italian economy after the war, while at the same time—it was hoped—it would reaffirm the Pirellis' commitment and loyalty to the city

Figure 5. Contemporary street view of the Pirelli Tower, constructed in the 1950s and officially opened in 1960. Photo by Luca Ruggiero.

78　CITY OF WORKERS

of Milan and to the local community (Irace, 1997). The Tower building originally hosted the company's headquarters. It was built on *Cascina Brusada,* the historical location of Giovanni Battista Pirelli's family home and first factory.

The location choice paid clear homage to the way in which the history of the Pirelli family was woven together with the history of Milan's economic development. Thanks to its iconic structure, design, and location, the Pirelli Tower became a symbol not only of the relationship between the company and the city but also of Milan's growing postwar economy as a whole. Being so high and so close to Milan's central station, Pirelli's Tower would also be the first building that new arrivals would notice, imposing Pirelli's powerful position in the city's economy, notably to the migrant workers who were flocking into Milan during the period of the city's "economic miracle" (Foot, 2001, p. 118). The Pirelli Tower's legendary status was accentuated further when it featured centrally in Luciano Bianciardi's novel *La vita agra* (The sour life), published in 1962. The novel's key character, an anarchist, moves from Tuscany to Milan with the intention to blow up the *Pirellone*; to him, it symbolizes a city that has transformed human beings into "ghosts." However, upon arrival in Milan, he is himself seduced by the Milanese high-society lifestyle and soon forgets his original aim.

Pirelli's cultural production offensive did not stop with the Pirelli Tower. During the same period, the company added new residential spaces for workers to Borgo Pirelli, and a purpose-built new refectory for workers, iconically designed by architects Minoletti and Chiodi (figure 6).

Pirelli also founded two significant cultural institutions during this period: the Pirelli Cultural Center and the *Rivista Pirelli* magazine. These were important gestures toward reaffirming Pirelli's prestige and acclaim in Milanese society in the postwar era. The aspiration was that the new cultural institutions would become icons for artistic and cultural expression that would reach far beyond the workers' community into the Milanese and broader Italian society (Bigazzi, 1996). Alberto Pirelli commented: "Our magazine [*Rivista Pirelli*] opens a dialogue between those who produce and those who consume, but it also aspires . . . to enact a dialogue that goes beyond discussions around the quality and price of our products" (A. Pirelli, 1948, p. 1).

Figure 6. The iconically designed workers' refectory at Bicocca. Copyright: Archivio del Moderno, Fondo Giulio Minoletti, Balerna, Switzerland (GMin Fot S 18/1/1). Reproduced with kind permission.

Both the *Rivista Pirelli* magazine (1948–72) and the Pirelli Cultural Center became successful venues and outlets for cultural exchange and intellectual debate, offering the Pirelli family a strong presence in the cultural scene of "the capital of Italian reconstruction," a name given to Milan because it was buzzing with cultural activities and hosting several magazines, publishing companies, bookshops, and theaters (Scotti, 2018, p. 27). The projects offered Pirelli heightened social acclaim, as the company's financial commitment to workers' housing and cultural projects for the City of Milan was highly publicized, notably in *Fatti e Notizie*, with articles featuring detailed descriptions, photos, and floor plans of the new cultural projects and workers' housing (Suffia, 2020, p. 153, 163).

But the impact of *Rivista Pirelli* and the Cultural Center went far beyond the original aim to showcase Pirelli's commitment to keep open

80   CITY OF WORKERS

the dialogue between workers, industrialists, and society as a whole. The magazine became one of Italy's most important forums for ideas about industrial production, city planning, social welfare, and broader sociopolitical issues (A. Pirelli, 1948; Bigazzi, 1996).

The importance that the Cultural Center and the *Rivista* gained in Italian political and cultural life crystallized the continuous presence of Bicocca as a space of radical social and political thought and praxis whose role expanded beyond the community of Pirelli's workers. The strong emphasis on Pirelli's successful cultural and social projects overshadowed the significance of the fact that Pirelli's workers handed back the means of production to factory owners during this same period. Nevertheless, these spatial and cultural projects were not inconsequential for class struggle; they stimulated an exchange of ideas between workers and the Italian left intelligentsia, which would become crucial for sustaining the imaginary (or fantasy) of Bicocca's land as workers' own space. As we shall see in the following chapter, sustaining this imaginary contributed greatly to the radicalization of workers' claims after the 1950s.

4 "Italy's Stalingrad" and the "Years of Lead"

RADICALIZING SOCIAL CLAIMS OVER INDUSTRIAL LAND (1945–EARLY 1970s)

The brief honeymoon period between capital and labor that characterized the end of the war ended abruptly, when repeated crises in industrial production and capital accumulation led to wage cuts, layoffs, and accentuated class struggle. This chapter documents the tumultuous period between 1945 and the early 1970s, which complexified further the role industrial land played in socioeconomic and political praxis. During this period, Pirelli's workers (now counting over twelve thousand) turned the Bicocca into a laboratory for more radical and innovative forms of class struggle and developed strong connections with the *Operaismo*, feminist, and students' movements. The chapter explains how the years of anti-Fascist resistance and the brief period of appropriation of the means of production immediately after the war ended were crucial for radicalizing social claims. Wildcat strikes, sabotage, and continuous protests extending to Milan's city center were combined with more symbolic forms of spatial appropriation during this period when labor militancy northeast of Milan became so strong that this area was promptly nicknamed "Italy's Stalingrad."

This chapter explains how these intense forms of class struggle overlapped with the "Years of Lead" and the "Strategy of Tension," one of the most troubled periods in recent Italian history, during which the combination of economic crisis and sociopolitical turmoil fed not only social struggles but also violent acts of kidnapping, bombing, arson, and murder that terrorized Italian society. The chapter draws attention to the fact that, when parts of the media started associating the workers' militant unions with these terrorist acts, these allegations, though never proven, started denting social support for the workers' struggles, dividing the unions internally, and weakening the labor movement as a whole. This, in turn, made it easier during the following decades for capital to perform the violent act of "land revanchism," which would catalyze the transition to new forms of capital accumulation.

CAPITAL'S DOUBLE VICTORY: WEAKENED UNIONS AND ECONOMIC "MIRACLES"

As we have seen in chapter 3, after World War II, corporations were eager to revoke the privileges and communal industrial management practices that many workers had achieved during the war. At first, corporations tried to restore class power through authoritarian practices by refusing to enter into dialogue with unions. The central Italian state became a strong ally in this strategy (Bianchi et al., 1970). The first post-Fascist elections in Italy, on April 18, 1948, brought the Christian Democratic Party to power, self-proclaimed as "the only party that could protect Italy against the danger of Bolshevism." The Christian Democrats received 48.5 percent of the vote, while the Popular Front, a prolabor Communist-Socialist coalition, came second with 30 percent (Anelli et al., 1985; Bellavite Pellegrini, 2017).

The Italian industrial world rejoiced in the electoral outcome, which renewed the role of the state as their ally against trade unionism. After the elections, aggressive industrial management strategies prevailed, and, with the support of the central state the industrial world gained a double victory over the working class. The first victory was that industries were able to implement extensive restructuring plans without substantial opposition from the unions. The second and perhaps more important victory followed suit: having managed to implement restructuring without involving the unions, corporations effectively undermined the unions' credibility and trust among workers themselves. Workers felt that their unions could no longer protect or support them in class struggle.

Along with the rest of the Italian industries, Pirelli took advantage of the favorable political climate to undo collaborative management and the involvement of workers' unions in industrial decision-making. In the 1950s Pirelli's management went further: they expelled all political-party representatives from Bicocca (the majority of whom belonged to the Communist and Socialist parties) and later suspended, transferred, or laid off many union representatives. Bianchi et al. (1970) and Bolchini (1985) document that during this period Pirelli also systematically refused to engage into dialogue with the largest, most powerful left-wing national union, the Confederazione Generale Italiana del Lavoro (CGIL). Instead, Pirelli's management signed separate labor agreements with two smaller and less radical labor organizations, the Confederazione Italiana Sindacati Lavoratori (CISL) and the Unione Italiana del Lavoro (UIL), which were close to the Christian Democrats.

Bolchini (1985) describes the crux of Pirelli's new authoritarian mode of running the factories in the 1950s: "The management would take a decision and would just implement it without prior communication with [the unions]; the unions then had to react and mobilize their members a posteriori in order to enter negotiations [from an already weakened position], a position in which the power balance was already set" (pp. 55–56). These practices were successful in keeping wages repressed and in significantly undermining the credibility and strength of the national union, the CGIL, which up until that point had been very powerful in negotiating industrial relations. Still, workers kept struggling throughout the 1950s. However, on top of class struggle, most Italian industries had to deal also with increased international competition. To overcome these difficulties, the Pirelli Group focused on expanding its national market base through a particular form of Italian corporatist Fordism. In a joint venture with the Italian automobile manufacturer FIAT, Pirelli instituted the Italian Road Initiative Company (Società per lo Sviluppo Delle Iniziative Stradali

Italiane, SISI). SISI commissioned a private planning proposal for the construction of a new highway network in Italy. The plan was adopted by the Christian Democratic government and became the basis for the construction of the Autostrada del Sole (Highway of the Sun), a five-hundred-mile-long highway that would connect Milan, Bologna, Florence, Rome, and Naples. The highway was completed in 1964. During the same period, the Christian Democrats further promoted private car ownership by lowering fuel prices and increasing the cost of public transport (Bolchini, 1967). This was something that was happening across the Western world. As Bolchini (1967) notes, "In order to convince Italians to buy more tires they first had to convince them to buy more cars. And for them to be convinced to buy more cars, more and better roads had to be constructed" (pp. 23–24).

Thanks mainly to state protectionism, indirect subsidies, and state-assisted expansion of the national tire market, but also thanks to the ability to keep salaries low, Pirelli was able by the early 1960s to recapture the growth numbers it had achieved during the war years and to launch itself toward what became known as Pirelli's "economic miracle." This was a period of strong economic growth for Italian industries as a whole—a period that brought the Italian economy back on track with the growth rates of other Western advanced economies. But Pirelli's economic miracle was short-lived.

THE EFFECTS OF RESTRUCTURING AND MECHANIZATION ON SPACE AND LABOR

In the 1960s Pirelli, alongside other Italian industries, underwent a new crisis, as protectionism and the expansion of the national market were no longer sufficient to offset stiffening international competition. As industrial restructuring, technological innovation, and further mechanization became necessary, this led to more authoritarian management and the concentration of command-and-control functions in the Pirelli Tower headquarters in the center of Milan. As in all other industries, restructuring and the introduction of increased mechanization and advanced production techniques at Bicocca intensified work rhythms, increased deskilling, and led to new rounds of layoffs and further suppression of salaries (Bianchi et al., 1970). As in other industrialized countries, restructuring in Italy led to a broader depreciation and banalization of the human input into the industrial production process. Even though at Pirelli automation levels remained relatively low, increased mechanization meant that the role of the worker at Bicocca's production line changed, as it did in the rest of the world. Many workers who in the past had been required to bring high levels of specialization and skills to the production process were now requested to perform only simple and repetitive tasks; they became generic, dispensable cogs rather than unique and indispensable components of the production process (Bolchini, 1985, p. 54). This was true for men and women, and particularly for the younger Pirelli workers, who complained that factory work no longer involved "learning a skill or a trade" (interview with worker, quoted in Bianchi et al., 1970, p. 72). As mechanization compartmentalized work into simple repetitive tasks that could be performed by unskilled labor, and the level of knowledge required from workers was minimized, it became easier to implement large-scale layoffs.

The increased mechanization and intensification of production also meant that in some departments at Bicocca workers were exposed to higher environmental risks and health hazards, as they now worked in "the permanent presence of [toxic] vapors, cellulose dust, and high temperatures" (Bianchi et al., 1970, p. 74). For this reason, many of the unions' actions during the 1960s and 1970s aimed explicitly at improving environmental and health conditions at factories. One of the key early environmental struggles was to fight against the corporate tendency to "monetize health hazards" with offers of meager financial compensation for health risks incurred on the factory floor (Ruzzenenti, 2020; Marchetto, 2014).

The last, but not least, side effect of mechanization and deskilling at Bicocca was the further depreciation of salaries. By 1968, salaries at Pirelli were lower than those offered by its competitors, CEAT and Michelin (Bianchi et al., 1970, p. 68). All the factors mentioned above (deskilling, lowered salaries, increased environmental and health risks, depreciation of work) contributed to high levels of dissatisfaction among workers at Pirelli, particularly the younger ones (Bianchi et al., 1970; Bolchini, 1967, 1985).

Pirelli's immediate and almost intuitive response to the workers' dissatisfaction was to offer a new round of paternalistic industrial practices, while insisting on the idea that workers and industrialists were part of the same "extended Pirelli family" (Bellavite Pellegrini, 2017; Bianchi et al., 1970). Pirelli's management believed that industrial conflict could—once again—be absorbed by an enhanced version of "enlightened" company policies (Bianchi et al., 1970, p. 71). But industrial paternalism had run its course, and the additional offer of schools, kindergartens, old people's homes, cultural centers, and sports and health care facilities was not enough to curb workers' dissatisfaction and counteract the negative effects on workers' lives and labor brought about by authoritarianism, the rationalization of production, and technological restructuring. A new and intense wave of class struggle was in the making across Italy, and Bicocca became its epicenter. And once again, the symbolic and material appropriation of land and factory spaces by workers had a very significant impact on this next phase of class struggle.

"ITALY'S STALINGRAD" AND THE "HOT AUTUMN" OF 1969: SPACES OF PRODUCTION AS SPACES OF RESISTANCE

Rationalization and technological innovation created an entirely new set of challenges for labor relations, as, in effect, they demanded, yet again, a new anthropological type of labor. Early industrial production had relied heavily on "professional factory workers" (*operaio professionale di mestiere*; Scavino, 2018, p. 56), who had to be highly skilled, highly disciplined, place-bound, and loyal to the company. The intensified mechanization of production, however, demanded that the professional factory worker be replaced by the "mass worker," an unskilled, flexible, and expendable worker who would be willing to accept a lower salary in return for work on dull and simple tasks within an automated production process (Scavino, 2018, pp. 53–56) and whose labor would be reduced to a simple "function for the capitalist" (*funzione del capitalista*; Filippini, 2011, p. 13).

There was growing discontent and resistance against becoming this new type of "mass worker," particularly among the younger generation of workers. However, it was not easy to articulate or express discontent over these new labor issues. The ideas and strategies that the labor movement had established over decades of class struggle were geared to serving the needs of the "professional factory worker" but could not respond effectively to the new needs of the new unskilled or deskilled "mass workers" who were required by capitalism's new phase (Panzieri quoted in Cengia, 2016, p. 240).

Moreover, the weakening and internal divisions of workers' unions that had preceded industrial restructuring, as described above, meant that traditional workers' organizations now lacked not only the know-how but also the capacity and even the willingness at times to fully understand and interpret—let alone respond to—the new situation. The result was that many official labor unions and organizations often ignored or underestimated the significance of industrial restructuring and instead remained stuck in fighting old battles and pursuing old issues, focusing mainly on bargaining over the conditions of renewal for annual labor contracts.

By the end of the 1960s, the twelve thousand men and women employed at Bicocca by Pirelli faced worsening working and wage conditions and increasingly authoritarian management, and started expressing discontent not only against the company but also against workers' unions, as they felt deprived of unionized support at the moment they needed it most (Bolchini 1967, p. 51; see also Renzo Baricelli, former CGIL union secretary, interview in Meyer 2008, p. 3). But at Bicocca, workers were endowed with an important asset that few other workers' groups possessed: historically embedded symbolic and material control over the spaces in and around factories. This symbolic and material appropriation of space at factories that had taken place during the war was still within the workers' living memory, and the close-knit network of support that workers had built during the war still endured. Moreover, the fact that Pirelli's restructuring at Bicocca brought mechanization but not full automation of production meant that Bicocca's workers still retained a level of control not only over social spaces but also over the shop floors, the operation of machines, and the production process as a whole. The combination of, on the one hand, weak union support and increased workers' discontent, and, on the other hand, a strong symbolic and material hold over land and social spaces at factories was key for Pirelli becoming the epicenter of a new and highly militant wave of industrial action during the late 1960s and early 1970s.

In January 1968, after trade unions signed yet another disappointing annual labor contract, Bicocca's workers mobilized the factory's spaces to initiate a series of intense discussions and debates, first, to understand their new conditions, and then to devise strategies to change them (Anelli et al., 1985). Pirelli's workers not only arbitrated their right to hold meetings in factories; they also invited Italy's most prominent intellectuals and members of the *Operaismo* movement to join them in these discussions (we shall discuss this in more detail in the next section). Soon Bicocca became the center and the symbol of a new phase and new forms of class struggle. The workers' meetings at Bicocca concluded that it was no longer possible to rely on official labor unions and organizations to propel direct class confrontation and that it was therefore imperative to develop alternative forms of class struggle. The idea that received strong support was to create entirely new militant workers' organizations that would be independent from the "traditional" unions and would operate outside their control and remit (Scavino, 2018).

The workers' control over spaces of production at Bicocca meant that Pirelli's workers were well positioned to turn ideas into praxis with immediate effect. And so it happened. As their economic and work conditions continued to deteriorate, Pirelli's workers drew upon the considerable experience and solidarity they had amassed during the years of resistance against Fascism and during the early postwar years and turned Bicocca once again into a hub for class struggle. During the late 1960s and throughout the 1970s, Bicocca and the entire industrial area northeast of Milan (the City of Factories) was nicknamed "Italy's Stalingrad" (Foot, 1999; Luciani, 1976).

In June 1968, Bicocca's workers formed the Comitato Unitario di Base (CUB), an umbrella organization for a set of grassroots workers' groups that operated outside the "official" remit of trade unions (Bianchi et al., 1970; Bianchi et al., 1971, p. 11; Bolchini, 1985). The Pirelli CUB has been described as "a masterpiece of workers' autonomy," and some Italian scholars have depicted it as the materialization of the autonomist ideas of the *Operaismo* movement of radical intellectuals (Bologna, 1988, p. 5), as these were spreading in Italian factories through the journals that forged collaboration between workers and intellectuals, including the *Quaderni Rossi* (Red Notebooks; 1961–65), *Classe Operaia* (Working Class; 1964–67), and *Potere Operaio* (Workers' Power; 1976–73).

Operaismo and its links with Bicocca's spaces will be discussed more extensively in the next section, but it is important to note here that one of the public intellectuals of the *Operaismo* movement, Sergio Bologna (1988, p. 5), disagrees that Bicocca's workers took their cue from *Operaismo*'s radical ideas. Instead, he credits the Pirelli CUB as "a fact that matured inside the Bicocca factory itself," with limited external influence from groups, ideologies, and theories. According to Bologna, the CUB "grew and developed all within the workers' own class consciousness" (p. 5), since its leaders were factory union figureheads with a past in the CGIL or the Communist Party, not young immigrant workers, as had happened in other factories influenced by *Operaismo*. Bicocca's CUB counted roughly one hundred members, who were called *Cubisti*, and whom the newspaper *Il Corriere della Sera* called, rather pejoratively, Bicocca's *Arrabbiati*, which translates as "the angry people of Bicocca" (Cervi, 1972a, p. 3). Women's participation in class struggle during this period was strong but is often obfuscated by language norms, as in this case, where only the plural male noun form (*Arrabbiati*) is customarily used even though female participants (*Arrabbiate*) were also involved. Bicocca's workers were actively spreading their ideas through leaflets and pamphlets, which they often distributed outside the factory gates (Cervi, 1972a, 1972b). Bologna (1988, p. 1) notes that "these pamphlets were, in fact, more significant than the actual official journal *Classe Operaia*" in raising workers' consciousness and getting them involved in industrial action because they were important sources of information and data regarding salaries, health and security conditions in the workplace, rhythms of work, and so on. The pamphlets called workers to engage in forms of class struggle different from those advocated by official trade unions. For example, a leaflet dated July 1968 encouraged workers to fight for increases in wages, slowing of factory rhythms, and abolition of harmful work conditions (Comitato Unitario di Base, 1968, p. 1). The same leaflet also advocated innovative forms of action: improvised strikes

90 CITY OF WORKERS

that would be decided ad hoc by workers on the factory shop floor, or continuous and prolonged demonstrations and strikes as an assertion of workers' power (Comitato Unitario di Base, 1968, p. 1).

The members of the radical Pirelli CUB organizations refused to hold meetings inside the offices of official trade unions (CGIL, CISL, UIL). Instead, they would hold meetings at the bar, the cooperative *trattoria,* or the *circoli operai* (workers' clubs) (Cervi, 1972a). They also held frequent *assemblee di marciapiede* (pavement assemblies) in the streets outside the factory. Soon, the official CGIL trade union leaders also started participating in these meetings, acknowledging the success of the initiatives (Bologna & De Mori 1969, p. 11). As Cervi (1972a) documents, every day, at the end of the main shift, both the bar and the trattoria would be full of workers discussing action strategies with the CUB, and those strategies would afterwards be presented at the workers' general assemblies for approval. As one of the members of the CUB stated: "At Pirelli-Bicocca we are few . . . but on occasion we can appear to be many, because we are able to drag a lot of others along. Sometimes we manage to have the majority of the workers' assemblies on our side and break the power of the unions" (interview in Cervi, 1972a, p. 3). For example, on September 13, 1968, "eleven departments went on strike, a total of 1,900 workers; a few days later, seventeen departments went on strike; and [by the end of September] twenty departments, that is, half the factory, was on strike" (Bologna & De Mori, 1969, p. 11).

The members of Pirelli CUB also established relations with the feminist movement (see next sections) and the student movement of Milan, which was strongly politicized after 1968. These movements "ignited the spark of revolt [but also] challenged the paternalism of trade unions, alongside the paternalism of employers" (Pieroni, 1971, p. 3). As the relationship between the leaders of the student movement and the workers' leaders was not always idyllic, the members of the CUB preferred to pursue relationships only with those students who were more willing to commit themselves to a long-term relationship. Together with select groups from other movements, the workers of Bicocca organized the *Gruppi di Studio* (study groups), which were meant to analyze the conditions of workers and the factors of exploitation at the Pirelli Bicocca factory. According to the students and workers of the CUB, this collaborative analysis of factory exploitation led to novel political and revolutionary discourses (Cervi, 1972a; Bologna & De Mori, 1969). "It was a matter of making ... [everybody] see that the elements presented as 'inevitable' components of factory work (intense rhythms, strict time management on the shop floor, hazardous environments, etc.) were nothing but elements of exploitation" (Bologna & De Mori 1969, p. 4). The political and class consciousness that these meetings forged led to identifying Bicocca during this period also as a "school of Communism" (anonymous student quoted in Cervi, 1972a, p. 3; "Pirelli Bicocca," 1971, p. 1).

Soon these emerging radical ideas turned into radical political praxis, and Bicocca's CUB became so distinguished for its militant particularism that it went down in history for its unique capacity to quickly devise original, imaginative, unconventional, but also at times violent types of industrial action that the industrial world had never seen or experienced before and certainly did not anticipate at this point (Bianchi et al., 1971, p. 11; Hayter & Harvey, 1993).

The new forms of radical industrial action at Bicocca included militant groups calling ad hoc meetings inside the factories without asking permission from the management or the unions, and without prior warning. In a way, these acts were mirroring the strategy that industrialists had followed after the 1950s when they made decisions completely ignoring workers' unions. Repeated on a regular basis, these ad hoc meetings and strikes turned the factory shop floor, the canteens, or the back yards into sites for industrial action "on the hoof" (Bianchi et al., 1971, p. 49).

Many Italian left intellectuals (notably those of the *Operaisti* movement) exalted the spontaneity and inventiveness of Bicocca's workers and glorified the members of Bicocca's CUB for instigating actions that distinguished them from official unions. Spontaneity and inventiveness were seen as the strategies that could overcome the paralysis of the unions and resist more effectively the management's top-down approach. These new forms of class struggle that were instigated from below, from the shop floor, were seen by many as reflecting the real everyday problems that workers faced and as a better way forward than the solutions suggested by official trade unions (Bolchini, 1985; Bianchi et al., 1970). In fact, Bicocca's CUB launched a direct polemic against the tactics of traditional

92   CITY OF WORKERS

workers' organizations and against left political parties' representatives at factories. But as Bicocca's tactics started yielding successful outcomes, the unions and the Italian Communist Party started paying attention. In December 1968, *Rinascita*, the Italian Communist Party's official magazine, enthusiastically described the spontaneous strikes at Pirelli: "All it took [to start a strike] was a worker in the vulcanization department to raise his hand with three fingers open, indicating the time when work would stop; then the whole department would spill out into the factory's inner yard . . . and soon the whole factory would join in for a plenary assembly, which would take place during working hours" (Coppola quoted in Bolchini, 1985, p. 57). According to Vincenzo Berardi (pseudonym), a veteran worker from Pirelli's cables sector and an active member of the CUB, it was in Bicocca that the idea and practice of industrial action "on the hoof" emerged:

> We would gather everyone together in each department at clocking off, and count. If we did not have a majority of at least 80 percent in favor of the strike, the strike in that department would be called off, and we would go straight back to work. If the strike was called off, there would be a second attempt in the same department during a different shift, or on a different day. This way, a shift in any specific department could reach 80 percent consensus in favor of industrial action even if the majority of workers in that shift did not belong to the [official trade unions] CGIL-CISL-UIL. (Berardi, interview, November 26, 2009)

These fragmented "autonomous" strikes that rotated continuously between different production departments and different shifts became the ultimate moment of appropriation of factory spaces on the part of workers. In contrast to the meetings of the official trade union, which were held outside the factories, the space appropriation inside factories that Bicocca's workers mobilized was the essential means for advancing their demands successfully. Vincenzo Berardi, again, recalls: "In the first few months of 1968, the CGIL [the official trade union] announced strikes for the region of Milan. But only 10–15 percent of the Pirelli workforce took part. Instead, we [Bicocca's CUB] talked directly to workers at meetings inside the factory and initiated strikes by simply shouting, 'Let's forget about trade union membership; let's strike for the things that matter

"ITALY'S STALINGRAD" 93

to us, right here and now, the things that affect us here, in this factory. Those present here who are representatives of an official trade union but not workers in this factory—GET OUT! NOW!'" (Berardi, interview, November 26, 2009; original emphasis).

The innovative forms of class struggle employed at Bicocca soon spread outwards, first to other factories around Milan and soon more widely, notably at FIAT's factories in Turin (Mirafiori, Lingotto, and Rivalta). The industrial action at FIAT's factories became more iconic, as FIAT's workforce at Turin (sixty-five thousand) was much larger than that of Pirelli's at Bicocca (twelve thousand) (Bolchini, 1967, p. 51; see also Berta, 1998). However, as Bologna (1998) records, it was the Bicocca and the CUB that acted as the avant-garde who directed, coordinated, and triggered the forms of struggle that soon spread to other factories and "foreshadowed the movements and grassroots unions of the 1970s" (p. 1). What Bicocca's workers started in 1968 was mirrored by FIAT's workers from 1969 onwards, with the same radical forms of industrial action: ad hoc strikes, unannounced assemblies, sabotage in parts of production. On November 4, 1969, the members of the Pirelli Bicocca CUB printed and distributed a leaflet praising the initiative of eight hundred FIAT workers who had blocked the supply of certain parts to assembly lines, thus paralyzing production. The leaflet also noted that FIAT workers were following many of the principles suggested by the Pirelli CUB (in June 1968) for "autonomous action from below, initiated during ad hoc departmental assemblies, without prior notice" ("Ondata di scioperi," 1969b, p. 3).

The new alliance of factory workers that was emerging outside the remit of official trade unions generated grave concern for company managers and the political establishment. This new common fighting spirit developing among factory workers at different locations was epitomized in the massive twin protests of Pirelli and FIAT workers in the streets of Milan and Turin in 1969. During those protests FIAT and Pirelli workers were singing in unison "Ladri gemelli" (twin thieves).

The autumn of 1969 became known as the "Hot Autumn" (*Autunno Caldo del '69*). During that autumn, the material and symbolic claims of Pirelli's workers over space extended beyond Bicocca itself: first to the wider industrial area around Bicocca and north of Milan, and later to Milan's city center itself. During that time, workers renamed streets after their partisan leaders and erected monuments to resistance workers (Dell'Agnese, 2005). The most iconic moment of those protests was when Bicocca's workers expanded their claims to social and political spaces beyond the Bicocca and picketed outside Pirelli's headquarters in the heart of Milan (figure 7). "In an affirmation of class consciousness, workers in white overalls, typical of the dirtiest jobs at Bicocca, linked arms in the open air outside Pirelli's headquarters. There was continuous picketing for three days and three nights, twenty-four hours a day. It was as if it were the 25th of April again [the end of Fascist rule in Italy]" (Berardi, interview, November 26, 2009). The Pirelli Tower, also known as the "company's brain," was paralyzed for three consecutive days ("Bloccato il grattacielo Pirelli," 1969a, p. 8).

With the Pirelli Tower Action, the perception of Bicocca's social space as a forum for free political and social expression for workers extended from the spaces of production to the spaces of management and from the industrial suburbs to the city center. The workers distributed leaflets across Milan that read: "We are picketing to stop intimidation and blackmail by Pirelli. We are here to stop managers from going to work, because some of them played a central role in creating a climate of psychological violence and authoritarian blackmail against workers and impeded our democratic right to freedom of expression" ("Bloccato il grattacielo Pirelli," 1969a, p. 8).

The Pirelli Tower Action is often cited as a decisive contribution toward the institution of the Workers' Statute in Italy in 1970. Strike actions were taking place across Italy and across the Western world at the same time. But many of these strikes (like the ones at the Renault factory in France) "hit workers and their wages really hard" (Bianchi et al., 1971, p. 49). By contrast, Pirelli's strikes succeeded in increasing workers' salaries by an astounding 70 percent between 1969 and 1974 (Bolchini, 1985). Furthermore, Pirelli's workers demanded and achieved the introduction of inflation-adjusted salaries and the reduction of weekly working hours. They also asserted the workers' right to hold meetings in factories before this right was officially sanctioned by law in the 1970 Workers' Statute (Bianchi et al., 1971). And some of the most radical groups demanded the introduction of productivity controls by workers' representatives (Giovanni Nassi, interview, February 22, 2007; Berardi, interview,

Figure 7. Claiming the city center: workers extending protests beyond factory doors, in front of the Pirelli Tower in Milan, October 9, 1969. Photo by Silvestre Loconsolo. © Archivio del Lavoro, n. 14184. Reproduced with kind permission.

96   CITY OF WORKERS

November 26, 2009; see also Cacciari, 1969; Bianchi et al., 1970, 1971; Sclavi, 1974; Montali, 2009; Bolchini, 1985).

BUILDING BROADER SOCIAL ALLIANCES: BICOCCA'S LAND AS LIVING LABORATORY FOR *OPERAISMO*, FEMINISM, AND THE STUDENTS' MOVEMENT

The struggles in the factories of the Italian North and the "Hot Autumn" of 1969 played a pivotal role in igniting demands for rights and democratization from a much broader social base, ranging from women and unwaged homemakers, students, military conscripts, and the unemployed to segments of the middle and professional classes (Cuninghame, 2008). These broader social demands were fed by and in turn fed into the workers' struggles, and for a brief time male and female workers, intellectuals, feminists, and students were allied under the banner of the *Operaismo* movement (Anelli et al., 1985; Bellavite Pellegrini, 2017; Bianchi et al., 1970, 1971; Bolchini, 1967, 1985; Cacciari, 1969).

Operaismo, which had a major impact on Italy's intellectual, social, and political life, was strongly influenced by the resurgent workers of Pirelli in Milan Bicocca, and FIAT in Turin. Intellectuals, together with workers and other social groups, would organize meetings in factories, during which they read about and discussed the issues troubling Italian society and labor. Volume 1 of Marx's *Capital* was particularly inspirational, as *Operaismo* considered it to be "both a piece of scientific work and a call to political action that could transform the objective reality of things" (Tronti quoted in Filippini, 2011, p. 8). The aim of these meetings was to analyze the dynamics of "modern factory" production and the role workers played within it and within the broader dynamics of "neocapitalism," as *Operaismo* termed the new phase of high-tech industrial capitalism (Filippini, 2011, p. 3; Scavino, 2018, 2021).

The ideas discussed in these meetings were published in journals that circulated widely across Italy, like the *Quaderni Rossi*, the *Classe Operaia*, and the *Potere Operaio* (Borio et al., 2005; Filippini, 2011; Perna, 1980; Scavino, 2018; Roggero, 2019; Tronti, 2009; Trotta & Milana, 2008). Technological restructuring and further rationalization of production were often held responsible in the *operaisti* journals' accounts for the "intensification of work, increased alienation, stronger integration of the worker into the capitalist production apparatus, the acceptance of the capitalist value system, and the abandonment of class antagonism" (Bonazzi, 2000, p. 34).

However, not everybody agreed with the pursuit of a direct link between intellectual labor and militant particularism, and the opinions appearing in *Operaismo*'s journals often contested those of trade unions and left-wing political parties on key labor issues, including the safety standards of factory work; the independence of trade unions; the link between productive modernization and labor relations; and the role of machinery in workers' alienation (Panzieri, 1961). *Operaismo* also entered into direct conflict with the Italian Communist Party (PCI). In fact, the term *operaisti* was originally a pejorative that the Communist Party used to describe activist groups who supported the revolutionary potential of the working class but refused to do so within the traditional remit of left-wing parties (Scavino, 2021). Moreover, *Operaismo* in itself was not a homogeneous movement (Filippini, 2011; Scavino, 2018; Trotta & Milana, 2008). The *Quaderni Rossi* group split up in 1965, and a more political praxis-oriented journal emerged, the *Classe Operaia* (Scotti, 2018).

One of the most important outcomes of the convergence of struggles of different social segments under the banner of *Operaismo* was the intense exchange of ideas and activist practices between the Lotta Feminista (Feminist Struggle) and workers, mainly around questions of unpaid household labor and sexual and physical violence. Key intellectuals and activists from the Lotta Feminista, including Leopoldina Fortunati, Mariarosa Dalla Costa, Giovanna Franca Dalla Costa, and many others, allied with feminist movements across the world, demanding wages for housework.

This call to place unpaid domestic work at the center of feminist and workers' debates was deeply influenced by, and influenced in turn, both *Operaismo* and the workers' movement. But the alliance was not easy. Many Italian feminists came to resent that the male-dominated *Operaismo,* and workers' movements failed to see beyond the centrality of factory labor. Giovanna F. Dalla Costa fiercely criticized *Operaismo* for wishing to conflate the "house worker" with the "factory worker" (cited in

Cuninghame, 2008, p. 6; see also Dalla Costa (1972, 2002), Della Porta (1996), and Federici (2019).

Operaismo's insistence that workers were the protagonists of class struggle par excellence led to an equally uneasy alliance with the student movement. Mario Tronti, one of the key intellectuals of *Operaismo*, recalls: "Faced with the [student] movement of 1968, I was filled with distrust. We, who believed in workers' struggles, were faced with students' struggles [instead]" (quoted in Filippini, 2011, p. 49). The rapprochement between the two movements was made possible only after the students agreed to give up their militant particularism (i.e., their fight only over university reforms or against academic authoritarianism) and join workers in the broader fight against the "entire plan of capital" (quote from *Potere Operaio*, cited in Scavino, 2018, p. 80). The students were also asked to acknowledge the influence that workers' struggles had had on the development of their own movement.

> The [students'] struggles that are sweeping society today have learned everything they know from the workers: the anti-*patron* goals, the demand for overturning capitalist accumulation, the generalized demand for student wages and training wages. . . . Nothing is invented here: a century of workers' experience is embedded within the current [student] struggles. The students, their existence, their movement, are the vindication of the revolutionary hegemony of the working class. (*Potere Operaio*, no. 9, 1968, quoted in Scavino, 2018, p. 81)

As it did with feminism, *Operaismo* allied with students only by recognizing their movement not as revolutionary force in its own right, but as an integral part of the workers' movement. Hence, students were accepted by the *operaisti* only after long internal deliberations and debates concluded that being a student was just a temporary social category before one became waged labor (Scavino, 2018, p. 55). This allowed *Operaismo* to consider students no longer as part of the "bourgeoisie" but as a fullfledged component of the "social labor force" itself (Scavino, 2021, p. 7). Higher education institutions were also depicted as part of capital's plan to produce a skilled labor force.

Despite the many contradictions and fights, the intense exchange of ideas and resistance practices between factory workers, students, feminists, intellectuals, unwaged laborers, political party members, and official trade unions, combined with the success of militant industrial action, led to a shared conviction that workers' demands were relevant to society as a whole. The fact that, compared to other Western countries, Italy's feminist and student movements were more closely aligned with labor demands, and factory issues, opened up debates and struggles around important issues like unwaged domestic and student labor, which remain relevant—and unresolved—today.

During this entire period, Pirelli's factories at Milan's Bicocca, alongside FIAT's factories at Turin, performed the role of living laboratories for these new ideas and experimental practices (Scavino, 2018). Industrial land acted as the material grounds on which it seemed—for a brief time—that a broader revolutionary social change might be possible (Scotti, 2018, p. 171). In Bicocca, the possibility for open exchange and cross-fertilization of ideas between workers, intellectuals, and other segments of the society during this period was facilitated by the long history of intellectual exchange and radical praxis that had been performed inside the social spaces of this land (Bolchini, 1985, p. 86). Bicocca's factories and workers' village carried a strong living memory of established practices for free circulation of ideas and praxis. As we have seen, even during the Fascist years, when free speech was banned and contacts outside Italy were limited, Bicocca had remained open to exchange of ideas and alternative social and political practices (Bigazzi, 1996).

The prominence of Bicocca in this period's events was also facilitated by the good rapport that workers maintained with Giovanni Pirelli, who was involved in one of the *Operaismo* journals, the *Quaderni Rossi* (Scotti, 2018). As we noted earlier, after the end of the war, Giovanni Pirelli decided not to take up any managerial roles in his family's factories but maintained direct contact with the workers and Socialist circles at Bicocca, despite the many contradictions and difficulties that this created for both sides.

THE "YEARS OF LEAD" AND "THE END OF CLASS STRUGGLE"

The involvement of *Operaismo* in the Pirelli and FIAT strikes contributed to effectively symbolizing these strikes as part of a much broader political moment of change (Bellavite Pellegrini, 2017; Tronti, 1963, p. 44). And it was not only "a bunch of lefties" arguing that; the board of directors of Pirelli agreed that the object of debates and negotiations with workers in "Italy's Stalingrad" had expanded from workers' salaries and working hours to "the very nature of corporations and to the economic and social meanings attributed to what . . . corporations represented" (Bellavite Pellegrini, 2017, p. 66). This shift in the objectives of class struggle, which was not only a local phenomenon but part of the "subversive seventies" (Hardt, 2023), is captured clearly in the minutes of the meeting of Pirelli's board of directors held on November 29, 1968: "The protests that began over a problem related to piecework have swelled into something much bigger and more violent, giving the distinct impression that our company is nothing but a pawn in a larger game, whose boundaries we are unable to see" (quoted in Bellavite Pellegrini, 2017, p. 66).

The radical industrial action of Pirelli's (and FIAT's) workforce caused broader uproar among the country's economic and political elites, but also among Italy's more established national trade union organizations. Bicocca became an emblem of the radicalization of Italian politics during that period. The workers' victories, however, did not mean that workers were freed from fear of retaliation. Vincenzo Berardi recalls that "we lived like thieves. There was constant fear of being sacked or of being sent to the 'black smoke,' the department that vulcanized the rubber mixture into tires by adding black smoke inside the liquid mix. But we kept going back there, every day, at five o'clock in the morning, distributing leaflets. . . . Many female workers who were heavily involved consumed their lives over this struggle" (Berardi, interview, November 26, 2009).

The workers' fear was not unfounded. Only two months after the strikes at the Pirelli Tower and while workers were already obtaining successful results, one of the most troubled periods in postwar Italian history began. The period went down in history as the "Years of Lead"—*Anni di Piombo*—and lasted from 1969 till 1980. During this period, a series of bomb attacks terrorized the country. They started on December 12, 1969, with a bomb explosion at the Piazza Fontana in Milan, which killed seventeen people. More bombs followed (140 in total). These attacks became known as the *Strategia della Tensione* (Strategy of Tension). No organization claimed responsibility, and speculative allegations were made against extreme left and extreme right groups. However, it was not long before conservative media and politicians pointed to radicalized workers and held them responsible. Workers' organizations denied the allegations and described them as a conservative conspiracy that aimed at discrediting their movement (Cento Bull, 2007). Nevertheless, the workers' movement and *Operaismo* were bruised heavily by these allegations of terrorism, and popular support for the labor movement dwindled significantly. In addition, the allegations of links with terrorist acts discouraged many workers and intellectuals from becoming further involved in political action, and most of them moved from willingness to participate in "heroic action" to "resignation and subordination" (De Luna, 2009, p. 50).

Bicocca was at the heart of the accusations, and this resulted in many workers distancing themselves from grassroots organizations. The "mainstream" national trade unions (reformist rather than revolutionary in demands and action), which had previously been overshadowed by Bicocca's grassroots groups, now regained strength and legitimation among Pirelli's workers. Thus, the "Strategy of Tension" signaled the beginning of a new era in class relations, where class conflict would become less overt. Characteristically, the number of strike hours, which had reached an average of 101.7 per Pirelli employee per year in 1969, decreased to 46.9 in 1975 and to 25.8 in the years between 1976 and 1981 (Bolchini, 1985, pp. 66, 121; Negrelli, 1983).

After this period, however, a small fraction of the workers' movement did indeed radicalize, and "New political formations arose who saw armed struggle as the only antidote to the decreased militancy and increased impotence of the workers' movement" (De Luna, 2009, p. 12). Prima Linea, one of the radical workers' groups that emerged during this period, was based in Sesto San Giovanni, part of the same industrial district northeast of Milan as Bicocca (Della Porta, 1984; Segio, 2005, 2006). But, according to Bolchini (1985), Bicocca also had its own share in this radical legacy:

> Some groups [at Bicocca] started to theorize violence as a form of political expression. . . . In marches and protests, human resources managers would often be forced out of the factory, shift managers would be beaten up, and workspaces would be occupied. . . . It was precisely at Pirelli where the first meetings of the Red Brigades [Italy's most notorious 1970s terrorist group]

were held ... and where groups linked to Lotta Continua [a radical extra-parliamentary movement] met. (Bolchini, 1985, p. 67)

Giovanni Nassi, son of a Pirelli worker, who lived through various stages of this history in different roles, supports these allegations: "The Bicocca did not only have the CUB. After the CUB, Pirelli had the Red Brigades. Bicocca is where the Red Brigades were born" (Nassi, interview, February 22, 2007).

Whether it is true or not that Bicocca was hosting clandestine extremist movements, the fact remains that the majority of Bicocca's workers withdrew from militant sociopolitical action after the "Strategy of Tension" and the allegations of links with terrorist groups. This withdrawal, as we shall see in the next chapters, had very significant effects on the claims over Bicocca's land as a social space in the decades that followed.

SPACES OF RESISTANCE AS SPACES OF INDUSTRIAL DECLINE

The capital-labor conflict that started in the 1960s and culminated in the early 1970s had a significant impact on Pirelli, as it "both fed into the firm's crisis and was fueled by it" (Bolchini, 1985, p. 69). While workers' total strike hours peaked, salaries increased by 70 percent between 1969 and 1974, thus doubling the company's payroll costs (Bolchini, 1985). The company also sustained significant material costs related to the workers' upheaval during the "Hot Autumn of '69." Nassi noted that "the word *destruction* is no exaggeration, it's a fact. They threw bolts into the works, broke and blew up machinery. The strikes, the fires ... Pirelli suffered three incidents of arson" (Nassi, interview, February 22, 2007).

Leopoldo Pirelli, who succeeded his father Alberto and his uncle Piero in 1965 during the intense class struggle period, insisted that the lack of "production recovery" for Pirelli was the direct outcome of "widespread industrial conflict, ... which was the cause of the lower yields in each production unit and the decrease of Pirelli's total productive capacity" (Leopoldo Pirelli quoted in Bolchini, 1985, p. 64). In the official 1971 Pirelli annual statement, Leopoldo Pirelli voiced "serious concern" about "the state of disorder and tension ... [and] the permanent state of conflict" that had "critically compromised the company's efficiency and ability to function in a normal manner" (Pirelli SpA, 1971, p. 5). Nassi also confirms that continuous industrial action was at the heart of Pirelli's crisis in the 1970s. But he also notes that "the 1970s crisis was mainly a crisis of technology. Pirelli was required to adapt product standards to those of its international competitors. To do this, significant investment was required to renew and replace existing equipment" (Nassi, interview, September 28, 2009).

In the early 1970s, the company found itself caught between several evils: increased labor costs, hikes in the international price of rubber, and fierce international competition over quality, which called for urgent and heavy investment in research, development, and technological adaptation. Pirelli had to address all this if it was to survive competition with international giants such as the French Michelin and the US Goodyear. Michelin was particularly threatening to Pirelli, with its strong investment in innovation and technology and the launch of a "new type of tire, the XZX belted radial, which "[caught] Pirelli off guard" (Nassi, interview, September 28, 2009). Pirelli was also unprepared to enter the growing sector of retreads, the recycling of old belted tires, that other companies were already using to compensate for the significant hikes in the international price of rubber (Bolchini, 1985). The economic predicament and market shrinkage that followed the 1974 oil crisis were added to the troubles. "Between 1971 and 1975, the loss of Pirelli's share in the global tire market translated into a decrease by 22,000 tons in national production, an equivalent to 20 percent of Pirelli's total production" (Bolchini, 1985, p. 71).

Pirelli had to fight at many fronts if it was to stay afloat. But as we shall see in the next chapter, Leopoldo Pirelli chose to focus on two issues: curbing workers' militancy and pursuing further growth. And the first thing he did to achieve these two goals was to claim Bicocca's land and social spaces back from workers. It was a strategy that became the beginning of the end of the role that industrial land played as workers' social space. This process, which we term "land revanchism," became the origin for reimagining and eventually producing industrial land as a financial asset that opened new pathways for the future of traditional industrial capital.

PART III City of Technology

LAND REVANCHISM AS A MEANS OF
TRANSITIONING TO HIGH-TECH
CAPITALISM (EARLY 1970S–EARLY 1990S)

5 Land Revanchism and the Unmaking of the Working Class (Early 1970s–1985)

In this chapter, we develop the notion of "land revanchism," the act of claiming back (through factory closures, relocations, and dispersal of production) the industrial land that working women and men had appropriated as their own social/insurgent space. We show how, between the early 1970s and 1985, land revanchism became a key strategy that traditional industrial capital used for overcoming both the technological crisis and workers' upheaval. The chapter exemplifies this by documenting how, in the early 1970s Pirelli launched an extensive plan to shut down production at Bicocca and relocate it to other parts of Italy, hoping to eliminate two internal "evils" in one stroke—labor militancy and the lackluster pace of technological innovation.

This act of land revanchism initiated a new round of class struggle in which workers tried to salvage the social role of land as a communal and political space. The chapter outlines how this new phase of class struggle over land involved the catalytic mediating role of state institutions (city and regional authorities) who supported the reorganization of industrial production into smaller, dispersed, "flexible" units across Italy. The struggle over industrial land now involved three parties: workers, industrialists, and state authorities. The outcome of the negotiations was a Pyrrhic

108   CITY OF TECHNOLOGY

victory for working men and women: their jobs were secured in return for handing back the land that was the centerpiece of their communal and political life and the launching pad for their class struggle. "Freed" from its material and symbolic association with labor struggles, Bicocca's land would be turned into a Technocity; and while workers condemned the dispossession of what had once been their living and working spaces, local and regional authorities welcomed the Technocity as an opportunity to mitigate the consequences of deindustrialization and to reinvent Milan as an international center for technological innovation.

LAND REVANCHISM: CLAIMING WORKERS' SOCIAL SPACES AS NEW SPACES FOR CAPITAL

As discussed in the previous chapter, the "Hot Autumn of '69" and the "Years of Lead" and "Strategy of Tension" that followed weakened and dented social support for militant class struggle. But workers' militancy was not the only problem that industrial elites had to handle while moving toward the 1970s. A global recession was underway, and a new crisis was brewing. In the case of Pirelli, between 1971 and 1975, the company's losses increased from 15 to 27 billion lire (from 140 to 251 million euros, converted with inflation to 2024 values) while production output declined by 20 percent (Bolchini, 1985, p. 71; Pirelli SpA, 1976). Although Leopoldo Pirelli insisted that the lack of "production recovery" was the direct outcome of "widespread class conflict" (Pirelli SpA, 1971, p. 5), militant industrial action was certainly not the only reason behind Pirelli's bad performance. In the 1970s the global tire industry was changing. After having expanded exponentially in the postwar years, mainly thanks to the expansion of motorization, it now had to adjust to increasingly specialized and segmented market demands, which could no longer be served by mass-produced, unspecialized products (Bolchini, 1985). Pirelli's main competition, the French Michelin, adapted early to the new market demands with an expansive policy that included investment in thirteen new factories in Europe; expansion of its market presence in the United States, Canada, and Latin America; and serious product innovation with the launch of the radial tire, featuring metal (rather than textile) casing, for greater resistance and durability (Manca, 2005; Bolchini, 1985). Importantly, Michelin established a close partnership with the French car manufacturer Citroen at the same time that FIAT ended its historical close partnership with Pirelli. Until then, FIAT was absorbing more than half of Pirelli's production (Manca, 2005, p. 25), but now it decided to equip all its cars with the new Michelin radial tire.

All this meant that, for Pirelli to become competitive again, serious investment in research and technology was necessary (Bolchini, 1985; Manca, 2005, p. 26). At first, Leopoldo Pirelli decided to finance technological innovation by increasing the volume of production and sales of Pirelli's existing product lines (Manca, 2005). To achieve this, he pursued new partnerships and acquisitions that would improve the company's share in international markets (Bolchini, 1985), and in 1970 he negotiated a merger with the British rubber company Dunlop that would create the third-largest tire company in the world, with an annual turnover of more than 1,300 billion lire and a total workforce of 180,000 employees (Colli, 2001; Bolchini, 1985; Cercola, 1984). Pirelli also increased capital flows through bank loans and issued new shares to expand the company's capital base: from 80 to 108 billion lire in 1979, and again from 108 to 179 billion lire in 1980 (Colli, 2001). Pirelli also introduced several innovations to the Group's organization, including delinking the role of the company's ownership from that of the company's management, roles that had been traditionally conflated in the same person, although Leopoldo Pirelli insisted on keeping his central position as the company's CEO.

In 1978, as part of its continuous quest for capital to finance technological innovation, Pirelli sold its landmark Pirelli Tower, the skyscraper in Milan's city center that had hosted the company's headquarters (Colli, 2001, p. 524). The building was bought by the Regional Government of Lombardy and became the seat of the Regional Council. The sale of Pirelli's iconic skyscraper was a rather abrupt move in search of a quick capital fix to finance the debt that the company had started accumulating, while expanding production. Nevertheless, the sale tarnished Pirelli's public image as it raised questions about the company's stability and

110   CITY OF TECHNOLOGY

liquidity; it also raised questions regarding the City Council's decision to buy the Tower and therefore offer direct cash flows to an ailing company (Colli, 2001).

The fears about Pirelli's future were confirmed in 1981, when the pursuit of the partnership with Dunlop collapsed, leaving Pirelli short of options for market expansion to finance the necessary technological innovation. Strapped for cash and with a financial and technological crisis added onto the company's labor crisis, Pirelli had little room to maneuver. It was during this moment of acute crisis that Leopoldo Pirelli turned to Bicocca's land in search of a survival strategy. In the early '80s, he launched a program for shutting down production at Bicocca and relocating it to other sites across the country, in order to turn Bicocca into a Technocity, a hub for high-tech industrial research and offices, a means to launch the company into a new phase of high-tech capitalism.

The Technocity proposal aimed to eliminate the company's two internal "evils" in one stroke. First, the cash flows from land rent that Pirelli could potentially obtain from leasing Bicocca to Technocity activities would enable the company to reinvest in new technologies (Perulli, 1986). But second, and perhaps more importantly, the Technocity project would reclaim Bicocca's land—symbolically and materially—from militant workers and their autonomist practices. It was an act of land revanchism. The land that had functioned originally as a condition of production, then as a means of mitigating social conflict, and later as a social/political space for Pirelli's workers would once again become the catalyst for change.

The revanchist act of moving production elsewhere would sever workers from the land that had become not only the hub of their industrial and political activity but also their social and communal space over time. Reclaiming this territory previously "lost" to workers would raise the capital for launching Pirelli into the high-tech tires sector (Perulli, 1986). While acknowledging Smith's (1996) concept of the "revanchist city," we employ the term *land revanchism* here in a more literal sense, closer to the origin of the word *revanchism* as defined in the *Oxford English Dictionary*: "a policy of seeking to retaliate, especially to recover lost territory."[1] The actual origin of the word goes back to nineteenth-century French Revanchists, a group of bourgeois nationalists who resolved to restore bourgeois order by reclaiming Paris from the Paris Communards. We use the word here to denote the process through which capital literally reclaimed territory previously lost to the workers' movement. This is exemplified here through the case of Bicocca, but it was a process that was taking place in several industrial locations across the Western world during the same period. With this act of land revanchism Pirelli literally reversed the company's territorial losses in the hope that this territorial gain would also become the lever for reversing also the company's economic losses and restoring its market share and competitive edge.

ENDING CLASS CONFLICT AND CREATING MILAN'S NEW UNDERCLASS

Leopoldo Pirelli's Technocity proposal came at a time of broader industrial decline and restructuring in Italy (and the entire Western world) and was therefore received with great enthusiasm by local and regional authorities, as it echoed their own vision for reinventing postindustrial Milan as an international center for finance, services, and technological innovation (Nepoti, 2003; Memo, 2007). Local authorities saw the Technocity as "a pilot scheme for launching similar initiatives in the future. . . . The proposed land use and planning arrangements for Bicocca represent the first step toward implementing a collaboration between public agencies and the private sector, in order to carry out an important operation that includes reorganization and renovation, job matching, and territorial restructuring in the metropolitan area of Milan" (Regione Lombardia, 1985, pp. 1-2).

Unsurprisingly, however, Pirelli's and the city authorities' enthusiasm for Milan's postindustrial future was not shared by the company's workers, since emptying the area of militant workers who had appropriated it as their own space was a precondition for the success of the scheme. The materialization of the Technocity would entail irreversible changes to labor relations and to the symbolic and material role of the land that they had come to perceive as belonging to them as much as it belonged to Pirelli. Therefore, the production of Bicocca as a Technocity generated another round of fierce class struggle.

112 CITY OF TECHNOLOGY

Initially (in 1981) Leopoldo Pirelli signed a memorandum of understanding with trade unions that the pursuit of the Technocity would not alter the occupational structure of Bicocca's production units (Perulli, 1986).[2] However, in October 1983 he arbitrarily announced to his workers his new plans for full technological and occupational restructuring at Bicocca by 1985. The rationale was that, in order to compete against Michelin and Goodyear in the new high-tech tires sector, Pirelli had to abandon the production of "traditional" textile tires and invest in the production of the new high-tech metallic tires. At that time, 60 percent of production at Bicocca was dedicated to textile tires, and this, according to Leopoldo Pirelli, meant that tire production at Bicocca had to be dismantled (Perulli, 1986). The new high-tech tire production should take place at Pirelli's plants at Settimo Torinese, near Turin, where the infrastructure and services were more up-to-date than those at Bicocca (Perulli, 1986; Giovanni Nassi, interview, February 27, 2007). In Leopoldo Pirelli's own words: "Bicocca ... boasts substantial historical value but is destined to undergo the evolution imposed by new products and new production processes, which require more modern, streamlined, radically different infrastructure. ... Especially in urban areas, the third industrial revolution—the one in which we find ourselves—will involve overthrowing models that are characterized by the concentration of investment and employment in a few larger plants" (Leopoldi Pirelli, personal statement in Pirelli, 1984, p. 3).

In order to convince worker unions that relocating industrial production and "freeing" up the land of Bicocca would be pursued in both the city's and the workers' best interests, Leopoldo Pirelli mobilized all his clout and powers of persuasion. He enrolled the Pirelli family's track record of commitment to both city and workers as a key argument to convince unions and the local authorities about the company's continuous ethical engagement with both. Giovanni Nassi recalls how eager Leopoldo Pirelli was to "create a socially credible reason why he was doing this. By creating the Technocity, Leopoldo Pirelli could claim he was offering a research and technology center to the city of Milan, the same way that his father had offered the Pirelli skyscraper to the same city" (Nassi, interview, February 22, 2007). Leopoldo Pirelli emphasized this same point in his personal statement that accompanied the company's 1984 annual report: "[The Technocity] is a social and cultural contribution that Pirelli would like to offer to the city of Milan, convinced, as we always have been, that economic progress cannot ignore [the social and cultural] dimensions of civic life" (Pirelli, 1984, p. 5).

But the workers remained unconvinced by this rhetoric. The arbitrary announcement of the plant closures at Bicocca sparked a new phase of class struggle. Trade unions suspended all negotiations and responded with strikes and a mass demonstration in Milan on November 4, 1983 (Perulli, 1986). However, the terms of engagement in this new period of class struggle were very different from those of the previous decade. After losing support and acclaim during the "Strategy of Tension," Bicocca's more radical workers' organizations (e.g., the CUB) had become marginalized. The CUB accused Pirelli of using the crisis as a pretext for reestablishing the power relations that had prevailed before the "Hot Autumn" of '69. But this time, Pirelli's opponent was not the CUB but the local representatives of the less radical national trade union (CGIL), whose executive member at the Consiglio di fabbrica Pirelli, Sergio Cofferati, had already stated in 1976 at a conference on the evolution of working-class struggle that "trade unions cannot contain the effects of the crisis by defending every single job and every single factory plant" (quoted in Bolchini, 1985, p. 119). Indeed, the CGIL union representatives at Bicocca opted for a more "pragmatic" approach. They acknowledged the crisis and declared their willingness to enter negotiations with Pirelli.

Both Pirelli and the unions had a lot at stake. For Pirelli, a consensual agreement over plant closures was highly desirable, as it would facilitate the smoother management of the difficult restructuring process; a consensual agreement would also be advantageous for Pirelli when it came to negotiating with local and regional authorities the terms for redeveloping Bicocca's spaces into a Technocity (Perulli, 1986).

For trade unions, not entering negotiations also incurred high risks. Around that time, in September 1984, Pirelli had made a separate local deal with the workers' unions at the Settimo Torinese plants that extended the workweek to Saturdays for five weeks per year for each worker (Perulli, 1986). This agreement had already created strong tension and fragmentation among Pirelli's unions at Milan and those at Turin, and was indicative of a new direction that class struggle would take from that moment onwards.

114   CITY OF TECHNOLOGY

After a long history of emblematic and radical struggles to redefine socially determined work and to claim places of work as places of freedom and expression, Bicocca's workers were now faced with the real threat of losing their status as Milan's working class par excellence. Contrary to the musings of Gorz (1982), who, at the time, celebrated the deindustrialization of European cities as an opportunity to turn the industrial proletariat into a liberated "privileged minority," Pirelli's workers knew that the rapid restructuring of Milan's economy would be the unmaking of the working class. Saying farewell to their status as Milan's industrial workers would not mean liberation or "privileges"; it would mean becoming Milan's economic underclass, "a class of unemployed, unemployables, and underemployed who are more and more hopelessly set apart from the nation at large and do not share in its life, its ambitions and its achievements" (Myrdal, 1963, p. 10). This would be an underclass not only in its strictly economic sense, as originally conceptualized by Myrdal (1963) but also as later developed by Wright (1994), namely, a class that had become economically "useless" for capitalism because their labor had become unworthy of exploitation (Myrdal, 1963, p. 10; see also Walker, 1978; Gans, 1993; Wright, 1994; Mingione, 1996).[3]

After having come as close to a vision of self-management as one could get under capitalism, Pirelli's workers were faced with the reality of capitalism's new phase: Keynesian practices were vilified, paternalism was banalized, neoliberalism was becoming mainstream, and the gradual individualization of social responsibility was settling in. Under these circumstances Pirelli's workers knew that they could no longer negotiate broader social change, as they had done in the past; the best they could expect from the new negotiations was to maintain some form of "control of their own personal economic circumstances" (Walker, 1978, p. 33).

A PYRRHIC VICTORY

In November 1984, Pirelli and workers' unions started an intense period of negotiations over Bicocca's jobs and spaces that lasted several months. The City Council, the provincial government, and the regional authorities played an important role as mediators and guarantors in this new phase

LAND REVANCHISM

of class struggle. On April 26, 1985, trade unions, Pirelli, and the local authorities cosigned a Declaration of Intentions Protocol, the *Schema di Protocollo di Intesa* (henceforth *Protocollo*). The agreement set the terms and conditions for the relocation of production away from Bicocca and outlined three basic rules for restructuring (Regione Lombardia, 1985).

First, the *Protocollo* stipulated that Pirelli would keep a small unit for cable production open at Bicocca. This production line had few employees and was considered to be more in line with the desire to reinvent Pirelli as a high-tech company. Second, the *Protocollo* specified that any new tire production plants would have to be located within a twenty-five-kilometer radius from Bicocca. Third, the *Protocollo* guaranteed employment for up to 1,700 of the 2,000 remaining Bicocca workers through a combination of early retirement offers, reemployment with the municipality or with companies affiliated with the municipality, and redeployment at a new plant that Pirelli had built at Bollate, near Milan (Pirelli, 1984, pp. 2–3; Perulli, 1986; Regione Lombardia, 1985, pp. 2–3; "Cassa per il Mezzogiorno," 1984; Anonymous 1986). The plant at Bollate would take on part of Bicocca's production and give employment to 600 workers who still lived in Bicocca but now had to commute to the new location (Perulli, 1986; Regione Lombardia, 1985, pp. 2–3). Around the same time that Pirelli was negotiating restructuring, the Italian government issued an incentives package for relocation of industrial activity to the Mezzogiorno.[4] There could not have been better timing for Pirelli. Taking advantage of the incentives, the company relocated the production of its diversified products lines to the South of Italy (Perulli, 1986; "Cassa per il Mezzogiorno," 1984).

The *Protocollo* agreement turned out to be a Pyrrhic victory for Pirelli's workers, as it rubber-stamped the demise of Bicocca's land both as an industrial production site, and as a space hosting a strong workers' community and its history. Although around one thousand of Bicocca's original workers/residents were allowed to continue living in their Bicocca homes, that which had made Bicocca emblematic, namely the large workers' community and the spaces of close-knit production and reproduction, would now be removed. Vincenzo Berardi (interview, November 26, 2009), a Bicocca worker and resident of the Bicocca village who was redeployed to the new plant at Bollate, talks of the agreement as a moment of "massive defeat" for workers. The reorganization of Pirelli's production units into dispersed, "flexible," and smaller-scale plants meant that trade unions lost their power to mobilize large masses of workers against central decision-making.

According to Murray (1983), decentralization of production in Italy as a whole dented the workers' movement, as it "created new divisions in the industrial working class by increasing the number of workers living and working in conditions that greatly differed from those of the mass-collective worker. The breakdown of large factories into small production units made collective action considerably more difficult" (p. 76). Indeed, although workers' unions succeeded in keeping part of the production lines at Bicocca, they did not foresee the effect that the new arrangements, the disassembling of production, the disengagement of Bicocca's land from the worker's movement, and the hollowing out of Bicocca's social spaces would have on class relations.

According to the same Pirelli veteran worker (Berardi, interview, November 26, 2009), it would be simplistic to explain the disassembling of Bicocca's factories only by the need for technological innovation. According to him, the transfer of production away from Bicocca was part of a strategy pursued by the "bosses" to "break up the workers' movement for good."

> They decided it was time to end class struggle. . . . They decided . . . to kill the factories. . . . Pirelli had been the fulcrum, the most eminent example of [class] struggle, of our determination to move from capitalism to socialism; we were very close to that change back then. . . . This cohort [of workers] that fought to foster socialism, this foothold consisting of thousands of workers, united and cohesive, and sharing a common vision, had to be dismantled. (Berardi, interview, November 26, 2009)

Indeed, the redevelopment of Bicocca as a technological pole became a catalyst for changing the historically established power relations between Pirelli and its workers. The workers' movement, which until then had drawn significant strength from the dense concentration of production and workers' dwellings and social spaces on a single site, received a harsh blow. The end of production at Bicocca shattered both the imaginary and the materiality and everyday practices of Bicocca as the social and political space for working women and men (Murray, 1983). The invention of a new spatial imaginary (Kaika, 2010) for Bicocca's land as Technocity became the catalyst for local capital to recapture its position of power by instituting a new relationship between capital and land: land would no longer be a condition of production, an investment that was bound to depreciate over time, a means to mitigate capital/labor conflict, or a site to launch and nurture class struggle. Instead, it would be mobilized as an asset that had to realize its full accumulation potential.

"Free" from its working women and men and "free" from production activities, Bicocca's land was now ripe to reach its full real estate potential and be transformed and reorganized into a technological center modeled after similar technological poles in the United States. The Technocity would be the first of its kind in Italy to host research centers, universities, businesses, and Pirelli's own research and development laboratories in one area and take advantage of the synergies arising from the concentration of high-technology services and research functions. The *Protocollo* agreement describes the project as "a renovation of the urban and residential structure of the Pirelli-Bicocca area, aimed at enabling and facilitating the development of a 'special service-production zone' . . . that will permit the implementation of a fairly large 'Integrated Multifunctional Technological Center'" (Regione Lombardia, 1985, p. 3).

This moment would mark the beginning of Pirelli's own "journey of perpetual search for enhanced future ground rents" (Harvey, 1982b, p. 368). Land could now be brought into the company's balance sheets according to the rent it would potentially yield in the real estate market. The next phase, planning for the Technocity, which we shall discuss in the following chapter, was the last instance when the company was forced to involve workers in decision-making. It was also the last display of place loyalty on the part of a family-owned company, as the transition from family-run to corporate capitalism had begun, using land revanchism as a vehicle.

6 The Eureka Moment

"DISCOVERING" INDUSTRIAL LAND AS ASSET (1985–EARLY 1990S)

Up to this point, the book has followed the metamorphoses of the social, economic, and material role of land since the beginning of industrialization: originally as a condition of production, a dead weight and a cost burden, subsequently as a means of mitigating class conflict, later as a social/political space, and during the 1970s as a means of recovering industrial production and stimulating growth. In this chapter we identify and explain what we call the Eureka moment: the moment when industrial capital reimagines and materially produces industrial land as an asset, a means of accumulation in its own right. In the following pages we shall document the economic, cultural, and social conditions that led to that moment, when land stopped being accounted for as dead weight or as a cost burden in industrial accounts and started being registered in annual balance sheets as a real estate asset that could be mobilized to recover from crisis. The land revanchism that preceded (analyzed in chapter 5), was key in activating this moment.

This chapter uses, once again, Bicocca's land as an emblematic case to elucidate this process. Pirelli's Eureka moment occured in the late 1980s, when the company's accounts were in the red, and it could not overcome international competition. At that moment, the company's management

118

realized that the entirety of its industrial land could be reimagined, and accounted for, as a real estate asset that could provide the cash flow necessary to rescue the ailing company. Until that moment, industrial land had featured in Pirelli's accounts at zero value, as an investment that was depreciating over time. But now, for the first time, the same land was brought into the company's accounts as an asset whose value was increasing, as it was calculated according to speculative international real estate prices. The effect was impressive and contributed to balancing the company's accounts. Initially, this was done through a "simple" act of creative accounting. But, as we shall explain in the following pages, from this moment onwards, industrial land became the centerpiece of a radically new corporate strategy that would redefine the ailing traditional industry's relationship to the production of (urban) space and would propel new forms of urbanity.

THE EUREKA MOMENT: DISCOVERING LAND AS A GROWTH ENGINE AND ACCUMULATION STRATEGY

In 1985, after the *Protocollo*, the agreement between local authorities, trade unions, and Pirelli's management, was signed, a few lines of production remained active at Bicocca, while the large plants closed down. But in 1987, Pirelli reached a new agreement with the unions to also transfer the remaining production lines away from Bicocca to plants in Bollate, an area fifteen kilometers west of Bicocca, and in Settimo Torinese, an area outside Turin. The reasons cited were technological but also spatial: the new, much larger machinery could not fit inside the old buildings. "We needed to first build the new equipment and then think of tailoring the clothing [the building] around it. First you have to build the equipment. Then the building" (Nassi, interview, February 22, 2007).

With the eviction of the last tire production lines from Bicocca, the act of land revanchism was completed. The ownership and management of Bicocca's land were transferred internally to a new daughter company, Progetto Bicocca SpA, which was set up explicitly to oversee land redevelopment and to manage real estate operations (Pirelli, 1986). An internal "sales" figure was set for this transfer of land ownership at 159.9 billion lire. The figure comprised two parts: first, the value of industrial land and buildings that would be retained as production sites, estimated at 46.4 billion lire; second, the value of "fixed tangible assets" (i.e., land and buildings that would be redeveloped as part of the Technocity project), estimated at 113.5 billion lire (Pirelli SpA, 1991, p. 70). The value of "fixed tangible assets" was calculated on speculative grounds from the potential land rent each plot could yield on the basis of "the permissible land use and gross floor areas specified for this plot in Technocity's Master Plan" (Pirelli SpA, 1992, p. 3).

Giovanni Nassi, who played a leading role in managing and delivering Bicocca's transformation as CEO of Progetto Bicocca, recalls with great enthusiasm the Eureka moment when he (and through him, Pirelli) realized that land is not just a condition of production, a dead weight, and a cost burden, but could become a means of accumulation in itself, a growth engine that could propel Pirelli into a new phase of accumulation. This was revolutionary, since

> up to that moment, the industrial world in Italy . . . held this rather stupid but convenient logic: whenever an area with a plant on it was no longer valuable as industrial land, they would say: "Let's sell the wretched thing right away for quick money" [*Vendiamola: pochi, maledetti, e subito*]. According to this logic, industrial land and industrial plants were bound to gradually depreciate in value until they ended up with a value of zero. Once the process of depreciation was completed, they considered the land paid off; they didn't consider its potential value as real estate asset. (Nassi, interview, February 22, 2007)

During the years when Pirelli was pursuing a merger with Dunlop, Nassi noticed that "Dunlop, in contrast to Pirelli, accounted [their abandoned land and plants] at market values in their balance sheets, and not at zero value, which is what we used to do at Pirelli. Well, I started to use Dunlop's very interesting logic and decided to create a "real estate within' . . . that would enable me to make the maximum profit in the long term" (Nassi, interview, February 22, 2007).

Indeed, until 1987, Pirelli treated its industrial land and buildings in its balance sheets the same way as machinery and industrial equipment:

namely, its value depreciated every year until it would eventually be considered to be "paid off." For this reason, until 1987, all land and buildings owned by Pirelli SpA in Italy (including Bicocca and other sites in Milan) was valued at 67.3 billion lire. In 1991, however, after the Eureka moment described above, the value of Bicocca's land and buildings increases in the balance sheets (under Progetto Bicocca SpA's ownership) at the staggering value of 159 billion lire. As land and buildings were brought into the accounts as real estate assets, their value jumped on speculative grounds, that is, on the basis of potential future real estate yields. The figure at which Bicocca's land was valued in 1991 was 2.36 times higher than the value at which the same land plus all other Pirelli's land holdings in Italy had been calculated four years earlier. From 1991 onwards, the speculative value of Bicocca's land featured into Pirelli's balance sheets as a new asset that helped shore up the company's accounts and its potential financial leverage.

By abandoning its traditional practice of treating industrial land as a condition of production and as an investment that depreciated over time, Pirelli reinvented its land not only as real estate, but as a "pure financial asset" (Harvey, 1982b, p. 347) that could now be brought onto the company's balance sheets according to the rent it would potentially yield in the real estate market. In short, Pirelli turned the rent gap, which was itself coconstituted by planning and related regulations, into "real" prices, thereby significantly contributing to enhancing the company's balance sheets. This new "accounting" tactic would soon be turned into the centerpiece of a radically new corporate strategy that would help launch Pirelli into a new phase of capitalism and would also redefine the company's relationship not only to its workers but also to urban space and local governance. Revolutionizing the way it perceived and "accounted" for its land and real estate assets marked the beginning of Pirelli's "journey of perpetual search for enhanced future ground rents" (Harvey, 1982b, p. 368).

The moment when Pirelli assetized its industrial land was also historically opportune. By the time Pirelli launched its redevelopment plans for Technocity, Bicocca was no longer a factory district at the periphery, but equally, "Milan was no longer a leading industrial city. Milan's authorities

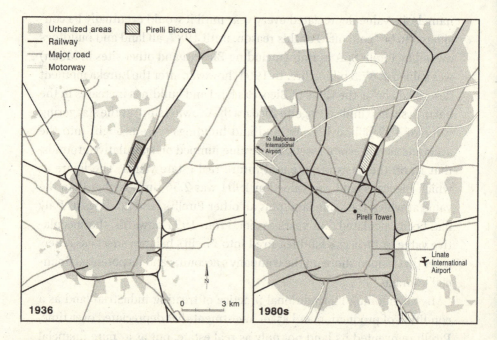

Figure 8. Milan's urban boundaries in 1936 versus the 1980s, showing urban growth in relation to Bicocca's geographical position. Compiled by the authors, drawing upon data from Pirelli (1999, p. 10), Pirelli SpA (1982-87), Bolocan Goldstein and Pasqui (2003), and Secchi (1984). Cartographic work by Graham Bowden. This figure was first published in Kaika and Ruggiero (2016).

aspired to build a new, finance- and service-oriented, urban economy" (Nassi, interview, February 22, 2007). As figure 8 shows, Bicocca had become integrated, both physically and cognitively, into the urban landscape, while Milan was aspiring to become an international finance and service center (Bolchini, 1967, pp. 23-24; see also Pirelli SpA, 1982-87). The historical and geographical conditions made this a ripe moment to mobilize land as a pure financial asset that would help launch Pirelli into the next phase of capitalism. The fact that Milan's economy was becoming increasingly internationalized meant that land rent in and around Milan could now potentially be determined no longer at the local but at the regional, national, or indeed international level (Haila, 1988). This way, the urbanization of land around Bicocca and the internationalization of Milan's economy acted as what Haila (1988, p. 92) terms a "stimulus condition" that prompted landowners, including manufacturing-based corporations, to treat their land as a pure financial asset. However, as we shall see in the following sections, before any piece of land or real estate becomes embedded in global real estate markets, its value first has to be produced at local level.

THE LOCAL PRODUCTION OF GLOBAL REAL ESTATE VALUES: WHAT LAND FINANCIALIZATION OWES TO "FLEXIBLE" PLANNING AND LOCAL STRATEGIC ALLIANCES

Originally, Bicocca and the surrounding area did not feature in Milan City Council's plans and visions for a postindustrial urban future (Riganti, 2003, 2007; Secchi, 1984; Bolocan Goldstein, 2007; Bolocan Goldstein & Pasqui, 2003; Balducci, 2003). The city's declining northeast industrial axis, where the Bicocca was located, was completely ignored in the 1984 *Progetto Passante: Documento Direttore* proposal, which demarcated instead the northwest-southeast axis as priority area for the city's new development. As figure 9 shows, the construction of a new rapid transit line along this axis, combined with land use revisions, would help propel new development projects (Riganti, 2003; Bolocan Goldstein, 2003a, 2003b, 2007; Bolocan Goldstein & Bonfantini, 2007; Healey, 2007; Vicari & Molotch, 1990; Secchi, 1984; Comune di Milano, 1984).

However, as Vicari and Molotch (1990) have detailed, the complexity and bureaucracy of local institutions (Healey, 2007, p. 92) and the inability to "identify US style growth machine dynamics," prevented swift change, and, in effect, impeded the development of a comprehensive plan out of the 1984 vision for a post-Fordist Milan. This left the city's redevelopment to ad hoc decisions through specific development projects, a process that Balducci (2003, p. 64) denotes as "planning by projects" (see also Bolocan Goldstein, 2003; Bolocan Goldstein & Pasqui, 2003; Balducci et al., 2011).

The lack of clear planning and direction on the part of local institutions proved advantageous for Pirelli. In 1985, following the signing of the

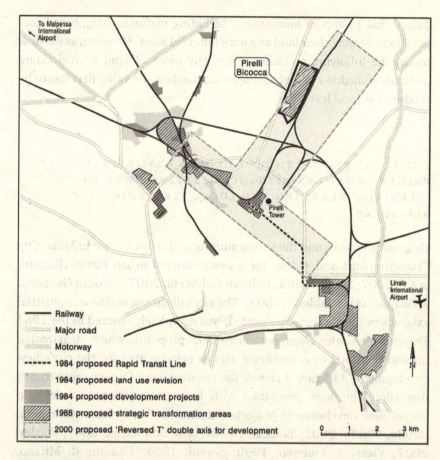

Figure 9. Bicocca's influence on Milan's post-Fordist development geographies. In 1984 the municipality ignores the northeast axis and prioritizes the northwest/southeast axis for development around a new rapid transit line, but in 1988, after Pirelli's Technocity proposal, Bicocca is identified as an Area for Strategic Transformation, and in 2000 it is assigned key priority development status as part of a "Reversed T" double axis. Compiled by the authors, drawing upon Comune di Milano (1984, 1988); Comune di Milano, Assessorato allo sviluppo del territorio (2001); Balducci (2003); Healey (2007); Riganti (2003, 2007); Bolocan Goldstein (2003b; 2002, p. 97; 2007, p. 177); Bolocan Goldstein and Pasqui (2003); Vicari and Molotch (1990); Secchi (1984); and Boatti (2011). Cartographic work by Graham Bowden. This figure was first published in Kaika and Ruggiero (2016).

Protocollo agreement, Leopoldo Pirelli appointed a consulting committee of high-profile experts in science and technology to outline a clear content and direction for his new Technocity (Nepoti, 2003). At the same time, Pirelli started negotiating, in Italy and abroad, the relocation at Bicocca of major high-technology research and production centers (Calabrò, 1989). At the national level, Pirelli approached CONFINDUSTRIA (the General Confederation of Italian Industry), the National Research Council (Consiglio Nazionale delle Ricerche, CNR), ENEA (National Agency for New Technologies and Sustainable Economic Development), and the University of Milan for the possible relocation of some of their activities to the new Bicocca Technocity. Pirelli also negotiated at the international level with IBM, Digital Equipment, and Rank Xerox (Nepoti, 2003) and initiated a public debate for the nomination of Milan (and of Bicocca as a deputed site) as the next host of the European Environmental Agency.

When Pirelli started negotiating its development plans with the local authorities, it was an act that would eventually change entirely the positionality of Milan's northeast industrial axis in the local authorities' cognitive map for the city's postindustrial future (Bolocan Goldstein, 2003a; Nepoti, 2003). It was an undisputed advantage for Pirelli that they were the first company to move toward brownfield site redevelopment with a very clear vision and a concrete plan (the Technocity) that resonated well with the local administration's own vision of what urban postindustrial development should involve (services and technology). In 1985, the Lombardy Regional Authority declared that the proposal for Bicocca Technocity was in accordance with the general "objectives for stimulating new and diffuse technological-productive trends; it guaranteed to match the job needs of northern Milan, which had undergone significant industrial restructuring, and it promoted modernization of the production processes that could sustain industrial competitiveness in highly developed regions" (Regione Lombardia, 1985, p. 1).

Pirelli had two distinct advantages in negotiating the development of the Technocity. First, the imaginary for morphing Bicocca into a high-tech Milanese center gave direction to the local authorities' desire to mitigate the consequences of deindustrialization. Second, the Technocity plan presented the City Council with the first comprehensive (albeit private) planning proposal for redeveloping a declining industrial area. Within this context local and regional authorities greeted Pirelli's proposal with great enthusiasm, since, in their own words, it represented "the first step toward collaboration between public agencies and the private sector on renovation, job matching, and territorial restructuring" (Regione Lombardia, 1985, pp. 1–2).

In 1986, Pirelli launched a closed international architectural competition in which twenty high-profile international studios were invited to prepare a "scheme for an integrated technological center on the site of Pirelli's Bicocca plant" (Pirelli, 1986, p. 13). The invited participants included Frank O. Ghery, Renzo Piano, Gae Aulenti, Vittorio Gregotti, and Richard Maier. The competition was promoted through a high-profile international publicity campaign that included a traveling public exhibition of the entries for the architectural competition. Nepoti (2003) notes:

> The commitment put into communicating and publicizing the project leads us to believe that Pirelli considered the transformation of Bicocca—at least initially—to be a massive image-building operation, in line with their long tradition, rather than a prospect for direct economic return. Throughout its history, Pirelli constantly demonstrated a concern for its public image, [which was exemplified] not only through its advertising campaigns and its strong presence at exhibitions and sporting and cultural events, but also through projects such as the construction of the Pirelli skyscraper, which served not only as management headquarters but also as a means to link the company's name to one of the most remarkable creations of modernist architecture. (pp. 88–89)

Pirelli tendered its comprehensive planning proposal for the redevelopment of Bicocca to the local authorities in 1987, and as figure 9 shows, the 1988 *White Paper for the Redevelopment of Abandoned Industrial Areas* (*Documento direttore delle aree industriali dismesse*) identified Bicocca as an "Area for Strategic Transformation" (*area di trasformazione strategica*) (Bolocan Goldstein, 2002, p. 97; Riganti, 2003, 2007; Bolocan Goldstein, 2007; Comune di Milano, 1988).

The building program for Bicocca Technocity included research centers, universities, and businesses, as well as Pirelli's own research and development laboratories (Bolocan Goldstein, 2003b; Nepoti, 2003). Like the early twentieth-century plan for the development of the Bicocca in the model of industrial paternalism, the late twentieth-century plan for transforming Bicocca into a Technocity drew inspiration from examples in the United States.

> During a visit to MIT, I came to the conclusion that technology was the natural way forward for redeveloping [the site]. When I went back to the United States, I realized there were two possible concrete solutions: a Scientific Park or a Technological Center. . . . It was the idea of creating something complex, either in the form of a business park, or in the form of a preconstituted urban settlement, that interested me. But we couldn't have a park because the area around Bicocca was already built up with residential blocks, neighborhoods constructed originally to accommodate factory and office workers. (Nassi, interview, February 22, 2007)

Bicocca's land was now ready for development, "freed" from labor, from production, and from the living memories of class struggle that had produced it as a sociopolitical space. Still, the transformation of social spaces and spaces of production into financial assets demanded more than the expulsion of labor and industrial production. As it turned out, this transformation necessitated one final yet significant step: the revision of the traditional terms of the relationship between local institutions and local capital. The mutually beneficial relationship between industrialists and local authorities that was firmly established under industrial paternalism, survived Fascism, and was sustained during Milan's Fordist years now had to be reaffirmed in order to launch Milan's elites and the Milanese economy into a post-Fordist globalized era. Promoting Milan as the "European capital of the advanced tertiary sector" necessitated a revision of institutions, planning tools, and regulations (Bolocan Goldstein, 2002, p. 90).

Indeed, local authorities did much more than just greet the Technocity proposal with enthusiasm; they contributed directly to the project's success with two key interventions. First, as noted earlier, and as shown in figure 9, they shifted the institutionalized geographies of Milan's postindustrial development to accommodate the Bicocca as a new axis of development. The previously ignored northeast axis would now become the key axis for developing postindustrial Milan.

The second intervention in support of the Technocity project culminated in the institution of new, and unprecedented, "flexible" planning regulations, which would apply only to large-scale brownfield site redevelopments.

128   CITY OF TECHNOLOGY

In recognition of the importance of Bicocca Technocity as a pilot scheme for Milan's urban future, the Regional Council (Giunta Regionale) agreed, in 1988, that in order to assist the realization of Pirelli's proposed technology and innovation pole, the council had to allow for

> a high level of flexibility and elasticity [in planning regulations] in order to facilitate the need for continuous adjustments to the plan, to accommodate the distinctive functions of a technological pole. . . . The Bicocca is therefore identified as a special zone, which allows for ample fluctuation of functions, land use, and square footage limits. The total allowance of built area has to be left open and negotiable, and so do the exact functions and land use. (Unità Tecnica di Pianificazione Regionale, 1988, p. 3)

In short, Milan's authorities established a new, "flexible" planning regime that would enable Pirelli to have any subsequent modifications of the original plan approved on an ad hoc basis and with little bureaucracy. On this basis, in 1988, the Regional Council of Lombardy (Giunta Regionale) approved a modification (*variante*) of the General Master Plan that declared Bicocca as "a Special Zone Z4" that would be governed under the rules for the "urban recovery zones" as those are set forth in Article 31 of Law No. 457 (Regionale Lombardia Variante al P.R.G. no. 2947, p. 27). Invoking a piece of legislation that dated back to 1978 (Unità Tecnica di Pianificazione Regionale, 1988, p. 27), Bicocca's redevelopment as a special "urban recovery zone" allowed "for ample fluctuation of functions, land use, and permissible gross floor areas (GFAs)" and left both land use restrictions and GFA limits "open to negotiation" (Unità Tecnica di Pianificazione Regionale, 1988, p. 3).

The modification of Milan's General Master Plan, with its "flexible" arrangements, gave Pirelli unprecedented powers over land zoning and redevelopment. It stipulated a very generous total permissible floor area and allowed Pirelli to use land at will and to easily increase or decrease permissible gross floor areas, within certain parameters, so as to better accommodate its future plans (see table 1) (Unità Tecnica di Pianificazione Regionale, 1988, p. 3; Delibera, 1258, July 20, 1987, Archivio Civico Milano). In effect the "flexible" urban development plan allowed the company to act as a planning authority itself with a large degree of freedom in reconstructing the Bicocca area. The Region of Lombardy justified the

THE EUREKA MOMENT 129

Table 1 Approved minimum and maximum permissible gross floor areas (GFAs) per land use type for the Bicocca Technocity Plan

Land use type	Permissible gross floor areas (GFAs)
Industrial production	Minimum 129,400 m^2
Residential	Minimum 60,000 m^2
Administrative functions	Maximum 145,000 m^2
Research, university, specialist education, and business services	Maximum 297,000 m^2
Urban green spaces	Minimum 100,000 m^2
Public services and parking	Minimum 80,000 m^2

SOURCES: Unità Tecnica di Pianificazione Regionale (1988, pp. 42–44) and Giovanni Nassi's personal archive. This table was first published in Kaika and Ruggiero (2016).

"flexibilization" of the planning regulations on the grounds of the complexity and innovation involved in transforming Bicocca into a technological pole. "The realization of the technology innovation pole [cannot be guided through traditional planning instruments]. It has to be regulated at each step, but [this regulation] should not undermine its most innovative and singular elements" (Unità Tecnica di Pianificazione Regionale, 1988, p. 18).

According to Nassi, the special treatment that the Technocity project received by Milan's planning authorities was justified by the importance and timeliness of the project. "There was great enthusiasm around the project. It was a magic moment.... Everybody recognized that it was something important and that it involved a well-established company in need of help.... It has always been like this. Pirelli would develop transport plans that would then be put in place by the municipality, as a favor to Pirelli, but also as a service to the workers who had to get to the factory" (Nassi, interview, February 22, 2007).

The importance that the elastic/flexible planning parameters under the Special Zone Z4 legislation had for making the Technocity project a financial success was indisputable, and this has been extensively analyzed in academic literature (Bolocan Goldstein, 2003a). Nassi, who was in charge of the project, confirmed that

130   CITY OF TECHNOLOGY

the modification of the general Master Plan was the first (and, thus far, the last) "flexible modification" to be authorized. This was instituted to handle a project that was not yet finished and was becoming bigger and bigger. Because we had in front of us a long period of elaboration, we needed, not a strict set of rules and regulations, but a flexible one, and the City Council did it for us. It had never done it before, nobody had ever conceived a flexible planning variant like that in Italy, and this became a decisive element for the success [of the Bicocca project]. For example, for the university buildings, . . . we could build more, but not less than the stipulated square footage. For the offices, [it was the reverse]: there was a maximum square footage of development allowed, and it was not possible to develop more than that [see table 1]. So, practically they fixed a reference point, and then said that for flats you can go above this point, for offices you can only go below this point, for the university you can go above, for research you can go above. These were the only parameters that were fixed, and they allowed us to keep our plans flexible and to change them along the way, while being respectful, at the same time, to the set rules. (Nassi, interview, February 22, 2007)

Bicocca's redevelopment through flexible planning processes did not go undisputed. Despite the exceptions, the redevelopment of each new plot still had to go through the standard planning application procedure, which involved institutionally a wider set of actors and civil society groups, who often voiced objections (Nepoti, 2003). For example, the planning permission for the Piano di Lottizzazione, the plan that outlined the perimeter for the construction of the first tower blocks at Bicocca, was contested and heavily criticized by many civil society groups. Moreover, as documented by Vicari and Molotch (1990) and Nepoti (2003), while planning permission application for the Piano di Lottizzazione was pending, the Milanese political elites plunged into deep crisis, following bribery allegations (*tangenti*) that conferred upon Milan the unattractive nickname *Tangentopoli*. The plan was finally approved in July 1992 (Nepoti, 2003). In the *2000 Municipal Urban Policies Framework* (*Documento di inquadramento delle politiche urbanistiche comunali*) (Comune de Milano, 2000), the Bicocca/City Center axis featured as one of Milan's new central development poles (as seen earlier, in figure 9).

REDEFINING MILAN'S NEW GEOGRAPHIES: THE ROLE OF "TRADITIONAL" LOCAL ELITES IN MAKING THE NEW URBAN ECONOMIES

By pursuing the transformation of Bicocca to a Technocity as part of its land financialization practices, Pirelli played a doubly important role in redefining the geographies of Milan's post-Fordist development (Bolocan Goldstein & Pasqui, 2003, p. 174; Camagni & Gibelli, 1986, 1992; Mingione, 1994). First, by being a powerful local player that could design and develop its own land according to its own interests, Pirelli further nurtured the City Council's unwillingness (or inability) to pursue a more comprehensive redevelopment strategy. The same complex bureaucracies that impeded innovation in planning institutions acted as facilitators for a "piecemeal approach" to planning (Balducci, 2003, p. 64) where only projects backed up by "powerful [local] private actors [who] had a strong motivation and held sites in a single ownership" proceeded to materialization (Healey, 2007, p. 93).

Second, by promoting the Bicocca internationally as an attractive real estate investment opportunity, Pirelli took a leading role in global placemaking for Milan as a whole (Bolocan Goldstein & Pasqui, 2003; Balducci, 2003, 2010; Bolocan Goldstein, 2007). Indeed, it was not the local government but Pirelli that acted as the city's international "ambassador" during this period, communicating to potential international investors the advantages of investing in Milan. Pirelli made international headlines with the design competition for Bicocca Technocity to which only worldrenowned architectural practices were invited (Pirelli, 1986, p. 13). The highly publicized exhibition of the competition's design tenders traveled from Milan's *Triennale* to Leningrad, London's Barbican, Brussels' Royal Museum of Fine Arts, New Jersey's Institute of Technology, and Barcelona's Urban Center (Pirelli, 1986; Manca, 2005).

The central role that Pirelli's land at Bicocca played as Milan's ambassador for remapping the geographies of the city's postindustrial future highlights the important—yet often neglected—role that traditional, place-loyal elites of the "parochial sort" (Molotch, 1976) have played in the transition of local economies. As we show here, it was loyalty precisely

132 CITY OF TECHNOLOGY

to these place-loyal traditional elites, and not to some abstract global capital flows, that incentivized local governance coalitions to modify plans and put in place the institutional arrangements that would assist the transformation of urban economies. In the case of Bicocca, the modification of traditional planning tools by local political elites granted Pirelli considerable powers to maximize potential rent gaps and thereby open up a process that permitted accelerated financialization of its land assets.

So, although redeveloping Bicocca was an enterprise that aimed to capture revenues from an emerging global real estate market, the success or failure of Bicocca Technocity owed at least as much to the specificities of the local labor-capital, capital-governance, and labor-governance relations as it did to global capital flows (Wood, 2004). The revision of the terms of these local alliances produced land as an asset that would assist struggling traditional elites to launch themselves as transnational players in a globalized finance-based economy. Subsequently, the locally produced land rents would become embedded in global capital markets as financial assets and would attract, it was hoped, new waves of international capital and elites to old industrial centers, thereby producing radically new forms of urbanity.

Pirelli's publicity campaign for Bicocca Technocity makes implicit reference to this dialectic between local and global: to the necessity for capital to renew its terms of engagement with its local alliances in order to compete globally. The campaign was Janus-faced; at the local level, it promoted Pirelli as a historical, place-bound, place-loyal company; at the international level, it promoted the company as a daring footloose global player. When addressing a Milanese audience, Leopoldo Pirelli would emphasize his commitment to "do good" for the city and compare his "contribution" of the Technocity to Milan's urbanity to his father's contribution of the Pirelli skyscraper to the same city: "[The new plans for Bicocca] are a social and cultural contribution that Pirelli offers to the city of Milan, convinced, as we have always been, that economic progress cannot ignore these two fundamental dimensions [cultural and social] of civil life" (Pirelli, 1984, p. 5). By contrast, when Leopoldo Pirelli addressed an international audience, the image of Pirelli as a place-loyal elite disappeared, morphing instead into that of a global player embarking on a new path of strategic capital investment: "The creation of a 'New Technological Pole' ... should help place the city in the vanguard of town planning and economic development, in line with similar experiments set in motion in recent years in the United States, France, and Great Britain" (Pirelli, 1986, p. 9).

The importance of planning institutions and local alliances for launching the new postindustrial urban economies has been extensively studied. However, as we document in this book, the process of propelling Western postindustrial urban futures could not even have started without the process of land revanchism that preceded: it was the "unmaking" of the working class and the destruction of land as social space (chapter 5) that enabled the production of industrial land as an asset that would help traditional elites move into high-tech capitalism and later (as we shall see in chapter 7) into financial capitalism. This "lived" dimension of land assetization (and later financialization) that we exemplify in this monograph through the side-by-side reading of the histories of Pirelli, its workers, and its land, and their relations to local institutions, offers a new critical understanding of the role that urban regeneration practices played in remodeling the architecture of global economies. As we continue the narrative in the following chapters, we shall show that although land revanchism, layoffs, and plant closures may have started out in earnest as a means to overcome problems with cash flows and outdated infrastructures (Bolocan Goldstein, 2003b), the significant economic returns reaped by the first phase of redeveloping industrial land soon led to the realization that, if properly managed, further plant closures could prove instrumental, not only for production recovery and innovation, but also for launching traditional capital into a new phase of financial capitalism by mobilizing land as a pure financial asset. This is what we shall discuss in the next chapter.

PART IV City of Finance

LAND AS PURE FINANCIAL ASSET
(EARLY 1990s–2020)

7 Land Financialization as a "Lived" Process

FROM INDUSTRIAL COMMODITY PRODUCTION TO THE PRODUCTION OF LAND AS FINANCIALIZED ASSET (EARLY 1990s–2000)

In this chapter, we shall discuss the final stages of the class struggle that eventually materially and symbolically produced industrial land as a pure financial asset across the Western world from the 1990s onwards. The chapter explores the embodied, "lived" dimension of this transformation. Although land financialization is often examined as a contemporary, macroeconomic phenomenon driven by global financial elites, we show here that land financialization is instead a deeply historicized, embodied, and spatially embedded process that owes as much to the long histories and specificities of local class struggle over land as it does to more recent global macroeconomic processes and capital flows.

Our analysis departs from the dominant focus[1] on the "usual" global suspects of land financialization (global real estate and financial elites, developers, urban governance) and centers instead on local traditional industrial elites and workers. The fact that these agents have thus far been considered a "more parochial sort" (Molotch 1976:317), we argue, has led to neglecting the significant role that they play in the transition to a financialized economy and to new forms of urban management.

The chapter focuses on the final act of the class struggle over Bicocca's land between labor and capital, to offer a historical-geographical account

137

138   CITY OF FINANCE

of the embodied strategies, and the shifts in conflict and alliances between labor, capital, and local governance through which the insertion of land in globalized financial capital, circulation unfolds. We shall document how, before land could be enrolled in circuits of global real estate markets, land rent had to be produced, locally, by turning production and reproduction spaces into real estate values.

This process unfolds during the 1990s, when Pirelli was caught between two interrelated forms of class conflict: international interclass conflict among industrial elites, involving aggressive antagonism; and local more "traditional" class conflict, involving further layoffs, factory closures, strikes, and demonstrations. After attempting a hostile takeover against its German competitor Continental, Pirelli came close to bankruptcy. But as the company was being forced into public administration, Progetto Bicocca (its daughter company managing the Technocity project) started yielding high profits, not from industrial innovation (as originally expected), but from real estate markets. Pirelli's new management seized the opportunity and turned real estate into a key activity for the then-troubled company. This time, reimagining new roles for industrial land was not simply an accounting exercise to help balance the company's books. Now all plans for production recovery were shelved, and even the Technocity project was abandoned. Released from all demands to host industrial production, Bicocca's land was finally "free" to become a proper real estate asset in its own right. Pirelli abandoned the Technocity project and launched a plan for redeveloping Bicocca as Milan's new "historical suburb," a highly speculative real estate venue mixing residential, office, cultural, and retail spaces. Importantly, the new imaginary and plans for the old industrial land were packaged as a financial asset whose stocks and shares were floated on the global market. In the speculative investment fever that followed, Pirelli made spectacular profits and the initially small real estate division that the company had established became its core business and was promptly renamed, from Milano Centrale Immobiliare (MCI) to Pirelli Real Estate (Pirelli RE).

However, as this chapter will explain, the switch from extracting value from industrial production to extracting value from real estate speculation demanded the revision of the terms of the historical relationship between labor, capital, and institutions, in three important ways. First, it required discharging land from the multiplicity of social roles it had acquired over time; this meant shutting down the final remaining production lines at Bicocca and a final round of layoffs. Second, it demanded the collaboration of local authorities, who added value to the project by keeping the allowances for "flexible" delivery deadlines and permissible gross floor areas they had instituted originally to facilitate the Technocity project. Third, land financialization demanded a radical revision of the mutually beneficial relationship between capital and local authorities that was firmly established under industrial paternalism, survived Fascism, and was sustained during Milan's post-Fordist years. In order to launch themselves into a new era of financial capitalism, local traditional elites still demanded that local authorities act as de facto facilitators for producing value and profit locally, but this time they promised nothing concrete in return to the city or its citizens/workers. As this chapter will document, while Bicocca was morphing into a luxury historical suburb, traditional local industrial capital was morphing into internationalized financial capital.

By detailing the changing relationship between Pirelli and its land assets at Bicocca, as the former was struggling to morph into a finance-led conglomerate, the chapter foregrounds how the socially embodied mobilization of land as a financial asset acted as catalyst for the "capital switch" from the "real" economy of goods and service production to a financialized form of global accumulation.

THE "CONTI AFFAIR" AND THE INVENTION OF THE NEW PIRELLI

As we saw in chapter 6, Pirelli mobilized the Technocity project in the late 1980s as a lever to launch itself as a leader of the global high-tech industrial sector. However, the revenues from its core tire business kept decreasing until they reached only 41 percent of the company's total revenues. By that time, the tire sector had become a restricted global oligopoly. While in the 1960s 80 percent of global tire production had been carried on by

140   CITY OF FINANCE

Table 2   The international market shares of the tire industry in 1990

Industrial Group	Global Tire Market Share (%)
Michelin	22
Goodyear	18
Bridgestone	16
Continental	8
Pirelli	7.5
Sumimoto	6.5
Other	22

SOURCE: Sicca and Izzo (1995).

about forty companies (Anelli et al., 1985), in the 1990s the same percentage was produced by only six large companies. Pirelli still featured in fifth place, but its global market share was just 7.5 percent and lagged considerably behind its competitors—Michelin, Goodyear, and Bridgestone (Sicca & Izzo, 1995; Anelli et al., 1985) (see table 2).

Unfazed by the failure of the earlier attempt to merge with Dunlop, Leopoldo Pirelli insisted that a strategy of mergers and acquisitions was still the best means to give Pirelli the economies of scale that its global competitors were enjoying (Zanetti, 2003, p. 15). So in the early 1990s Pirelli pursued the acquisition of its key German competitor, Continental. If successful, the acquisition would create a group that would be highly competitive against the top global pneumatics producers (Michelin, Goodyear, and Bridgestone) in production volume, geographical coverage, and sales (Zanetti, 2003, p. 15; Nepoti, 2003; Turani, 1992a, 1992b). In support of the merger, Leopoldo Pirelli stated, in an address to Pirelli's shareholders,

> Pirelli is convinced that global geographic coverage is increasingly important in the field of pneumatic tires. In a context where the automobile industry is itself globalized, in order to compete effectively, it is necessary to be able to rely on a magnitude similar to that of our major competitors. The merger between Continental and Pirelli would create a company with a global market share equal to 16 percent and a total annual turnover of 10,000

billion lire [approximately 5 billion euros after inflation correction]. (Leopoldo Pirelli, letter to shareholders, February 4, 1991, in Pirelli SpA, 1991, p. 6)

Continental's management, however, identified the operation as a hostile takeover, while the German workers' unions voiced fear of layoffs in the German factories (Boarini, 1995). In response, significant actors of the German industrial and financial establishment (Deutsche Bank and the three key German automobile producers BMW, Daimler-Benz, and Volkswagen) made a united countermove to defend Continental's independence. For the German automobile companies, the maintenance of a national pneumatics producer represented strength and independence. Despite the German opposition, Pirelli did manage to acquire 50 percent of Continental's shares with the support of its group of financial partners in Italy.

However, the acquisition that was expected to be so profitable to Pirelli instead triggered the deepest financial and managerial crisis in the company's history, which became known as "the Conti Affair." A clause in Continental's statutes that had been overlooked by Pirelli's advisers offered each Continental shareholder voting rights of up to 5 percent, regardless of the number of shares they held in the company. Removing the clause would require approval by a qualified majority (75 percent) of members, which Pirelli did not have after the acquisition (Sicca & Izzo, 1995). As a result, despite acquiring 50 percent of Continental's shares, Pirelli could not take control of the company (Sicca & Izzo, 1995).

The blow that the Conti Affair dealt to Pirelli was heavy both in financial terms and in terms of reputation. Importantly, the impact of the acquisition failure became further intensified because Leopoldo Pirelli had made a commitment to reimbursing his financial partners in the takeover, even if the takeover proved to be unsuccessful. Originally, this agreement was not disclosed to the board of directors of Pirelli. But Leopoldo Pirelli had to disclose it immediately after the failed acquisition (Turani, 1992b).

It is now clear that the prospects for a merger between the Pirelli and Continental groups ... are nonexistent. The [Pirelli] group had agreed to compensate (by December 31, 1991) any financial losses and costs sustained by the investors who backed up the Continental acquisition operation

142   CITY OF FINANCE

if by November 30, 1991, the merger was not completed. The group must therefore honor its commitment to the original investors. Further costs and depreciation sustained directly by the group must be added to this obligation. (Leopoldo Pirelli quoted in Sicca & Izzo 1995, p. 119)

The fact that Leopoldo Pirelli was determined to keep his commitment to the investors was honorable, but it made the Conti Affair a complete financial disaster for Pirelli. In its annual statement of December 31, 1991, Pirelli SpA reported "a total deficit of 670 billion lire: 100 billion from ordinary operations; 350 billion from costs, compensation, and depreciation connected with the Continental operation; and 220 billion from restructuring costs" (Leopoldo Pirelli quoted in Sicca & Izzo, 1995, p. 119; Pirelli SpA, 1991, 1992).

THE END OF FAMILY-RUN, PLACE-LOYAL CAPITALISM

After Pirelli SpA reported a total deficit of 670 billion lire in December 1991, it was placed under public administration and the guardianship of Mediobanca, a major Italian investment bank (Zanetti, 2003, p. 32; Pirelli SpA, 1992; Sicca & Izzo, 1995, p. 119). Mediobanca imposed radical changes in the operations, management, and structure of Pirelli, ranging "from the redefinition of core businesses and activities, to rethinking the company's identity" (Zanetti, 2003, p. 32; Sicca & Izzo, 1995, p. 88), in order to safeguard "the company's growth and the promotion of sustainable competitive advantages" (Sicca & Izzo 1995, p. 7).

The financial and managerial restructuring that Mediobanca imposed included a separation between ownership and management. This in effect dictated a shift away from Pirelli's traditional family-run and -owned structure. The company's manager, who had always been a member of the Pirelli family, would now be replaced by a CEO, who would be appointed by the company's shareholders.

Although Leopoldo Pirelli was keen to take up the position of CEO under this new structure, he was "strongly advised" by Enrico Cuccia, director of Mediobanca, to step down (Turani, 1992a). For the first time in Pirelli's history, the company would have a CEO appointed who was not a direct Pirelli family member (Turani, 1992a, 1992b; Pirelli SpA, 1992, 1993; Sicca & Izzo, 1995; Zanetti, 2003; Nepoti, 2003). Thus the Pirelli family, a paradigmatic example of local traditional industrial capitalists, entered (somewhat belatedly) the process of global intraclass competition that from the 1970s onwards became dominant in many Western economies, notably the United States (Scott, 1988; Pollard & Storper, 1996; Lever, 1991; Pinto, 1998). This moment is emblematic and could be said to mark the end of Italian industrial paternalism that was characterized by the central role of big industrial families such as Pirelli, Olivetti, Falck, Marelli, and Agnelli. In an interview that Leopoldo Pirelli gave in 1999 to Eugenio Scalfari, editor-in-chief of *La Repubblica*, one of the most important Italian newspapers, he lamented the end of an era of family-owned industrialism, as to him that era represented a form of capitalism that tried to combine ethical principles with the logics of profit and industrial efficiency (L. Pirelli, 1999). In the same interview Leopoldo Pirelli juxtaposed his personal entrepreneurial vision against that of the new generation of CEOs that were now running the global economy:

> A lot of things have changed in the industrial world: the size of industrial groups, technology, the relationship with employees, the very nature of capital, the parameters that measure efficiency. Today—as in the past—the CEO is appointed by the shareholders; but I have always thought that appointment implied a responsibility toward a much wider world. [It implied seeing] the workers as human beings.... trying to understand their personality, not ignoring their problems, even the ones that occupied them outside work.... It also implied forging a privileged relationship with the city of origin, but also with all the new places where we went to build industrial plants in Italy, and in the rest of the world.... [By contrast], the main duty of the entrepreneur today is to produce as much economic value added as possible. EVA [economic value added] is a gentle name, almost seductive. It is a necessary measure, but it is a cruel measure.... Moreover, for a large-scale company, listed in the stock exchange, the capital is scattered among small savers, funds, banks, et cetera. The entrepreneur does not even know who the shareholders are. He only knows that he will be evaluated on the basis of EVA. He has to decide quickly on a daily basis, and for this reason his world risks becoming constituted more by economic parameters than by faces and souls. (L. Pirelli, 1999)

Indeed, the new strategic vision that Pirelli developed under Mediobanca's administration differed significantly from Leopoldo Pirelli's vision. It included "shelving the pursuit of a quantitative leap in the tire sector altogether, concentrating production in fewer and smaller units, reducing drastically the workforce, and selling all 'nonprofitable' activities" (Bertelè, 1993, p. 65; see also Pons, 2008; Fumagalli & Mocera, 2007; Zanetti, 2003). "The unsuccessful outcome of the Continental operation marked the end of a long cycle that was dominated by a major strategic project: to gain a leading position in the tire sector, in which the group had traditionally operated. The change in the company's management involved the redefinition of its strategic objectives and the end of its ambition to become a global competitor, in favor of simply consolidating the position it had already acquired since the end of the '70s as producer of medium- to high-end products" (Zanetti, 2003, p. 31).

Inevitably, the new management's strategic vision brought drastic changes in labor/capital relations. Selling off all "nonprofitable" units meant drastically reducing the workforce (see table 3) (Pons, 2008; Bertelè, 1993, p. 65; Fumagalli & Mocera, 2007; Zanetti, 2003). But layoffs were not the only change. Fabio Fumagalli and Gianmario Mocera (2007), who were union representatives for Filcem CIGL (the Pirelli workers' union for the chemical, rubber, and plastics sectors), wrote a book about Pirelli's 1990s crisis. According to them, the change in management curtailed the possibility for a dialogue between the unions and the company (Fumagalli & Mocera, 2007). According to Federico (pseudonym), a Pirelli trade unionist during the 1990s, the change in the company's management significantly reduced the range of issues that could be discussed and negotiated: "The loss of Leopoldo at Pirelli was clearly perceptible. . . . With the Pirelli family members, it had been possible to negotiate and discuss production, working hours, investments, and responsibilities. . . . That certainly does not mean that before the nineties, there had not been harsh confrontations and conflict. But [with the new Pirelli management] the only thing it was possible to talk about was money" (Federico, interview, September 29, 2009).

The similarity between the workers' comments and Leopoldo Pirelli's statement is striking. Both parties observe that the new phase of capitalism—financial capitalism—confines class struggle to negotiations over money. For workers, the shift of focus from industrial production to financial returns tilted the scales of power definitively in favor of capital, as it meant the loss of any negotiating capacity for workers over social and

LAND FINANCIALIZATION AS A "LIVED" PROCESS   145

Table 3   Pirelli Group finances, 1991–93

Pirelli Group finances	1991	1992	1993
Number of industrial plants	102	90	80
Number of employees	51,572	45,726	42,132
Net annual losses (in billion lire)	673	154	96
Net total financial debt (in billion lire)	3,204	2,632	2,106

SOURCE: Compiled by the authors, based on data from Pirelli & C. (1994). This table was first published in Kaika and Ruggiero (2016).

spatial relations in and around the spaces of production. It was a heavy blow to the workers, who were now perceived, more than ever before, as useless and irrelevant in capital's perpetual pursuit of growth.

FINDING LAND'S ROLE AS "PURE" FINANCIAL ASSET

The financial "cure" that supervised restructuring suggested for Pirelli soon started yielding positive economic results. The reduction of the workforce and the sale of key production lines were welcomed by global financial markets and had a positive effect on the group's balance sheets. As table 3 shows, by 1992, although the group's balance sheets were still in the red (by 154 billion lire), the net financial debt decreased from 3,204 to 2,632 billion lire (from 2.8 million euros to 2.3 million euros, after inflation correction).

Global financial markets and analysts approved strongly of the "cure" offered to Pirelli and encouraged the new management to pursue further restructuring (Bertelè, 1993, p. 63). "Once out of the tunnel, Pirelli rediscovers a taste for profit," wrote *Il Sole 24 Ore*, an important economic newspaper ("La cura Tronchetti," 1994). Analysts from Pro UBS Phillips and Drew also noted that "Pirelli is back on track" (quoted in Bertelè, 1993, p. 63), while Morgan Stanley commented on the positive effects brought by shifting focus away from production and into the creation of a "New Pirelli" brand (quoted in Bertelè, 1993, p. 66). This was the 1990s, a time of much hype around speculative brand creation and reinvention.

Pirelli appears to represent the exception to received wisdom in the industrial world, namely that tire companies need to be large and must keep growing in order to cover the ever-higher R&D costs. Pirelli's experience suggests the opposite. . . . The main structural change undergone by Pirelli since the Conti affair has been the decision to drop [production] in areas where the company had a marginal presence and concentrate instead on [production] areas where the company's medium size is more appropriate. This strategy aimed to build on Pirelli's main strength, its brand name in high-performance tires for fast cars. (Mitchener 1993)

However, the story untold by the global financial commentators was that much of the success in Pirelli's balance sheets was due to the drastic reduction of the workforce and the closure of industrial plants (see table 3). Giorgio (pseudonym), Pirelli worker and trade unionist in the 1990s, depicts selling off "perfectly functioning units" like the diversified rubber products division (the ProDi) as part of "a financial operation, part of a strategy of dismissals [in Pirelli's workforce]. [The sale] by no means covered the huge debt accumulated from the failed Continental acquisition. Approximately 3.7 billion lire in debt weighed on the company, and the sale of the ProDi brought in less than 1 billion lire. Still, many—if not all—saw it as a necessary operation and it remained unchallenged" (Giorgio, interview, September 29, 2009).

Zanetti (2003) also notes that the international praise for Pirelli's restructuring overlooked important aspects of the long-term effects of the restructuring operation.

Although the restructuring allowed Pirelli to show sufficient profit in its balance sheets, the new focus on manufacturing top-end quality products turned out to be problematic, because it involved a competitive disadvantage for Pirelli. Although [its competitors] could support the necessary investment in expensive R&D through consistently high sales volumes, Pirelli instead tried to do this . . . through severe cuts in labor costs and through the intensification of the exploitation of the production apparatus. As a result, Pirelli's structural disadvantage significantly increased pressure on the labor factor. (pp. 31–32)

But even though Zanetti's analysis focuses on labor relations, it fails to account for the huge significance that land financialization alongside labor layoffs played in Pirelli's rescue strategy.

The untold story that this book narrates is that at the end of the day, what saved the company from full bankruptcy in the 1990s, together with layoffs and the sale of key production lines, was what was delivered by Progetto Bicocca, Pirelli's daughter company that was responsible for redeveloping Bicocca's land into a Technocity. The completion of the first Technocity redevelopment project in 1993 yielded high real estate prices and further entrenched the "capital switching" from industrial production to the production of land rent and financialization. Pirelli's industrial land at Bicocca provided a key solution and opened a new chapter that enabled Pirelli to increase financialization practices in its operations by adding real estate to tire production.

FROM TIRES TO REAL ESTATE AND FROM TECHNOCITY TO "HISTORICAL CENTER IN THE SUBURBS"

While Pirelli was being forced into public administration and restructuring, the first plot at Bicocca that was redeveloped under the Technocity plans was delivered. It comprised seven office buildings on a seventy-five-thousand-square-meter site that was used during the war for recycling copper and rubber. Pirelli's workers had nicknamed the site "Albania" because it was separated from the other plants by the main road (via Chiese), the way Albania is separated from Italy by the Adriatic Sea. "Albania" was reputed to be Bicocca's most polluted and unpleasant site. Gloria, a veteran Pirelli worker, remembers that "being sent to do work in 'Albania' was considered to be a kind of punishment" (Gloria, interview, November 16, 2007; Giovanni Nassi, interview, February 22, 2007).

Up until that point, real estate had been a marginal activity for Pirelli: a "necessary evil," as Giovanni Nassi put it (Nassi, interview, February 22, 2007), that had to be performed to deal with dead capital. The redevelopment of Bicocca's "leftover spaces" was expected to generate some cash flow, but the broader aim remained originally to boost Pirelli's Research and Development operations through the Technocity. Hence, the redevelopment of the first seven office buildings on the "Albania" site was done within a "cheap production and swift delivery" logic that could yield quick, albeit modest returns (Giovanni Nassi, interview, February 22, 2007).

148   CITY OF FINANCE

However, the economic return that these first office buildings yielded exceeded expectations so much that it prompted Pirelli's new management to have a closer look at further exploiting land as real estate asset. The results whetted Pirelli's appetite for further real estate experiments, and although the Technocity project started out as a strategy to overcome problems with outdated infrastructure and technology and with militant labor, the high economic returns of the first redevelopment phase led to the realization that, if properly managed, the plant closures and the "capital switching" from industrial production to the production of land rent could prove instrumental for launching Pirelli into the new era of speculative and financial capitalism. Drawing on the experience accumulated by the development of the "Albania" site, the company established a financing mechanism for the redevelopment of the rest of Bicocca through smaller "target companies," each corresponding to one building block at Bicocca (Nassi, interview, February 22, 2007). "The company's new management was very eager. They said, 'Bring us more ideas to redevelop the remaining 680,000 square meters of this land!'" (Nassi, interview, February 22, 2007).

In 1992, Pirelli's management regrouped all the company's real estate activities (including Progetto Bicocca and Bicocca Technocity) under Milano Centrale Immobiliare (MCI) (see figure 10). MCI incorporated all of Pirelli's ongoing real estate ventures (namely Progetto Bicocca plus two smaller companies, Vitruvio and Iniziative Agricole Commerciali Italiane [IACI]), which up to that point had been dealing mainly with relocating Pirelli's industrial activities (Memo, 2007).

Real estate was becoming an important part of the Pirelli Group. In November 1992, Pirelli's MCI became the exclusive representative in Italy of Knight Frank & Rutley, a major international real estate agency with global coverage ("Immobili, accordo," 1992). One year later, on June 3, 1993, MCI was floated on the Italian stock market and 74 percent of Progetto Bicocca's shares were sold for over 110 billion lire (Sicca & Izzo 1995). By holding on to the remaining 26 percent of the shares of Progetto Bicocca, Pirelli (via MCI) retained control of the management of the Bicocca project and maintained an "exclusive and mandatory role as the planning, administrative, and commercial coordinator of the project" (Pirelli SpA, 1993, p. 6; Modolo, 1993). "Pirelli's share would never fall

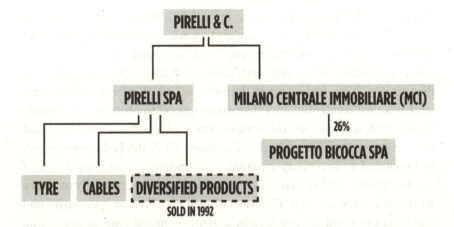

Figure 10. Structure of the Pirelli Group in 1993. Diagram by authors, drawing upon information in Pirelli & C. (1994). This figure was first published in Kaika and Ruggiero (2016).

below 25 percent, thus securing that Pirelli would be able to direct the project and maintain control over the operations" (Nassi, interview, February 22, 2007).

In theory, the capital raised from selling Progetto Bicocca's shares could have helped production recovery for Pirelli. However, the idea of financing industrial recovery was now shelved. The capital raised by floating MCI in the stock market was mobilized instead to finance further development projects and real estate ventures (Modolo, 1993). During the second half of the 1990s MCI became one of the most important Italian real estate companies through important acquisitions (Unim) and further exclusive agreements (Morgan Stanley Real Estate Funds). In the 1996 International Meeting of Real Estate Companies in Cannes, MCI presented Bicocca as one of the most important European urban transformation projects.

A HISTORICAL CENTER IN THE SUBURBS

By the mid-1990s, the redevelopment of Bicocca had become a pure real estate speculative venue, and the Technocity project had been abandoned

150   CITY OF FINANCE

altogether. The Technocity vision, articulated around innovation, new forms of manufacturing, creative high-technology production, and social investment, was deemed too demanding in technical expertise and economic resources. What replaced Technocity was a plan to redevelop Bicocca as a "historical center in the suburbs," which reinvented Bicocca's land as a new residential area that would appeal to Milan's young highly skilled professionals and the creative class, by combining cultural and entertainment facilities with office functions. While the Technocity project had included an imaginary articulated around innovation, new forms of manufacturing, and creative high-technology production, the imaginary for turning Bicocca into a "historical suburb" centered on speculative real estate ventures and the production of rent. Giancarlo (pseudonym), who worked as an architect for both the "Bicocca Technocity" and the "Bicocca historical center in the suburbs" projects, recalls: "The program moved toward something resembling urban design; it included a theater, a university, and apartments, and [we] redefined it with a slogan as 'a historical center in the periphery,' a place where historical social and physical characteristics would blend seamlessly with high culture functions" (Giancarlo, interview, November 14, 2007).

"Liberated" from Leopoldo Pirelli's commitment to redevelop Bicocca as a high-tech industrial project with social functions, Pirelli was finally free to focus uniquely on extracting short-term profit from Bicocca's real estate ventures. Unlike the earlier Technocity project, these ventures were linked neither to a broader strategy for industrial innovation and recovery nor to any broader social project. By now, they had turned into a self-propelling carousel (Nepoti, 2003) in which capital and land were tightly knitted together in intricate and mutually reinforcing speculative circulation processes. Bicocca's land stopped being the medium to launch Pirelli as an international leader in high-tech tire production; it now became the means in its own right to raise short-term profits and accumulate knowledge and expertise for future real estate ventures.

Importantly, however, though the new plan was very different in scope and aims from the Technocity project, the favorable and "flexible" planning regulations that were essential to maximize rent extraction remained intact. The only difference was that Pirelli now had to pay higher *oneri di urbanizzazione* (urbanization charges). Giorgio (pseudonym), a Pirelli worker and elected union leader during the 1990s, explains: "According to the urban planning rules, urbanization charges are something like a fee that Pirelli had to pay to local authorities—a higher price for redeveloping industrial land into an urban area—[but] after you have paid these, you can do whatever you like on the land" (Giorgio, interview, September 29, 2009).

Once again, Bicocca's mutation into Milan's new emblematic urban area could not have happened without the collaboration of local but also national authorities, who did more than just grant "flexible planning" arrangements for Pirelli. Around that time the Italian state authorized the State University of Milan to "decongest" its *mega-ateneo* (mega-university) structure by creating an "offspring" university for thirty-five thousand to forty thousand students. This presented a great opportunity for Pirelli, who suggested Bicocca's land as the site for this new university. There was another site competing for the role, an abandoned freight yard at Porta Vittoria that belonged to the state-owned Railway Company. The City Council of Milan chose Bicocca. In 1994, the University of Milan acquired around 40 percent of Bicocca's land and buildings from Pirelli. A 1992 law (Legge 498/92—Funds for University Real Estate Needs) decreed that at least 25 percent of the funds required for real estate development for university expansions should be provided by national insurance and social security institutes. In effect the redevelopment of Bicocca was partly subsidized through public funds with the assistance of local authorities (Vicari & Molotch, 1990). This period coincided with the first time that the Northern League (Lega Nord) gained control of Milan's City Council (Nepoti, 2003).

Thanks to keeping "flexible" planning regulations in place, Bicocca could morph easily to accommodate the new university functions alongside the new housing and office developments that Pirelli envisioned. The new university acted as an important image-making tool to help Bicocca transform its public image from industrial district to a lively new urban center. For Giancarlo, the architect who worked on both Bicocca Technocity and Bicocca historical suburb projects, the new Bicocca represented a positive compromise between a standard real estate investment and a scientific and technology research pole. "This was also a request on the part of the City Council, who wanted an increased quota for housing.

The mix of functions changed, new services came in, like the university"
(Giancarlo, interview, November 14, 2007).

Before long, cultural projects came to add further cultural capital to
Bicocca's public image: the Hangar Bicocca, a contemporary art gallery
inside an old industrial building, and the Arcimboldi theater and opera,
an iconically designed building that can accommodate 2,400 people.
Together with the university, these buildings added prestige and connec-
tivity to Bicocca, increasing the speculative value of the residential and
office developments to come. Soon after its completion in 2002, the
Arcimboldi theater was chosen for the relocation of the opera productions
of Milan's emblematic Teatro alla Scala when La Scala had to close
temporarily for a period of renovations. The relocation of La Scala's opera
productions to Bicocca "forced" the Milanese bourgeoisie to visit Bicocca
and witness firsthand the transformation of an area that up to that
moment had been linked in their cognitive maps only to polluted industrial activity and working-class activism. The new university, the
Arcimboldi opera house, the art gallery, all acted as attractive image-
making tools promoting Bicocca's transformation from industrial land
and workers' village to historical suburb, catering to Milan's elites and
emerging "creative class."

THE LOCAL TERMS FOR PRODUCING LAND
AS A GLOBAL FINANCIAL ASSET

The new incarnation of Bicocca as a historical suburb demanded a further
revision of the special terms of the relationship between Pirelli, labor, and
local institutions. As we have seen, Leopoldo Pirelli's earlier Technocity
project had gained enthusiastic support from the local authorities, partly
because it offered a direction for Milan's post-Fordist development.
Moreover, it obtained the reluctant support of Pirelli's workers on the
grounds that it was expected to "combine ethical principles with the logic
of profit making and industrial efficiency" (L. Pirelli, 1999, p. 39). But
abandoning the Technocity project in favor of pure and speculative real
estate development marked the end of the long era when each new venture on the part of place-loyal elites would be accompanied by a promise

for delivering matching social projects and assuming a certain ethical responsibility for the city and its working population.

The philosophy underlying Bicocca's new development was more aligned to the now well-established rules of engagement of neoliberal capitalism: what was good for business had to be, by default, good for the city too. Under these new terms of rapport between business and the local government, the latter became simply a facilitator rather than an equal partner to economic growth. In the case of Bicocca, Milan's authorities maintained flexible planning rules and facilitated the relocation of central functions at Bicocca, all of which enhanced the value of real estate ventures. These "facilitating" acts were in line with the long-standing history of the reciprocal relationship between capital and local government. The difference was that this time the government's enabling strategies were performed without guarantees for concrete returns in jobs or welfare provision, but only under the vague expectation that some of the economic benefits of good corporate performance would somehow eventually trickle down to the local community. As Professor Alavanti (pseudonym) put it, this was "a real estate valorization, realized at the public's expense, which allowed Pirelli to sell the apartments at the price of semicentral areas. . . . While the public sector was pushed to create an attractive pole, Pirelli reaped the benefits of the valorization of the land at Bicocca" (interview, November 15, 2007).

In short, the shift from family-owned industrial to corporate financial capital in the 1990s changed irrevocably not only the terms of engagement between labor and capital but also those between urban governance and capital. Under the new terms of the relation between capital, labor, and institutions, land lost the multiplicity of symbolic and material roles it had acquired over one and a half centuries of acting as the centerpiece of capital-labor disputes. It could no longer function as the means to mitigate capital/labor conflict or as a means to renegotiate and regulate the conditions of production and reproduction. From that moment onwards, land was produced solely as an asset, whose full accumulation potential had to be realized in order to launch corporations into a new era of financialized capitalism with the aid of broader local and regional power alliances.

Shedding light on the often-neglected, yet prime, role that local struggles and alliances over land between traditional industrial elites, local

154   CITY OF FINANCE

authorities, and workers played in turning industrial land into a (financial) asset, enables us to understand the prime role that class struggle over land played in enabling ailing local industrial capital to launch itself into a new phase of global finance capitalism, ultimately shaping the architecture of a now-financialized global economy. Empirically grounding the central role that the mobilization of industrial land as a financial asset played in the transition to a financialized economy also asserts that financialization, as Harvey (2012) suggests, is a profoundly urban process.

The historical and embodied analysis presented in this chapter offers three key insights. First, it shows that the renegotiation of historical alliances over industrial land between workers' unions and industrial elites with the mediation of urban governance is a key component of the financialization of land and urban economies at large. Second, by detailing how land financialization enabled local traditional elites not only to survive crisis but, more importantly, to launch themselves into a new financialized phase of urban capitalism, we show that mobilizing industrial land as a financial asset performed not just a *coordinating* but also a *transformative* role in the transition from industrial to financial capitalism. Third, by documenting how changes in urban governance arrangements are a response, not to the needs of disembodied international elites or abstract "global" forces, but to the needs of locally embedded traditional elites that desperately tried to re-image their role and explore new forms of capital accumulation, we affirm that, even though real estate may now be embedded in global capital markets as a financial asset (Rutland 2010), its value still needs to be produced at the local level (Wood 2004: 119).

8 Decaffeinated Urbanity

FINANCIALIZED LAND AS NO-MAN'S-LAND
(2000–2020)

This final chapter focuses on the socio-spatial implications of discharging industrial land from the multiplicity of social roles it had acquired over time in order to reinvent it as a financial asset. As the previous chapter detailed, the reimagining and production of Bicocca's industrial land as a "historical city in the suburbs" marked the final act of reclaiming this land from workers both symbolically and materially. This chapter will discuss how this act eradicated the spatial imprints of the one-and-a-half-century-long history of class struggles that produced and emblematized the multifaceted and coexisting imaginaries and uses for this land: city of workers and showcase of industrial paternalism in the early twentieth century; hub for anti-Fascist resistance during the Second World War; exceptional case of appropriation of the means of production by workers after the end of the war; "Italy's Stalingrad" and inspiration for the *Operaismo* movement in the 1960s and 1970s; exemplary case of land revanchism in the 1980s.

This chapter will document how the spaces produced to turn Bicocca into a "historical center in the suburbs" created ruptures across the place's history. The social spaces that once emblematized Pirelli's land as an arena for radical political thought and praxis were eradicated; the very few

155

156   CITY OF FINANCE

remaining original residents were segregated and excluded. The rupture from the land's industrial past is accentuated by the monumentality of Bicocca's new buildings. Both old and new residents, as well as university students and academics, share the same conviction: that the reinvention of Bicocca as a mixed-use space turned the area into a "no-man's-land."

The material we shall present in this chapter documents how the reinvention of Bicocca's industrial space as a dehistoricized middle-class suburb (Vicari Haddock et al., 2005) offered upgrades in infrastructure facilities. At the same time, however, it produced a new type of "decaffein-ated" urbanity, "freed" from the requirement to serve industrial produc-tion, but also "cleaned" from the imprints of the rich history of class alliances and conflicts that produced it over time. We shall argue that in this new urbanity, use and access rights are no longer up for grabs; they are granted only on the basis of property rights. Bicocca's new architec-ture, its residential and office buildings, the new university complex (Milano Bicocca), the opera theater, and the art gallery, all successfully perform a breach with the multilayered social dynamics, imaginaries, and materialities that this land had hosted over time.

This chapter offers evidence that, like many other redevelopment projects across the world, the eradication of the history and memory of class struggle that originally produced the Bicocca was key for the eco-nomic success of the assetization and financialization of this land.

ERASING BICOCCA'S CLASS HISTORY: DRESSING DEAD CAPITAL WITH GLITTERING, NEW ARCHITECTURAL FORMS

The 2000 Strategic Plan for Milan (Comune di Milano, 2001) that acknowledged the importance of the northeast axis for the city's future rubber-stamped the submission of Bicocca's land to radically new forms of urbanity. As the previous chapter detailed, by the year the Strategic Plan was issued, Pirelli's real estate ventures were yielding such high profit margins that Pirelli decided to make real estate one of its core activi-ties. In 2007 Pirelli commissioned a new iconic building for its headquarters at Bicocca to Gregotti Associati, an Italian architectural firm with international acclaim. The spectacular design comprises an oversized glass cylinder that literally engulfs Bicocca's old cooling tower inside (figure 11). The cooling tower was part of the autonomous thermal power system that Pirelli built on site after the Second World War (in 1950) to secure continuous production. During our conversation with one of the designers of the new Bicocca, the architect stated that the new headquarters building was deliberately designed to be "the most accentuated element inside the new Bicocca. There, both Pirelli's past and present coexisted harmoniously. We wanted to keep and make visible the cooling tower within the [new glass] building because this way the building became symbolic of a shift from the industry to the service sector. Both elements would coexist [inside one single building]" (Vincenzo [pseudonym], interview, November 14, 2007). Indeed, dressing dead industrial capital (the cooling tower) in a glittering new attire, the building becomes an eloquent signifier of the strategic role that real estate played in the Cinderella-like transformation of the Bicocca from a manufacturing site to an international real estate value producer.

The "Great Bicocca," the name that the Bicocca historical suburb project acquired more recently, became an economic success. Both the new university and the Arcimboldi theater received intense local and national media coverage and featured centrally in Pirelli's advertising campaigns promoting Bicocca as an attractive residential district. The campaigns targeted high-income young professionals and the local and international "creative" class (Vicari Haddock et al., 2005). The motto for the luxury loft accommodation at "Edificio 16" was "*Imagine living in Soho or Chelsea. The difference is: it is pronounced 'Bicocca.'*" Bicocca's master planners declared that they were committed to producing a socially responsible plan for Bicocca through what they termed "neutral" architectural forms that would allow inhabitants and users of the area to "mold" it according to their own needs. One of the project's key architects recalls:

> [At Bicocca] we opted for neutrality: exactly the opposite of the spectacular effects of contemporary architecture.... The idea was that, by being neutral, architecture leaves space open to those who live in the area; it allows the district to be molded [by the users]. If you do something sufficiently

Figure 11. The old Pirelli concrete cooling tower, now functioning as a conference hall, is "engulfed" by the new glass and steel headquarters building. Photo by Luca Ruggiero.

ordered and clear, then that space will become very receptive to social intermediation. Instead, if you want to interpret social intermediation through architecture, if you try to create the social portrait of the area in built form, you'll be able to make a portrait of that precise moment, but ten minutes later this portrait will be useless. One has to do something with a level of critical detachment from what goes on during that particular moment. This is what we tried to do here. Everybody accused us of having been Stalinists, Soviets, but it is exactly the opposite. We just used a bit of understatement. Today, all the architects make monuments as if they were images of a brand. Well, the Bicocca is something else. (Vincenzo, interview, November 14, 2007)

However, according to Giovanni Nassi, who was the CEO of the project, the modular character of the designs was chosen not for social or architectural but for purely economic reasons: a modular project was chosen, not because the architecture could be "molded" by the new inhabitants but because its modular character secured flexibility for the project's implementation as it developed over time to accommodate different economic needs and strategies. Nassi noted that he personally had preferred the design proposal submitted by the Gabetti-Isola Studios; but that proposal had to be rejected because it would be "very difficult to modify as the project was progressing. The design produced by Gregotti Studio was chosen among twenty other proposals because it presented a modular urban project that was easier to implement, compared to other competition entries. This suited us best, as the project was expected to be realized gradually" (Nassi, interview, February 22, 2007).

THREE RUPTURES IN PHYSICAL AND SOCIAL SPACE

Despite the declared intention of the new Bicocca design team to deliver a socially adaptable architecture, the new Bicocca inevitably created a series of ruptures in physical and social space at different scales. The first was a rupture in the physical fabric and the urban tissue of the area, best perceptible at the scale of urban design and planning and most visible in maps and bird's-eye view representations of the area (figure 12). Unlike similar redevelopments in other cities (like Soho or Chelsea) during the same

Figure 12. A ruptured urbanity. Bicocca's workers' village, on the lower left side, juxtaposed to the much larger-scale contemporary office and residential buildings. Authors' depiction, based on an archival photo provided by Giovanni Nassi.

time, which were integrated in the city's (New York's and London's) existing urban fabric, the redevelopment of new Bicocca, as figure 12 shows, created a space dislocated equally from the old workers' village and from the main urban fabric of the city of Milan (Vicari Haddock et al., 2005).

The second rupture that the new Bicocca created is experienced at a more intimate scale, at the street and eye level. As one walks the streets to and from the area, the monumentality of the new Bicocca's architecture and the empty spaces there (figure 13) contrast starkly with the more humble architectural forms of the historical workers' village that once were buzzing with vibrancy.

However, the most significant rupture that the new Bicocca produced is not in physical space; it is a rupture in the social spaces of Bicocca. The newly created living blocks alongside the new art and entertainment spaces may have been successful in attracting part of the city's emerging "creative" or middle and lower-middle classes, but they alienated and marginalized Bicocca's historical residents. At the time when the new Bicocca project was delivered, around one thousand active or retired

Figure 13. Monumental architecture and "decaffeinated" urbanity. Photo by Luca Ruggiero.

workers and their families were still living at the historical housing plots of the Borgo Pirelli workers' village. Juxtaposing Bicocca's historical working-class dwellings with high-end apartments, a new university, and office and art functions created an entirely new social mélange that eradicated forever the working-class homogeneity that used to be the key characteristic of the area.

A DECAFFEINATED URBANITY: WHERE THE INCIPIENT CREATIVE CLASS MEETS THE REAL CREATIVE CLASS

The active or retired workers and their families who still live in the Borgo Pirelli, some of whom we interviewed, do recognize the upgrades in infrastructures and old derelict buildings as an improvement brought about by the redevelopment of Bicocca's industrial space as a middle-class "historical

162   CITY OF FINANCE

suburb" (Vicari Haddock et al., 2005). Nonetheless, they cannot come to terms with the erasure of their historical social spaces and landmarks and the eradication of spatial references to their life histories. The social spaces and services that had been produced through decades of intense class struggle were in one brushstroke replaced with a new type of urbanity: "It is true that they have built these beautiful universities, but Bicocca has now become a dormitory city. On Saturdays and Sundays there is nothing around; when the twenty-seven thousand students leave, there is nothing left here" (Alberto, historical resident, interview, October 1, 2009).

Other inhabitants remember Bicocca—with a good dose of nostalgia— as vibrant, buzzing with a constant flow of workers milling around. Antonio remembers the area around the Borgo Pirelli "continuously swarming with workers going to and from the bar, where they would have their discussions over a glass" (Antonio, interview, October 2, 2009). Similarly, Maria, the owner of one of the few original shops that resisted transformation, remembers "an incessant movement of buses that used to stop just in front of my shop and take the workers to the factory, every day of the week, even on Sundays. . . . Workers would come here during their lunch breaks, with their working coats still on, to buy a shirt or something. Many shops are closing down now, as students don't buy here anymore" (Maria, interview, October 2, 2009).

Although Bicocca's new art and entertainment spaces offer valuable services to new residents and attract visitors from Milan, they nevertheless marginalize those whom Wilson and Keil (2008) aptly term the "real creative class": workers and their families, those whose labor, resourcefulness, and struggles molded Milan's urbanity over the decades. Characteristically, but perhaps not surprisingly, none of Bicocca's historical residents who were interviewed for this research project had even heard of the new art gallery, Hangar Bicocca, which is in the immediate vicinity of their homes.

In a desperate attempt to keep alive at least some of the symbolic elements of Bicocca's history, one of Pirelli's retired workers who was still living in the Borgo Pirelli during our fieldwork sent a letter to the City Council of Milan on January 27, 2008, pleading for at least "renaming the new squares or streets after Pirelli's workers who [opposed Fascism] and were deported to concentration camps in 1944" (Vincenzo Berardi [pseudonym], veteran Pirelli worker, copy of letter in authors' archive).

Bicocca's new urbanity is one from which the rich history of alliances and conflicts that originally produced these spaces has been removed. Bicocca's "neutral" architecture that was supposed to enable new and old residents to "mold" the area to their own social needs in fact eradicated the area's historical memory. But this, in turn, became key to the project's economic success (Smoltczyk quoted in Lehrer, 2006, p. 336). The alienation of historical residents was the expected—maybe desired, even—collateral damage. What is interesting, however, is that Bicocca's new residents feel equally alienated. The replacement of Bicocca's socio-spatial memory by "neutral" architectural forms does not sit well with new users either, who comment negatively on the area's lack of character and vibrancy. Casa Loca, the *centro sociale* on Viale Sarca that offers cheap meals and accommodation for students, reflects this attitude by describing itself in its advertising leaflets as "a colorful and rebellious place" within "a sea of cement and nonplaces" (i.e., the rest of Bicocca).

During interviews, residents of new apartment blocks, office workers, and university staff and students often described Bicocca's new spaces as empty and "alienating" (figure 13). Most open spaces are in effect private (D'Amico, 2007). The *grandeur* and monumentality of the new architecture combined with the presence of security guards and surveillance cameras discourage socializing or "hanging around" (Terragni quoted in Bordieri, 2001). Veronica, a researcher at the University of Bicocca, speaks of the area as a "space of controlled social activity, a space in which urban design incorporates the fear of the stranger." She adds that "even the benches and some other aspects of the original Gregotti urban furniture had to be rearranged in order to encourage some form of socialization" (Veronica, interview, November 15, 2007). University students, who constitute the main part of Bicocca's daytime population, also feel alienated. "The Bicocca is [now] a nine-to-five city. When, at sunset, the offices and the university close, the area gets desolate, and when we finish studying we don't know where to go. In the district there is not a single bar or club for students" (Marco, student at the University of Bicocca, interview, October 9, 2008).

But the privatization of social spaces and the lack of character and vibrancy are not the only issue. Old and new residents and users share the same concern over the area's lack of basic social services. As Bicocca became reinvented as a mixed-use district, access to social services that used to be granted by virtue of belonging to a community of workers were lost for old and new inhabitants alike. As Serena Vicari Haddock et al. (2005) document, Bicocca's old and new inhabitants may now have access to art spaces, a theater, and a new university, but they lack basic social and welfare services, from food shops and meeting spaces to schools, health centers, churches, and police stations.

As one new resident eloquently put it: "You can only find pizza and photocopying shops here. But one cannot live on pizza and photocopies" (Mario, interview, October 2, 2009). Antonio remembers the rich provision of social services to Bicocca's residents that are now gone: "As tenants, we used to have special treatment. There was free healthcare here. We also had resident doctors for the workers" (Antonio, interview, October 2, 2009). Equally, some of the old inhabitants still remember attending Pirelli's pioneering Montessori nursery school, which was located inside the magnificent historical Arcimboldi residence. "My mum used to work at the factory; as a result, my brothers and I attended nursery school there. They used the Montessori Method, which, at that time, was quite innovative, a luxury really. It was one of the very few schools that used this method [in Italy]" (Carla, interview, October 2, 2009).

Since 2008, when we conducted our first interviews with local users and residents, the district has become more urbanized, with the completion of new residential and office building blocks and services added. However, Lupo's (2020, pp. 68–69) research in the area in 2020 documented that residents and users still expressed the same perceptions of the space as alienating: "You don't have the feeling you walk in Milan, but in an aseptic space without a past: a test-tube district. If you want to feel everyday life pulsing ... you have to leave behind ... this architecture."

When Bicocca lost its working-class character to become a middle-class suburb, it became a no-man's-land. The eradication of the area's historical memory produced a "decaffeinated" urbanity, "freed" from the struggles, alliances, and rich history that had originally produced this space. As in most postindustrial redevelopment projects across the Western world, the eradication of an area's social history was perceived to be key to the project's economic success (Smoltczyk cited in Lehrer, 2006, p. 336).

Today, Bicocca's land is no longer up for grabs through social struggles. It is now properly enclosed by being assetized and privatized, echoing Harvey's (1982b, p. 361) aphorism that "only the kind of land ownership that treats the land as pure financial asset will do." However, Harvey's aphorism fails to acknowledge an important element of the function of land as pure financial asset: that ownership is not enough to turn land into a financial asset. As we have shown in this book, land first has to be socially *produced* as a financial asset locally, before it is embedded in global circuits of financial capital, and this is an embodied and deeply historically embedded process.

Epilogue

FINANCIALIZATION AS "LIVED" PROCESS:
MOVING THE FIELD FORWARD

This book is a theoretical intervention on land financialization, as well as an in-depth case study and a peopled story. But it is also a call to explore further and empirically substantiate financialization as a "lived" process. Throughout the book, we read the histories of Milan's working class, Milan's industry, and Milan's industrial land at Bicocca side by side to demonstrate something that is almost counterintuitive, namely that the nineteenth century's dynamics of class struggle over land are deeply implicated in the twentieth and twenty-first centuries' land financialization processes.

The story of Bicocca's land and labor has functioned here as a heuristic device for exemplifying the ways in which land financialization is not a present-time novelty, driven by invisible or unreachable global actors. Our book shows that the financialization of land is a deeply historicized, slow-burning process that involves countless everyday actors and livelihoods—a "lived," socially embodied, and geographically grounded process through which historical and present dynamics of local class struggle over production and over land are inextricably linked with the global dynamics of accumulation and circulation of (financial) capital.

167

168   EPILOGUE

Our analysis followed one and a half centuries of class struggle around Bicocca's land as social space—versus Bicocca's land as accumulation strategy—to show how this struggle over a piece of land catalyzed every single stage of the evolution of capitalism, of labor relations, and of Bicocca itself (and Milan). From simply being an industrial production site in the late nineteenth century, Bicocca was transformed into a workers' village in order to mitigate labor/capital conflict (early twentieth century). During World War II, the same piece of land became the stronghold of workers' resistance against Fascism; and later (in the 1950s and 1960s) it turned into the laboratory for some of the most radical forms of industrial trade unionism that Europe had seen thus far. During the industrial downturn of the 1970s, we followed Bicocca's landowner (Pirelli) undertaking an act of land revanchism and reclaiming the land and social spaces from militant workers through industrial restructuring and layoffs (1980s). When production was moved away from Bicocca, a new imaginary for this land emerged as a Technocity, a pad to launch the company onto the road to high-tech capitalism. Later, in the 1990s, under severe economic strain, Pirelli mobilized the same piece of land as pure financial asset through a speculative real estate enterprise that reinvented Bicocca as a "historical suburb" of Milan with mixed-use residential, office, cultural and educational spaces (1990s–2000s). In its most recent symbolic and material function, the same piece of land played a transformative role in capital accumulation as it catalyzed Pirelli's morphing from a traditional, place-loyal, family-owned industrial tire-manufacturing company into a transnational holding company and a global player in high-tech industry, but also in financial capitalism and real estate.

As industrial capital diversified to real estate and financial practices in the 2000s, the century-long class struggles that had been waged around the production-reproduction nexus of industrial capitalism shifted decidedly. Under financial capitalism, capital in the form of money and financialized speculative activities replaced production/reproduction relations as the new axes around which class struggle was waged. By losing their grip over land, Bicocca's workers lost their negotiating class power. Soon they turned from Milan's working class par excellence into Milan's underclass: a class that nobody was interested in exploiting any more. So it was not just Bicocca's land that became assetized, financialized, and offered to the global carousel of real estate value extraction. The very livelihoods of the people who had historically made this land their social and working space were equally placed on the altar of real estate value extraction; without that offering (i.e., without layoffs and relocations) the land financialization at Bicocca would have been impossible. Ironically, the real estate value extracted from reinventing Bicocca's land as a "historical suburb" was produced precisely through the added value that the histories of these workers' livelihoods had engrained into this land through their historical labor and struggles. As these stories entered advertising and real estate promotion narratives, the workers' bodies and lives were thrown out as the "rubble" of land assetization. This is stark proof that the struggles against the dire socio-environmental outcomes of the financialization of space and livelihoods are always embodied and fought at the level of *production*.

We maintain that the stories of urbanization, (de)industrialization, and regeneration across the world, from London's South Bank (Baeten, 2009; Imrie et al., 2009) to Baltimore's waterfront (Merrifield, 1993) and Copenhagen's harbor (Desfor and Jørgensen, 2004), could—and *should*—be retold bringing into sharp focus this "lived" dimension of struggles of neglected actors: of the working class and other marginalized social groups. To do this, the concept of the "working class" itself needs to be revisited, widened, historicized, and understood not only as an antiquated notion depicting those who work in manufacturing, mining, or agriculture but also in a broader sense that includes all those producers and "professionals" who are, as Stefania Barca puts it, subjected to a violent separation from their means of subsistence (Barca, 2020; see also Huber, 2022).

The ongoing displacement processes at Sao Paolo, Rio, Mumbai, Jakarta, Lebanon, Athens, Barcelona, Manchester, or Copenhagen cannot be understood simply as processes of gentrification for the production of real estate values. These stories have to be retold as processes that produced financial assets through fierce class struggle around the social, material, and economic and environmental role of land. From Copenhagen to Manila and from Accra to Lisbon, it is important to shed light on the neglected, yet prime, role that historical struggles between traditional elites and industrial labor, as well as contemporary class, ethnicity and gender struggles and alliances over land, play in crafting a new phase of global finance capitalism.

170   EPILOGUE

Our analysis of land financialization as a lived process also calls for bringing back the state (at all levels) as a significant and central player in enacting the lived process through which financialized landscapes and livelihoods are created. In academic research over the last two decades, the role of the local, regional, and national state (which had once been central in urban studies) has been treated as more marginal, or depicted as a more passive agent compared to the dominance of global financial interests. In this book we show how fundamental the role of the state (local, regional, and national) has been for the conversion of Bicocca from an industrial site into a workers' village and finally into a financial asset. We call for integrating further the role of the state into studies of lived financialization.

A CHALLENGE: MOVING THE FIELD BEYOND SUPREMACIST NARRATIVES

The research agenda we set in this book calls for broadening our conceptual apparatus and our empirical knowledge of financialization as a lived process. We call for more in-depth and critical understanding of how alliances and antagonism among neglected localized actors produce global real estate values and shape in important ways the architecture of a now-financialized global economy and its associated crisis dynamics.

We hope this book can inspire and generate further research that brings "names and addresses" to the still largely disembodied financialization debates. Much empirical work needs to be done to document the struggles, political practices, and power relations that enable land financialization to take place; and significant conceptual work needs to be undertaken to theorize further the real material effects on livelihoods of supposedly "immaterial" financial processes. Over the past five years, a growing body of research that employs qualitative and ethnographic methods to study financialization has emerged.

But the approach we suggest here, and the shift of focus we advocate—away from macroeconomic processes and away from what we call the "usual suspects of financialization" (transnational global elites, foreign developers, etc.)—pose major epistemological and methodological challenges that question dominant academic practices. At the moment, there are two key directions in land financialization research and literature. The first—and dominant—direction represents research that focuses on financialization practices in the Global North and still neglects the "lived" aspect of financialization as it remains embedded within a macroeconomic framework analysis and narratives around financial flows or international actors (developers, architects, bankers).

But there is a second, still nascent, more critical, body of research that employs mostly qualitative or ethnographic methods, some of which builds on our conceptual work (Kaika and Ruggiero 2016) on "lived" financialization. This research is conducted mainly by authors from, or focusing on, the so-called Global South, or the European "Periphery" (Klink & Stroher, 2017; Mosciaro, 2018). We celebrate the emergence of this more critical analytical framework. But at the same time, we are somewhat apprehensive that this significant shift of analytical focus mainly occurs when researching financialization in places other than the core Global North and is often driven by the underlying assumption that "peripheral" actors and environments are (and therefore should be researched as) victims, and not active agents of financialization processes. By adhering to this unsubstantiated (and perhaps ideological) assumption, critical perspectives risk becoming locked into the dominant supremacist narrative that depicts financialization as a top-down, Western-driven process, to which actors and practices in (semi)peripheral regions are *insignificant*.

We hope that, by examining land financialization as a lived, embodied process within a conceptual-methodological framework to which no actor is insignificant, this book will inspire further research that can go beyond supremacist ideologies and narratives. We hope that our book will encourage scholars to expand their important research on the localized social impacts of financialization in places like Mexico, China, Morocco, Poland, Spain, Greece, and Italy, and to research the ways in which local actors, elites, and power relations are central for enabling and accelerating the global financialization of everyday life (Reis, 2017; Büdenbender & Aalbers, 2019; Di Feliciantonio, 2016, 2017; Kutz, 2018; Zhang, 2018; Aalbers, 2019; García-Lamarca, 2022).

Finally, we hope that our conceptual-methodological framework that examines financialization as a lived and embodied process will be

172   EPILOGUE

expanded beyond examining the financialization of land (Kaika and Ruggiero, 2016; Swyngedouw & Ward, 2022; Haila, 2015; Christophers, 2015). It is urgent to systematically research the ways in which global financial capitalism is reproduced through embodied finance-led practices that engage millions of livelihoods in pension fund investments (French et al., 2011; Krippner, 2005); mortgage deals (García-Lamarca & Kaika, 2016); and the development and use of key infrastructures such as water (Loftus et al., 2016), healthcare (Luke & Kaika, 2019; Mosciaro et al., 2024), and energy (Christophers, 2022), in the age of climate change (Kaika et al., 2023; Barca 2024).

As this book represents the first monograph that performs a timeful, longitudinal historically and geographically grounded analysis of land financialization as a lived and embodied process, we hope it will act as inspiration to tell the stories of other places and people through this lens and to foreground actors, power relations, and processes that have been neglected or ignored for too long in financialization literature. We also hope that further ethnographic research and life histories can offer a more granular understanding of the gender and intersectional dimensions of these embodied processes, which are often obfuscated by the very language of archival material. Our driving motive for conducting this research and writing this book was the need to understand how land financialization as a historically specific, geographically embedded, and lived process affects everyday lives and is affected by them in return. As financialization of land, water, energy, soil, minerals, and other vital resources displaces and dispossesses further livelihoods, we need to expand further this framework with more in-depth historical-geographical accounts of the embodied strategies and the shifts in conflicts and alliances between an ever wider range of global and local social actors through which financialization and its insertion in globalized capital circulation unfolds. As this book has shown, these localized practices and actors play not just a *coordinating* but a *transformative* role in the transition to financial capitalism and in the transformation of livelihoods across the world.

Notes

INTRODUCTION

1. Many thanks to Ioannis Iliopoulos for bringing this book to our attention.

2. Many thanks to the anonymous referee for pointing out that there is uniqueness in this contribution.

3. Among the most notable critical scholarship that has addressed the issue of space and class struggle over time are Thompson (1964); Castells (1984); Tilly (1986); Katznelson (1982); Gould (1995); Negri (2018); Mitchell (1996); Harvey (2003); and, more recently, Mitchell (2012).

4. As early as 1939, August Lösch, one of the founding fathers of economic geography, posited the necessity of considering both time and space in economic analysis: "If everything occurred at the same time, there would be no development" (Garretsen & Martin, 2010, p. 130). More recently, there have been calls in regional studies and economic geography (Graziano & Ruggiero, 2023) to consider time and history when explaining the evolution of regional economies in order to capture their multiple and evolving spatial configurations (Castigliano, 2018; Garretsen & Martin, 2010; Henning, 2019; Kolasa-Nowak, 2019; Zarycki, 2007). This call to counter the tendency to take "snapshots" focuses on the crucial role the past can play in constructing and shaping identities, images, brands, and spatial configurations of contemporary cities and regions (Castigliano, 2018; Hincks et al., 2017; Hincks & Powell, 2022; Hoole & Hincks, 2020; Paasi, 2023; Vall, 2011).

173

174   NOTES

5. We first coined the term *land financialization as a lived process* in Kaika & Ruggiero (2016). See also Kaika & Ruggiero (2015).

CHAPTER 3

1. The term *Gappisti* comes from GAP (Gruppo di Azione Patriottica)—Patriotic Action Group member.

2. The term *Sappisti* comes from SAP (Squadre di Azione Patriottica)—Patriotic Action Squad member.

CHAPTER 5

1. www.oxforddictionaries.com/definition/english/revanchism.

2. The "Accordo tra Industrie Pirelli SpA e segreteria nazionale della Federazione unitaria lavoratori chimici (Fulc)" was signed on October 7, 1981, in Rome (Archivio Ires-CGIL Lombardia, cited in Perulli, 1986, pp. 60–73).

3. Although a full account of the long, heated, and important debate over the definition of the underclass lies outside the scope of this chapter, we are specifying how we use the term.

4. Legge 1 marzo 1986 n. 64, Disciplina organica dell'intervento straordinario nel Mezzogiorno, Comma 4, Agenzia per la promozione dello sviluppo del Mezzogiorno.

CHAPTER 7

1. While generating great insight, the main body of the growing research on land financialization still focuses on finance-centered or governance-centered accounts of urban change. Notable exceptions are, among others, the work of Haila (1988, 2000, 2007, 2015); Moulaert et al. (2002); Moulaert and Sekia (2003); Moulaert and Nussbaumer (2005); Beauregard and Haila (2008); Wood (2004); Oosterlynck et al. (2011); Christophers (2018, 2022); and Ward (2022).

References

Aalbers, M. B. (2019, June 11). Financial geography III: The financialization of the city. *Progress in Human Geography, 44*(3). https://doi.org/10.1177/0309132519853922.

Accornero, A. (2002). *Il mondo della produzione: Sociologia del lavoro e dell'industria.* Bologna: Il Mulino.

Agnelli, E. (1930). L'industria automobilistica. In *Industrie italiane illustrate dai loro capi: Lezioni tenute ad iniziativa della R. Scuola di Ingegneria di Pisa, sotto gli auspici della Confederazione generale fascista dell'industria italiana* (pp. 269–311). Livorno: Edizioni della rivista L'Unione Industriale.

Amin, A., Cameron, A., & Hudson, R. (2002). *Placing the social economy.* London: Routledge.

Anelli, P., & Bonvini, G. (1985). Fra ricostruzione e autunno caldo: Gli anni dello scontro a Bicocca. In P. Anelli, G. Bonvini, & A. Montenegro (Eds.), *Pirelli, 1914–1980: Strategia aziendale e relazioni industriali nella storia di una multinazionale:* Vol. 1, *Dalla prima guerra mondiale all'autunno caldo* (pp. 89–127). Milan: F. Angeli.

Anelli, P., Bonvini, G., & Montenegro, A. (1985). *Pirelli 1914–1980: Strategia aziendale e relazioni industriali nella storia di una multinazionale:* Vol. 1, *Dalla prima guerra mondiale all'autunno caldo.* Milan: F. Angeli.

Baeten, G. (2009). Regenerating the South Bank: Reworking the community and the emergence of post-political regeneration. In R. Imrie, L. Lees, &

176 REFERENCES

M. Raco (Eds.), *Regenerating London: Governance, sustainability and community in the global city* (pp. 237–253). London: Routledge.

Balducci, A. (2003, January 1). Policies, plans and projects: Governing the city-region of Milan. *DisP—The Planning Review, 39*(152), 59–70.

———. (2010). Strategic planning as a field of practices. In M. Cerreta, G. Concilio, & V. Monno (Eds.), *Making strategies in spatial planning* (Vol. 9, pp. 47–65). Dordrecht: Springer Netherlands.

Balducci, A., Fedeli, V., & Pasqui, G. (2011). *Strategic planning for contemporary urban regions: City of cities: A project for Milan*. Farnham: Ashgate.

Barca, S. (2020). *Forces of reproduction: Notes for a counter-hegemonic Anthropocene*. Cambridge: Cambridge University Press.

———. (2024). *Workers of the earth: Labour, ecology and reproduction in the age of climate change*. London: Pluto Press.

Beauregard, R. A., & Haila, A. (2008). The unavoidable continuities of the city. In P. Marcuse & R. van Kempen (Eds.), *Globalizing cities* (pp. 22–36). Oxford: Blackwell.

Bellavite Pellegrini, C. (2017). *Pirelli: Technology and passion*. London: Profile Books.

Benenati, E. (1998, Spring). Americanism and paternalism: Managers and workers in twentieth-century Italy. *International Labor and Working-Class History* (53), 5–26. www.jstor.org/stable/27672454.

———. (1999). Cento anni di paternalismo aziendale. In S. Musso (Ed.), *Tra fabbrica e società: Mondi operai nell'Italia del Novecento* (pp. 43–81). Milan: Feltrinelli.

Berta, G. (1998). *Conflitto industriale e struttura d'impresa alla FIAT, 1919–1979*. Bologna: Il Mulino.

Bertelè, U. (1993). Pirelli: Cronaca di un turnaround annunciato. *L'impresa*, (3), 63–66.

Bertrand, C. L. (1982). The *biennio rosso*: Anarchists and revolutionary syndicalists in Italy, 1919–1920. *Historical Reflections/Réflexions Historiques, 9*(3), 383–402. www.jstor.org/stable/41298794.

Bertucelli, L. (1999). *Il paternalismo industriale: Una discussione storiografica*. Modena: Università di Modena.

Bianchi, G., Frigo, F., Merli-Brandini, P., & Merola, A. (Eds.). (1971). *I CUB: Comitati Unitari di Base. Ricerca su nuove esperienze di lotta operaia: Pirelli-Borletti-Fatme*. Rome: Coines edizioni.

Bianchi, G., Frigo, F., Merli-Brandini, P., Merola, A., & Musazzi-Cella, M. (Eds.). (1970). *Grande impresa e conflitto industriale: Ricerca su quattro casi di conflitto sindacale: FIAT—Pirelli—Marzotto—Italcantieri*. Rome: Coines edizioni.

Bianciardi, L. (2013). *La vita agra*. Milan: Feltrinelli.

Bigatti, G. (2015). Tecnici e imprenditori. In S. Musso (Ed.), *Storia del lavoro in Italia. Il Novecento: 1896–1945:* Vol. 1, *Il lavoro nell'età industriale.* Rome: Castelvecchi.

———. (2018). The short time of industry: The Bicocca district and its transformations. In G. Bigatti & G. Nuvolati (Eds.), *Story of a district. Milano-Bicocca: people, places, recollections.* Milan: Scalpendi Editore.

Bigazzi, D. (1996). Le permanenze del paternalismo: Le politiche sociali degli imprenditori italiani tra Otto e Novecento. In M. L. Betri & D. Bigazzi (Eds.), *Ricerche di storia in onore di Franco Della Peruta* (pp. 36–63). Milan: F. Angeli.

Bjornerud, M. (2018). *Timefulness: How thinking like a geologist can help save the world.* Princeton, NJ: Princeton University Press.

Bloccato il grattacielo Pirelli. (1969, October 9). *Il Corriere della Sera.*

Boarini, F. (1995). *Ristrutturazione finanziaria dei gruppi industriali ed evoluzione dei capitalismi avanzati.* Milan: Università Commerciale Luigi Bocconi.

Boatti, G. (2011, December 12). Milano, PGT: Privati Gestiscono Tutto. *Quaderni di Italia Nostra,* (29), pp. 60–68.

Bolchini, P. (1967). *La Pirelli: Operai e padroni.* Rome: Samonáa e Savelli.

———. (1985). *Pirelli, 1914–1980: Strategia aziendale e relazioni industriali nella storia di una multinazionale.* Vol. 2. *Il gruppo Pirelli-Dunlop: gli anni più lunghi.* Milan: F. Angeli.

Bolocan Goldstein, M. (2002). Governo locale e operazioni urbanistiche a Milano tra gli anni 80 e 90. *Urbanistica,* (119), 90–112.

———. (2003a). La Pirelli a Milano: Cenni di storia urbana e vicende recenti. In M. Bolocan Goldstein (Ed.), *Trasformazioni a Milano: Pirelli Bicocca direttrice nord-est* (pp. 27–43). Milan: F. Angeli.

———. (Ed.). (2003b). *Trasformazioni a Milano: Pirelli Bicocca direttrice nord-est.* Milan: Franco Angeli.

———. (2007). Confini mobili: Sviluppo urbano e rapporti territoriali nel milanese. In M. Bolocan Goldstein & B. Bonfantini (Eds.), *Milano incompiuta: Interpretazioni urbanistiche del mutamento. Quaderni del Dipartimento di Architettura e Pianificazione* (pp. 169–184). Milan: Franco Angeli.

Bolocan Goldstein, M., & Bonfantini, B. (Eds.). (2007). *Milano incompiuta: Interpretazioni urbanistiche del mutamento. Quaderni del Dipartimento di Architettura ed Pianificazione.* Milan: Franco Angeli.

Bolocan Goldstein, M., & Pasqui, G. (2003). Nord Milano: Temi e prospettive di sviluppo territoriale. In M Bolocan Goldstein (Ed.). *Trasformazioni a Milano: Pirelli Bicocca direttrice nord-est* (pp. 151–175). Milan: F. Angeli.

Bologna, S. (1988, November). 1968 Memorie di un operaista. 1968. Alle porte del 1969. L'autunno degli operai. *Supplemento de "il Manifesto,"* (10), 1–10.

REFERENCES

Bologna, S., & De Mori, R. (1969). Lotta alla Pirelli. Milano giugno-dicembre 1968. [Document of the Comitato Unitario di Base Pirelli]. *Linea di massa,* 1–32. Machina online archive. www.machina-deriveapprodi.com/post/linea-di-massa.

Bonazzi, G. (2000). *Sociologia della FIAT: Ricerche e discorsi, 1950–2000.* Bologna: Il Mulino.

Bonelli, F. (1978). Il capitalismo italiano: Linee generali d'interpretazione. In *Storia d'Italia annali:* Vol. 1, *Dal feudalesimo al capitalismo* (pp. 1246–1255). Turin: Einaudi.

Bordieri, A. (2001, May 26). Sulla Bicocca, dieci anni dopo. *Arch'it, rivista digitale di architettura.* http://architettura.it/sopralluoghi/20010526/index.htm.

Borio, G., Pozzi, F., & Gigi, R. (2005). *Gli operaisti.* Rome: DeriveApprodi.

Boudreau, J. A., & Kaika, M. (2013). Reflections on the academic and economic environment. *International Journal of Urban and Regional Research, 37*(6), i-v.

Büdenbender, M., & Aalbers, M. B. (2019). How subordinate financialization shapes urban development: The rise and fall of Warsaw's Służewiec business district. *International Journal of Urban and Regional Research, 43*(4), 666–684. https://doi.org/10.1111/1468-2427.12791.

Buntrock, D. (1996). Without modernity: Japan's challenging modernization. *Architronic, 5*(3), 1–5.

Cacciari, M. (Ed.). (1969). *Ciclo capitalistico e lotte operaie: Montedison, Pirelli, Fiat, 1968.* Padua: Marsilio Editori.

Cafagna, L. (1990). *Dualismo e sviluppo nella storia d'Italia.* Venice: Marsilio.

Calabrò, A. (1989, June 9). La fabbrica dei Miliardi. *La Repubblica.* https://ricerca.repubblica.it/repubblica/archivio/repubblica/1989/06/09/la-fabbrica-dei-miliardi.html.

Camagni, R., & Gibelli, M. C. (1986). *Il progetto Bicocca nel quadro di una strategia di riqualificazione del Nord Milano.* Milan: Irer Regione Lombardia.

———. (Eds.). (1992). *Alta tecnologia e rivitalizzazione metropolitana: Uno studio di inquadramento economico e territoriale per il progetto di polo tecnologico nell'area Pirelli-Bicocca a Milano.* Milan: Franco Angeli.

Caprotti, F. (2007). *Mussolini's cities: Internal colonialism in Italy, 1930–1939.* Youngstown, NY: Cambria Press.

Caprotti, F., & Kaika, M. (2008). City and nature: Ideology and representation in Fascist New Towns. *Social and Cultural Geography, 9*(6), 613–634.

Cassa per il Mezzogiorno. (1984, November 17). *Piano della Cassa per il Mezzogiorno.* Rome: Cassa per il Mezzogiorno.

Castells, M. (1984). *The city and the grassroots: A cross-cultural theory of urban social movements.* Los Angeles: University of California Press.

REFERENCES 179

Castigliano, M. (2018). Report on inaugural workshop RSA ReHi-Network
"Interdisciplinary connections between history and regional studies."
Planning Perspectives, 33(2), 289–292. https://doi.org/10.1080/02665433
.2018.1441068.
Cavallari, A. (1952). Dinastie operaie alla Bicocca. *Pirelli: Rivista di
Informazione e di Tecnica,* (3), 36–38.
Cengia, A. (2016). Le lotte operaie nello sviluppo capitalistico secondo Raniero
Panzieri. *Consecutio Rerum, 1*(1), 239–250. www.consecutio.org/wp-content
/uploads/2021/11/CR1.pdf.
Cento Bull, A. (2007). *Italian neofascism: The strategy of tension and the
politics of nonreconciliation.* New York: Berghahn Books.
Cercola, R. (1984). *L'intervento esterno nello sviluppo industriale del Mezzo-
giorno.* Naples: Guida Editori.
Cervi, M. (1972a, March 31). Gli arrabiati della Bicocca. *Il Corriere della Sera.*
———. (1972b, April 15). La Pirelli dietro la facciata. *Il Corriere della Sera.*
Cherry, G. E. (1996). Bournville, England, 1895–1995. *Journal of Urban
History, 22*(4), 493–508. https://doi.org/10.1177/009614429602200403.
Christophers, B. (2015). The limits to financialization. *Dialogues in Human
Geography, 5*(2), 183–200. https://doi.org/10.1177/2043820615588153.
———. (2018). *The new enclosure: The appropriation of land in neoliberal
Britain.* London: Verso.
———. (2022). *Rentier capitalism: Who owns the economy, and who pays for it.*
London: Verso.
Cipolla, C. M. (1981). *La macchina del tempo.* Bologna: Il Mulino.
Ciuffetti, A. (2004). *Casa e lavoro: Cillaggi e quartieri operai in Italia tra Otto e
Novecento.* Perugia: Crace.
Colli, A. (2001). Cent'anni di "grandi imprese" lombarde. In D. Bigazzi &
M. Meriggi (Eds.), *Le regioni dall'unità a oggi:* Vol. 16, *La Lombardia*
(pp. 481–529). Storia d'Italia. Turin: Einaudi.
Comitato Unitario di Base. (1968). Sciopero alla Pirelli e democrazia operaia.
Leaflet. Machina online archive. www.machina-deriveapprodi.com/post
/linea-di-massa.
Comune di Milano. (1984). *Progetto Passante: Documento direttore.* Milan:
Comune di Milano.
———. (1988). *Linee programmatiche per il Documento direttore sulle aree
dismesse o sottoutilizzate.* Milan: Comune di Milano.
Comune di Milano. Assessorato allo sviluppo del territorio. (2001). *Ricostruire
la grande Milano: Documento di inquadramento delle politiche urbanistiche
comunali.* Milan: Il Sole 24 Ore.
Conca Messina, S. A. (2017). Alle origini del welfare aziendale: Industria,
manodopera e opere sociali degli imprenditori nell'Italia dell'Ottocento. In
P. Battilani, S. A. Conca Messina, & V. Varini (Eds.), *Il welfare aziendale in*

180 REFERENCES

Italia fra identità e immagine pubblica dell'impresa: Una prospettiva storica (pp. 37–95). Bologna: Il Mulino.

Cuninghame, P. (2008). Italian feminism, workerism and autonomy in the 1970s: The struggle against unpaid reproductive labour and violence. *Amnis: Revue de Civilisation Contemporaine de l'Université de Bretagne Occidentale, 8*, 1–10.

La cura Tronchetti produce 55 miliardi di utile e una netta riduzione dei debiti. (1994, September 24). *Il Sole 24 Ore*, p. 1.

Dalla Costa, M. (1972). *The power of women and the subversion of the community*. London: Falling Wall Press.

———. (2002). The door to the garden [Paper presentation]. Operaismo a Convegno, Rome.

Dalmasso, E. (1970). *Milano capitale economica d'Italia*. Milan: F. Angeli.

D'Amico, P. (2007, November 9). Il futuro visto dalla Bicocca: Basta cantieri, più servizi. *Il Corriere della Sera*, p. 6. https://archivio.corriere.it/Archivio /interface/view.shtml#!/MTovZXMvaXQvcmNzZGF0aW1ldGhvZGUxL0A0 MjY0OA%3D%3D.

Daumas, M., & Payen, J. (Eds.). (1976). *Evolution de la géographie industrielle de Paris et sa proche banlieue au XIXe siècle* (Vol. 1). Paris: Centre de documentation d' histoire des techniques.

De Grazia, V. (1981). *Consenso e cultura di massa nell'Italia fascista*. Rome: Laterza.

Dell'Agnese, E. (2005). Costruzione e ri-costruzione di un paesaggio simbolico. In E. Dell'Agnese (Ed.), *La Bicocca e il suo territorio: Memoria e progetto* (pp. 12–22). Milan: Skira.

Della Porta, D. (Ed.). (1984). *Terrorismi in Italia*. Bologna: Il Mulino.

———. (1996). *Movimenti collettivi e sistema politico in Italia, 1960–1995*. Rome: Editori Laterza.

De Luna, G. (2009). *Le ragioni di un decennio, 1969–1979: Militanza, violenza, sconfitta, memoria*. Milan: Feltrinelli.

Desfor, G., & Jørgensen, J. (2004). Flexible urban governance: The case of Copenhagen's recent waterfront development. *European Planning Studies, 12*, 479–496.

Detti, T. (1978). Biennio rosso. In F. Levi, U. Levra, & N. Tranfaglia (Eds.). *Il mondo contemporaneo* (Vol. 1), Storia d'Italia (pp. 46–61). Florence: La Nuova Italia.

Dewhirst, R. K. (1960). Saltaire. *Town Planning Review, 31*(2), 135–144. https://doi.org/10.3828/tpr.31.2.d123q46810014113.

Di Feliciantonio, C. (2016). Subjectification in times of indebtedness and neoliberal/austerity urbanism: Subjectification in times of indebtedness. *Antipode, 48*(5), 1206–1227. https://doi.org/10.1111/anti.12243.

———. (2017). Spaces of the expelled as spaces of the urban commons? Analysing the re-emergence of squatting initiatives in Rome. *International*

Journal of Urban and Regional Research, 41(5), 708–725. https://doi.org/10.1111/1468-2427.12513.

Di Paola, P. (2009). Biennio rosso (1919–1920). In I. Ness (Ed.), *The International Encyclopedia of Revolution and Protest* (pp. 1–3). Malden, MA: Wiley-Blackwell.

Einaudi, L. (1924, August 6). Il silenzio degli industriali. *Il Corriere della Sera.*

Federici, S. (2019). Social reproduction theory. *Radical Philosophy, 2*(4), 55–57.

Filippini, M. (2011). Mario Tronti e l'operaismo politico degli anni Sessanta. *Cahiers du GRM*, (2). https://doi.org/10.4000/grm.220.

Fondazione Pirelli. (2020). Nascita di un simbolo: Il Grattacielo Pirelli. www.fondazionepirelli.org/it/iniziative/nascita-di-un-simbolo-il-grattacielo-pirelli/.

Foot, J. M. (1999). Mass cultures, popular cultures and the working class in Milan, 1950–1970. *Social History, 24*(2), 134–157. http://dx.doi.org/10.1080/03071029908568059.

———. (2001). *Milan since the miracle: City, culture, and identity.* Oxford: Berg.

French, S., Leyshon, A., & Wainwright, T. (2011). Financializing space, spacing financialization. *Progress in Human Geography, 35*(6), 798–819.

Fumagalli, F., & Mocera, G. (2007). *Chi vuole uccidere la Pirelli? Indagine sulla crisi di una grande azienda italiana.* Mursia, Milan.

Galdo, A. (2007). *Fabbriche.* Turin: Einaudi.

Gallino, L. (1978). Tempo e tempo libero. In L. Gallino (Ed.), *Dizionario di sociologia.* Torino: UTET.

Gans, H. J. (1993). From underclass to undercaste: Some observations about the future of the postindustrial economy and its major victims. *International Journal of Urban and Regional Research, 17*(3), 327–335.

García-Lamarca, M. (2022). *Non-performing loans, non-performing people: Life and struggle with mortgage debt in Spain.* Athens: University of Georgia Press.

García-Lamarca, M., & Kaika, M. (2016). "Mortgaged lives": The biopolitics of debt and housing financialisation. *Transactions of the Institute of British Geographers, 41*(3), 313–327. https://doi.org/10.1111/tran.12126.

Garretsen, H., & Martin, R. (2010). Rethinking (new) economic geography models: Taking geography and history more seriously. *Spatial Economic Analysis, 5*(2), 127–160. https://doi.org/10.1080/17421771003730729.

Gluck, S. B., & Patai, D. (1991). *Women's words: The feminist practice of oral history.* New York: Routledge.

Gorz, A. (1982). *Farewell to the working class: An essay on post-industrial socialism.* London: Pluto Press.

Gould, R. V. (1995). *Insurgent identities: Class, community, and protest in Paris from 1848 to the Commune.* Chicago: University of Chicago Press.

182 REFERENCES

Graziano, T., & Ruggiero, L. (2023). From periphery to growth pole (and back again?): Late industrialism, smart strategies and tourism in south-eastern Sicily. *Regional Studies, Regional Science, 10*(1), 89–105. https://doi.org /10.1080/21681376.2023.2168211.

Guiotto, L. (1979). *La fabbrica totale: Paternalismo industriale e città sociali in Italia*. Milan: Feltrinelli.

Guizzi, C. (2003). *Archivio Storico Pirelli: L'archivio della direzione centrale amministrativa-secreteria-Inventario*. (Publication No. 542643) [Master's thesis, Università degli Studi di Milano].

———. (2012). *La governance di una grande impresa: Pirelli, 1872–1972* [Unpublished doctoral dissertation]. Università degli Studi di Milano.

———. (2015). Pirelli propaganda, 1872–1972. In G. Ginex (Ed.), *The Muse in the wheels—Pirelli: A century of art at the service of its products* (pp. 53–89). Milan: Corraini Edizioni.

Haila, A. (1988). Land as a financial asset: The theory of urban rent as mirror of economic transformation. *Antipode, 20*(2), 79–101.

———. (1997). The neglected builder of global cities. In O. Kalltorp, I. Elander, O. Ericsson, & M. Franzen (Eds.), *Cities in transformation—Transformation in cities* (pp. 51–64). Aldershot, UK: Ashgate.

———. (2000). Real estate in global cities: Singapore and Hong Kong as property states. *Urban Studies, 37*(12), 2241–2256. https://doi.org/10.1080 /00420980020002797.

———. (2007). The market as the new emperor. *International Journal of Urban and Regional Research, 31*(1), 3–20. http://dx.doi. org/10.1111/j.1468-2427.2007.00703.x.

———. (2015). *Urban land rent: Singapore as a property state*. Oxford: John Wiley.

Hall, S. M. (2023). Oral histories and futures: Researching crises across the life-course and the life-course of crises. *Area, 56*(1), e12904. https://doi.org /10.1111/area.12904.

Hardt, M. (2023). *The subversive seventies*. Oxford: Oxford University Press.

Harvey, D. (1982a). Land rent and the transition to the capitalist mode of production. *Antipode, 14*(3), 17–25. https://doi. org/10.1111/j.1467-8330.1982.tb00035.x.

———. (1982b). *The limits to capital*. Oxford: Blackwell.

———. (2003). *Paris: Capital of modernity*. New York: Routledge.

———. (2012). The urban roots of financial crises: Reclaiming the city for anticapitalist struggle. *Socialist Register, 48*, 1–35.

Hayter, T., & Harvey, D. (1993). *The factory and the city: The story of the Cowley automobile workers in Oxford*. London: Mansell.

Healey, P. (2007). *Urban complexity and spatial strategies: Towards a relational planning for our times*. London: Routledge.

Henning, M. (2019). Time should tell (more): Evolutionary economic geography and the challenge of history. *Regional Studies, 53*(4), 602–613. https://doi.org/10.1080/00343404.2018.1515481.

Hincks, S., Deas, I., & Haughton, G. (2017). Real geographies, real economies and soft spatial imaginaries: Creating a "more than Manchester" region. *International Journal of Urban and Regional Research, 41*(4), 642–657. https://doi.org/10.1111/1468-2427.12514.

Hincks, S., & Powell, R. (2022). Territorial stigmatisation beyond the city: Habitus, affordances and landscapes of industrial ruination. *Environment and Planning A: Economy and Space, 54*(7), 1391–1410. https://doi.org/10.1177/0308518X221107022.

Hise, G. (2001). "Nature's workshop": Industry and urban expansion in Southern California, 1900–1950. *Journal of Historical Geography, 27*(1), 74–92. https://doi.org/10.1006/jhge.2000.0270.

Hoole, C., & Hincks, S. (2020). Performing the city-region: Imagineering, devolution and the search for legitimacy. *Environment and Planning A: Economy and Space, 52*(8), 1583–1601. https://doi.org/10.1177/0308518x20921207.

Huber, M. T. (2022). *Climate change as class war: Building socialism on a warming planet.* London: Verso.

Hunecke, V. (1978). *Classe operaia e rivoluzione industriale a Milano, 1859–1892.* Bologna: Il Mulino.

Immobili, accordo tra la Pirelli e la Knight Frank e Rutley. (1992, November 18). *Il Corriere della Sera,* p. 19.

Imrie, R., Lees, L., & Raco, M. (Eds.) (2009). *Regenerating London: Governance, sustainability and community in the global city.* London: Routledge,

Irace, F. (1997). L'architettura. In G. Vergani, S. Romano, U. Colombo, E. Tadini, & F. Irace (Eds.), *Pirelli, 1872–1997: Centoventicinque anni di imprese* (pp. 139–167). Milan: Scheiwiller.

Kaika, M. (2010). Architecture and crisis: Re-inventing the icon, re-imag(in)ing London and re-branding the city. *Transactions of the Institute of British Geographers, 35*(4), 453–474. https://doi.org/10.1111/j.1475-5661.2010.00398.x.

Kaika, M., Keil, R., Mandler, T., & Tzaninis, Y. (2023). *Turning up the heat: Urban political ecology for a climate emergency.* Manchester, UK: Manchester University Press.

Kaika, M., & Ruggiero, L. (2015). Class meets land: The social mobilization of land as catalyst for urban change. *Antipode, 47*(3), 708–729. https://doi.org/10.1111/anti.12139.

———. (2016). Land financialization as a "lived" process: The transformation of Milan's Bicocca by Pirelli. *European Urban and Regional Studies, 23*(1), 3–22. https://doi.org/10.1177/0969776413484166.

184 REFERENCES

———. (2018). The academic article as a collective "labour of love." In N. Gregson, M. Crang, J. Botticello, M. Calestani, A. Krzywoszynska, M. Kaika, & L. Ruggiero, *Winners of the 2017 Jim Lewis Prize, European Urban and Regional Studies, 25*(1), 3–7. https://doi.org/10.1177/0969776417751503.

Katznelson, I. (1982). *City trenches: Urban politics and the patterning of class in the United States.* Chicago: University of Chicago Press.

———. (1992). *Marxism and the city.* Oxford: Clarendon Press.

Klink, J., & Stroher, L. E. M. (2017, December). The making of urban financialization? An exploration of Brazilian urban partnership operations with building certificates. *Land Use Policy, 69*, 519–528.

Kolasa-Nowak, A. (2019). The importance of history in regional studies: The role of the past in Polish regional sociology after 1989. *Ruch Prawniczy, Ekonomiczny i Socjologiczny, 81*, 239–252. https://doi.org/10.14746/rpeis.2019.81.4.18.

Krippner, G. R. (2005). Financialization of the American economy. *Socio-Economic Review, 3*(2), 173–208.

Kutz, W. (2018). Financialization interrupted: Unwilling subjects of housing reform in Morocco. *City, 22*(4), 568–583. https://doi.org/10.1080/13604813.2018.1507109.

Lanaro, S. (1988). *L'Italia nuova: Identità e sviluppo, 1861–1988.* Torino: G. Einaudi.

Lehrer, U. (2006). Willing the global city: Berlin's cultural strategies of interurban competition after 1989. In N. Brenner & R. Keil (Eds.), *The global cities reader* (pp. 332–338). London: Routledge.

Lever, W. F. (1991). Deindustrialization and the reality of the postindustrialist city. *Urban Studies, 28*(6), 983–999. https://doi.org/10.1080/00420989120081161.

Lewis, R. D. (2000). *Manufacturing Montreal: The making of an industrial landscape, 1850 to 1930.* Baltimore: Johns Hopkins University Press.

———. (2001). A city transformed: Manufacturing districts and suburban growth in Montreal, 1850–1929. *Journal of Historical Geography, 27*(1), 20–35. https://doi.org/10.1006/jhge.2000.0267.

———. (2004). *Manufacturing suburbs: Building work and home on the metropolitan fringe.* Philadelphia: Temple University Press.

Llewellyn, M. (2003). Polyvocalism and the public: "Doing" a critical historical geography of architecture. *Area, 35*(3), 264–270.

Loftus, A., March, H., & Nash, F. (2016). Water infrastructure and the making of financial subjects in the south east of England. *Water Alternatives, 9*(2), 319–335.

Luciani, A. N. (1976). *Movimento politico e lotte operaie alla Pirelli dal 1943 al 1946.* Milan: Università degli studi di Milano.

REFERENCES 185

Luke, N., & Kaika, M. (2019). Ripping the heart out of Ancoats: Collective action to defend infrastructures of social reproduction against gentrification. *Antipode, 51*(2), 579–600. https://doi.org/10.1111/anti.12468.

Lupo, G. (2020). *Le fabbriche che construirono L'Italia.* Milan: 24 Ore.

Macchione, P. (1987). *L'oro e il ferro: Storia della Franco Tosi.* Milan: Franco Angeli.

Manca, G. (2005). *Sul filo della memoria: Cinquanta anni di Pirelli e dintorni.* Milan: EGEA.

Marchetto, G. (2014). "Come ci difendevamo": Le lotte per la salute in fabbrica nei ricordi di un operaio Mirafiori. In G. Gallozzi (Ed.), *Il lavoro o la vita Cinema, salute, ambiente,* Annali, Archivio audiovisivo del movimento operaio e democratico (pp. 57–62). Arcidosso (GR), Italy: Effigi edizioni.

Melograni, P. (1980). *Gli industriali e Mussolini: Rapporti tra Confindustria e fascismo dal 1919 al 1929.* Milan: Longanesi.

Memo, F. (2007). I nuovi city builder nello sviluppo immobiliare di Milano. [Unpublished doctoral dissertation]. Università degli Studi Milano Bicocca.

Merli, S. (1972). *Proletariato di fabbrica e capitalismo industriale.* Florence: La Nuova Italia.

Merrifield, A. (1993). The struggle over place: Redeveloping American Can in Southeast Baltimore. *Transactions of the Institute of British Geographers, 18,* 102–121.

Meyer, L. (2008, February). Intervista a Renzo Baricelli, protagonista sindacale di allora: A 40 anni dal fatidico '68 gli operai della Pirelli ricordano. *Zona Nove, Giornale di Niguarda—Ca' Granda—Bicocca,* 1–3.

Mingione, E. (1994). Life strategies and social economies in the postfordist age. *International Journal of Urban and Regional Research, 18*(1), 24–45.

———. (1996). *Urban poverty and the underclass: A reader.* Oxford: Blackwell.

Mitchell, D. (1996). *The lie of the land: Migrant workers and the California landscape.* Minneapolis: University of Minnesota Press.

———. (2012). *They saved the crops: Labor, landscape, and the struggle over industrial farming in Bracero-era California.* Athens: University of Georgia Press.

Mitchener, B. (1993, June 8). Pirelli's new approach mirrors changes in Italy. *New York Times.* www.nytimes.com/1993/06/08/business/worldbusiness /IHT-pirellis-new-approach-mirrors-changes-in-italy.html.

Modolo, G. (1993, June 4). Immobili e finanza aiutano Pirellina. *La Repubblica,* 52.

Molotch, H. (1976). The city as a growth machine: Toward a political economy of place. *American Journal of Sociology, 82*(2), 309–332. www.jstor.org /stable/2777096.

186 REFERENCES

Montali, E. (2009). *1968: L'autunno caldo della Pirelli: Il ruolo del sindacato nelle lotte operaie della Bicocca*. Rome: Ediesse.

Montenegro, A. (1985). La Pirelli fra le due guerre mondiali. In P. Anelli, G. Bonvini, & A. Montenegro (Eds.), *Pirelli, 1914–1980: Strategia aziendale e relazioni industriali nella storia di una multinazionale:* Vol. 1, *Dalla prima guerra mondiale all'autunno caldo* (pp. 19–85). Milan: F. Angeli.

Mosciaro, M. (2018). *The real estate/financial complex: The cases of Brazil and Italy* [Unpublished doctoral dissertation]. Politecnico di Milano and KU Leuven.

Mosciaro, M., Kaika, M., & Engelen, E. (2024). Financializing healthcare and infrastructures of social reproduction: How to bankrupt a hospital and be unprepared for a pandemic. *Journal of Social Policy, 53*(2), 261–279. https://doi.org/10.1017/S004727942200023X.

Moulaert, F., & Nussbaumer, J. (2005). The social region: Beyond the territorial dynamics of the learning economy. *European Urban and Regional Studies, 12*(1), 45–64.

Moulaert, F., Rodríguez, A., & Swyngedouw, E. (2002). *The globalized city: Economic restructuring and social polarization in European cities*. Oxford: Oxford University Press.

Moulaert, F., & Sekia, F. (2003). Territorial innovation models: A critical survey. *Regional Studies, 37*(3), 289–302.

Muller, E. K. (2001). Industrial suburbs and the growth of metropolitan Pittsburgh, 1870–1920. *Journal of Historical Geography, 27*(1), 58–73. https://doi.org/10.1006/jhge.2000.0269.

Mumford, Lewis. (1934). *Technics and civilization*. London: Routledge and Kegan Paul.

Murray, F. (1983). The decentralisation of production: The decline of the mass-collective worker? *Capital and Class, 7*(1), 74–99.

Musso, S. (2023). Tempo di lavoro, tempo di vita: Qualche riflessione dalla storia. *Lavoro Diritti Europa*, (2), 2–8.

Myrdal, G. (1963). *Challenge to affluence*. New York: Pantheon Books.

Negrelli, S. (1983). *Sindacato, strategia d'impresa, produttività: Il caso Pirelli*. Milan: Fondazione regionale Pietro Seveso.

Negri, A. (2018). *From Factory to Metropolis*. London: Polity.

Nepoti, D. (2003). Cronaca della trasformazione di un'area industriale. In M. Bolocan Goldstein (Ed.), *Trasformazioni a Milano: Pirelli Bicocca direttrice nord-est* (pp. 61–92). Milan: F. Angeli.

Nurra, P. (1910). Un nuovo grande quartiere a Milano nella zona compresa tra Milano e Sesto San Giovanni. *Le Case Popoplari e le Città Giardino, 1*(6), 161–173.

Ondata di scioperi alla Pirelli. (1969, November 5). *Il Corriere della Sera*.

Oosterlynck, S., Van den Broeck, J., Albrechts, L., Moulaert, F., & Verhetsel, A. (2011). *Strategic spatial projects: Catalysts for change*. London: Routledge.

Paasi, A. (2013). Regional planning and the mobilization of "regional identity": From bounded spaces to relational complexity. *Regional Studies, 47*(8), 1206–1219. https://doi.org/10.1080/00343404.2012.661410.

Pajetta, G. C. (1945, August 25). La Pirelli dopo il 25 aprile. *L'Unità*. ISEC Archive, Milan.

Panzieri, R. (Ed.). (1961). *Quaderni rossi 1. Lotte operaie nello sviluppo capitalistico*. Milan: Edizioni Avanti.

Pavese, C. (1997). I caratteri originali dell'insediamento: Un tentativo di analisi comparata. In L. Trezzi (Ed.), *Sesto San Giovanni, 1880–1921: Economia e società: La trasformazione* (pp. 129–148). Milan: Skira.

Perna, C. (1980). *Classe, sindacato, operaismo al Petrolchimico di Porto Marghera: Appunti sull'autunno del '69 attraverso i volantini di fabbrica*. Rome: Editrice sindacale italiana.

Perulli, P. (1986). *Pirelli, 1980–1985: Le relazioni industriali. Negoziando l'incertezza*. Milan: F. Angeli.

Pieroni, A. (1971, May 8). I gruppuscoli in tuta da lavoro. *Il Corriere della Sera*.

Pinto, N. (1998). Finance capital revisited. In R. Bellofiore (Ed.), *Marxian economics: A reappraisal. Essays on volume III of Capital* (pp. 216–232). Basingstoke: Macmillan.

Pirelli. (1984). *Progetto Bicocca: Invito alla progettazione urbanistica e architettonica di un centro tecnologico integrato*. Milan: Electa.

———. (1986). *Progetto Bicocca*. Milan: Electa.

———. (1999). *Progetto Bicocca: 1985–1998*. Milan: Skira.

Pirelli & C. (1994). *Relazioni e bilancio al 31 dicembre 1991–1993*. Milan: Ufficio studi Pirelli.

———. (2010). *Annual Financial Report at December 31, 2010* (Vol. 1). www .annualreports.com/HostedData/AnnualReportArchive/p/OTC_ PPAMY_2010.pdf.

Pirelli SpA. (1971). *Relazione e bilancio al 31 dicembre 1970*. Archivio Storico Fondazione Pirelli, Milan.

———. (1976). *Rapporto su ricerca e sviluppo*. Archivio Storico Fondazione Pirelli, Milan.

———. (1982–87). *Bilancio Industrie Pirelli, 1982–1987*. Archivio Storico Fondazione Pirelli, Milan.

———. (1991). *Relazioni e bilancio al 31 dicembre 1990*. Archivio Storico Fondazione Pirelli, Sezione Bilanci Collection, Milan.

———. (1992). *Relazioni e bilancio al 31 dicembre 1991*. Archivio Storico Fondazione Pirelli, Sezione Bilanci Collection, Milan.

188 REFERENCES

———. (1993). *Relazioni e bilancio al 31 dicembre 1992*. Archivio Storico Fondazione Pirelli, Sezione Bilanci Collection, Milan.

Pirelli, A. (1946). *La Pirelli: Vita di una azienda industriale*. Milan: Industrie Grafiche A. Nicola.

———. (1948, November). Questa nostra rivista. *Pirelli: Rivista di Informazione e di Tecnica*, (1), 8.

———. (1984). *Taccuini, 1922/1943*. Bologna: Il Mulino.

Pirelli, B. E. (Ed.). (2002). *Alberto e Giovanni Pirelli: Legami e conflitti. Lettere, 1931-1965*. Milan: Rosellina Archinto.

Pirelli, G. (1990). Qualche mese a Berlino (1942). In N. Tranfaglia (Ed.), *Giovanni Pirelli: Un mondo che crolla. Lettere, 1938-1943* (pp. 181-221). Milan: Rosellina Archinto.

Pirelli, G. B. (1907). "Relazione sulla Società Anonima Quartiere Industriale Nord Milano." Archivio storico Fondazione Pirelli.

Pirelli, L. (1999, October 27). Il rimorso di un grande imprenditore. *La Repubblica*. Interview by E. Scalfari. https://ricerca.repubblica.it/repubblica /archivio/repubblica/1999/10/27/il-rimorso-di-un-grande-imprenditore .html.

Pirelli, P. (1930). L'industria della gomma e dei conduttori elettrici in Italia. In *Industrie italiane illustrate dai loro capi: Lezioni tenute ad iniziativa della R. Scuola di Ingegneria di Pisa, sotto gli auspici della Confederazione generale fascista dell'industria italiana* (pp. 33-53). Livorno: Edizione della rivista L'Unione industriale.

Pirelli Bicocca: Scuola di comunismo. (1971, December 11). *Servire il popolo*. Archivio Storico Pirelli (no. 17, "Brigate Rosse e proteste," year 1971/72, N. 194004), Milan.

Pirola, D., & Magistroni, A. (Eds.). (2008). *Pirelli racconti di lavoro: Uomini, macchine, idee* [Pirelli, stories of work: Men, machines and ideas]. Milan: Mondadori Electa.

Polese, F. (Ed.). (2003). *Giovanni Battista Pirelli: Viaggio di istruzione all'estero: Diario, 1870-1871*. Venice: Marsilio.

Pollard, J., & Storper, M. (1996). A tale of twelve cities: Metropolitan employment change in dynamic industries in the 1980s. *Economic Geography, 72*(1), 1-22. https://doi.org/10.2307/144499.

Pons, G. (2008, November 24). Ascesa e declino dell'uomo che sognava di essere l'Avvocato. *La Repubblica*. https://ricerca.repubblica.it/repubblica/archivio /repubblica/2008/11/24/ascesa-declino-delluomo-che-sognava-di-essere .html?ref=search.

Regione Lombardia. (1985). *Schema di protocollo di intesa per la ristrutturazione dell'area Pirelli Bicocca e relativi processi di rilocalizzazione e di nuovo insediamento*. Milan: Regione Lombardia.

Reis, N. (2017). Finance capital and the water crisis: Insights from Mexico. *Globalizations, 14*(6), 976–990. https://doi.org/10.1080/14747731.2017.1315118.

Riganti, P. (2003). Progetto Bicocca: Il sistema della mobilità. In M. Bolocan Goldstein (Ed.), *Trasformazioni a Milano: Pirelli Bicocca direttrice nord-est* (pp. 115–131). Milan: Franco Angeli.

———. (2007). Mobilità senza rete: Usi del suolo e trasporti nella regione urbana. In M. Bolocan Goldstein & B. Bonfantini (Eds.), *Milano incompiuta: Interpretazioni urbanistiche del mutamento. Quaderni del Dipartimento di Architettura e Pianificazione* (pp. 97–106). Milan: Franco Angeli.

Riley, M., & Harvey, D. (2007). Talking geography: On oral history and the practice of geography. *Social and Cultural Geography, 8*(3), 345–351. https://doi.org/10.1080/14649360701488765.

Rimoldi, L. (2017). *Lavorare alla Pirelli-Bicocca: Antropologia delle memorie operaie.* Bologna: Clueb.

Roggero, G. (2019). *L'operaismo politico italiano: Genealogia, storia, metodo.* Rome: DeriveApprodi.

Rohse, M., Day, R., & Llewellyn, D. (2020, March). Towards an emotional energy geography: Attending to emotions and affects in a former coal mining community in South Wales, UK. *Geoforum, 110*, 136–146. https://doi.org/10.1016/j.geoforum.2020.02.006.

Rutland, T. (2010). The financialization of urban redevelopment. *Geography Compass, 2*(6), 1–12. https://doi.org/10.1111/j.1749-8198.2010.00348.x.

Ruzzenenti, M. (2020). Dossier "1970": Le radici operaie dell'ambientalismo italiano. *Altronovecento,* (43). https://altronovecento.fondazionemicheletti.eu/dossier-1970-le-radici-operaie-dellambientalismo-italiano/.

Scavino, M. (2018). *Potere operai: La storia, la teoria.* Rome: DeriveApprodi.

———. (2021). L'operaismo italiano dagli anni Sessanta agli anni Settanta: Continuità e metamorfosi di un fenomeno di classe. In M. Thirion, E. Santalena, & C. Mileschi (Eds.), *Contratto o rivoluzione! L'autunno caldo tra operaismo e storiografia.* Turin: Accademia University Press.

Sclavi, M. (1974). *Lotta di classe e organizzazione operaia: Pirelli Bicocca Milano ('68-'69), OM-FIAT Brescia ('54-'72).* Milan: Mazzotta.

Scott, A. J. (1988). *Metropolis.* Berkeley: University of California Press.

Scotti, M. (2018). *Vita di Giovanni Pirelli: Tra cultura e impegno militante.* Rome: Donzelli.

Scotto di Luzio, A. (2001). L'industria dell'informazione. In D. Bigazzi & M. Meriggi (Eds.), *Le regioni dall'unità a oggi: Vol. 16, La Lombardia,* Storia d'Italia (pp. 331–384). Turin: Einaudi.

Secchi, B. (Ed.). (1984). *Progetto Bicocca: Invito alla progettazione urbanistica e architettonica di un centro tecnologico integrato.* Milan: Pirelli SpA.

190 REFERENCES

Secchia, P., & Frassati, F. (1965). *Storia della Resistenza*. Rome: Editori Riuniti.

Segio, S. (2005). *Miccia corta: Una storia di Prima Linea*. Rome: Derive Approdi.

———. (2006). *Una vita in Prima Linea*. Milan: Rizzoli.

Sicca, L., & Izzo, F. (1995). *La gestione dei processi di Turnaround: Un caso esemplare: La Pirelli S.p.A*. Naples: Edizioni Scientifiche Italiane.

Smith, N. (1996). *The New Urban Frontier: Gentrification and the Revanchist City*. New York: Routledge.

Società italiana Pirelli. (1925, September 2). *Verbale assemblea straordinaria della Società italiana Pirelli* (d. 1423). Archivio Storico Fondazione Pirelli, Milan.

Soldini, A. P. (1952). Tranquilli a Induno i vecchi della Pirelli. *Pirelli: Rivista di Informazione e di Tecnica*, (5), 38–39.

Sombart, W. (1967). *Il capitalismo moderno*. Torino: Utet.

Stovall, T. (2012). *Paris and the spirit of 1919: Consumer struggles, transnationalism, and revolution*. Cambridge: Cambridge University Press.

Suffia, I. (2020). *"Fatti e Notizie" di welfare alla Pirelli (1950–1967)*. Milan: Franco Angeli.

Swyngedouw, E., & Ward, C. (2022). Land as an asset. In M. Hyötyläinen & R. Beauregard (Eds.), *The political economy of land: Rent, financialization and resistance* (pp. 40–55). London: Routledge.

Thompson, E. P. (1964). *The making of the English working class*. New York: Pantheon Books.

———. (1981). *Società patrizia, cultura plebea: Otto saggi di antropologia storica sull'Inghilterra del Settecento*. Torino: Einaudi.

Tilly, C. (1986). *The Contentious French*. Cambridge, MA: Harvard University Press.

Tranfaglia, N. (Ed.). (1990). *Giovanni Pirelli: Un mondo che crolla. Lettere, 1938–1943*. Milan: Rosellina Archinto.

———. (2008). Un "Romanzo industriale e marinaro": La formazione di Alberto Pirelli e la Pirelli nei primi trent'anni. *Studi Storici, 49*(3), 667–753. www .jstor.org/stable/20568084.

Tronti, M. (1963). Il piano del capitale. *Quaderni Rossi*, (3), 44–73.

———. (2009). *Noi operaisti*. Rome: DeriveApprodi.

Trotta, G., & Milana, F. (Eds.). (2008). *L'operaismo degli anni Sessanta: Da Quaderni Rossi a classe operaia*. Rome: DeriveApprodi.

Tsoukalas, K. (1981). *The Greek tragedy*. Athens: Nea Synora—Livani.

Turani, G. (1992a, February 16). E cuccia disse a Pirelli: Meglio lasciare. *Il Corriere della Sera*, 15.

———. (1992b, January 19). Quelle critiche a Pirelli e le mosse per il rilancio. *Il Corriere della Sera*, 14.

Unità Tecnica Pianificazione Generale. (1988). Variante al Piano Regolatore Generale vigente. In *Deliberazione della Giunta Regionale Lombardia*, no. 29471. Milan: Regione Lombardia.

Vall, N. (2011). *Cultural region: North east England, 1945-2000*. Manchester: Manchester University Press.

Valota, G. (2008). *Streikertransport: La deportazione politica nell'area industriale di Sesto San Giovanni, 1943-1945*. Milan: Guerini Associati.

Varini, V. (2012). Costruire un'impresa: Il welfare alla Pirelli tra Otto e Novecento. In L. Trezzi & V. Varini (Eds.), *Comunità di lavoro: Le opere sociali delle imprese e degli imprenditori tra Ottocento e Novecento* (pp. 115-142). Milan: Edizioni Angelo Guerini e Associati.

———. (2023). Eccitare il lavoro: Il welfare aziendale, una trama di lungo periodo. *Impresa Sociale*, (2), 19-31.

Vergani, G., Romano, S., Colombo, U., Tadini, E., & Irace, F. (1997). *Pirelli, 1872-1997: Centoventicinque anni di imprese*. Milan: Scheiwiller.

Vergopoulos, K. (1975). *The agricultural question in Greece*. Athens: Hexantas.

Vicari, S., & Molotch, H. (1990). Building Milan: Alternative machines of growth. *International Journal of Urban and Regional Research, 14*(4), 602-624. https://doi.org/10.1111/j.1468-2427.1990.tb00159.x.

Vicari Haddock, S., Tornaghi, C., & Mugnano, S. (2005). New visions of the territory: Urban renewal and new public spaces. In E. dell'Agnese (Ed.), *La Bicocca e il suo territorio: Memoria e progetto* (pp. 166-193). Milan: Skira.

Walker, R. A. (1978). Two sources of uneven development under advanced capitalism: Spatial differentiation and capital mobility. *Review of Radical Political Economics, 10*(3), 28-38.

———. (2001). Industry builds the city: The suburbanization of manufacturing in the San Francisco Bay Area, 1850-1940. *Journal of Historical Geography, 27*(1), 36-57. http://dx.doi.org/10.1006/jhge.2000.0268.

Walker, R. A., & Lewis, R. D. (2001). Beyond the crabgrass frontier: Industry and the spread of North American cities, 1850-1950. *Journal of Historical Geography, 27*(1), 3-19. http://dx.doi.org/10.1006/jhge.2000.0266.

Ward, C. (2022). Land financialisation, planning informalisation and gentrification as statecraft in Antwerp. *Urban Studies, 59*(9), 1837-1854. https://doi.org/10.1177/00420980211028235.

Ward, C., & Swyngedouw, E. (2018). Neoliberalisation from the ground up: Insurgent capital, regional struggle, and the assetisation of land. *Antipode, 50*(4), 1077-1097. https://doi.org/10.1111/anti.12387.

Wilson, D., & Keil, R. (2008). The real creative class. *Social and Cultural Geography, 9*(8), 841-847.

Wood, A. (2004). The scalar transformation of the U.S. commercial property-development industry: A cautionary note on the limits of globalization.

192   REFERENCES

Economic Geography, 80(2), 119–140. https://doi.org/10.1111/j.1944-8287 .2004.tb00304.x.

Wright, E. O. (1994). *Interrogating Inequality: Essays on Class Analysis, Socialism and Marxism.* New York: Verso.

Zanetti, A. M. (2003). *I lavoratori dell'impresa globale: Le relazioni di lavoro in Pirelli tra strategie globali e destini locali.* Milan: F. Angeli.

Zarycki, T. (2007). History and regional development: A controversy over the "right" interpretation of the role of history in the development of the Polish regions. *Geoforum, 38*(3), 485–493. https://doi.org/10.1016/j.geoforum .2006.11.002.

Zhang, Y. (2018). Grabbing land for equitable development? Reengineering land dispossession through securitising land development rights in Chongqing. *Antipode, 50*(4), 1120–1140. https://doi.org/10.1111/anti.12390.

Index

Accornero, Aris, 33

advertising: international advertising campaigns, 26, 53, 159; promoting Bicocca, 157, 163, 169; public image in, 126; tire industry and, 2; workers' histories used in, 169

aestheticization: industrial discipline and, 8; of spaces of production, 38–41

Agnelli, Edoardo, 57

Agnelli, Giovanni, 55–56

Agnelli family, 143

"Albania" (Bicocca recycling site), 147, 148

alliances: building broad social alliances, 96–99; class alliances, 17, 156; local strategic alliances, 123–30, 132–33, 153–54; over land, 169; regional power alliances, 153; renegotiation of historical alliances, 154, 163, 164; shifts in global and local alliances, 138, 170, 172; understanding of, 170

antagonism: between capital and labor, 33; class antagonism, 14, 42, 97, 138; small scale enterprises and, 27–28; understanding of, 170

anti-Fascist resistance: Bicocca and, 6, 10, 16, 45, 67, 71, 155; collaborative management and, 72–74; cultural space and, 75–80; factory villages and, 63;

67; land as space for, 10–11, 67–68; production spaces as spaces for, 68–72; restoration of corporate power and, 72, 74–75; working class and, 1. *See also* CLN (Comitato di Liberazione Nazionale) (National Liberation Committee); Fascism

architectural order: of Bicocca, 8, 19, 39–41, 156–59; Bicocca Technocity and, 126–27, 131, 150, 151; of Borgo Pirelli, 59; decaffeinated urbanity and, 16–17, 161–63; of global financial sector, 5; historical suburb projects, 151; importance of, 59; Pirelli Tower, 76–78; ruptures in physical and social space, 159–61

Arcimboldi manor house, 35, 164

Arcimboldi theater, 17, 35, 38, 150, 152, 157, 164

arson incidents, 12, 82, 102

art gallery, 17, 152, 156, 162

art spaces, 160, 161, 162, 164

Arturo Soria y Mata's Linear City (Ciudad Lineal) (Madrid), 37

assetization: economic success of, 17, 156; of industrial land, 2, 13–14, 43, 118–21; of land and workers in Bicocca, 169; lived dimension of, 133; transformative role of, 4, 156

193

INDEX

asset(s): industrial land as, 3, 7, 13–14; land as a financial asset, 2, 4, 7, 13–14; production of land as financialized asset, 5, 7, 14–16; real estate assets, 4, 14, 15, 16, 118–19, 138, 148. *See also* financial asset(s); land revanchism

auto industry, 84, 140–41. *See also* BMW; FIAT; Volkswagen

Autostrada del Sole (Highway of the Sun), 84

Banca Commerciale Italiana, 36
Banca Feltrinelli, 35, 36
Banca Pisa, 36
Barca, Stefania, 169
Benenati, E., 58–59
Benjamin, Walter, 47
Berardi, Vincenzo (pseudonym), 92, 100, 115
Bianchi, G., 83, 85
Bicocca: about, 1; anti-Fascist activism and, 6; assetization of land and workers, 168; class struggle around, 168; Cultural Center, 10–11, 68, 78–80; evolution of, 168; financialization of land and workers, 168; fundamental role of government in conversion of, 170; as industrial production site, 168; industrial trade unionism in, 168; land as accumulation strategy around, 168; land financialization at, 169; land financialization in, 167; as living laboratory for radicalization, 11; *Operaismo* movement and, 6–7; Pirelli's acquisition of, 8, 35–36; production lines at, 13; real estate value extraction in, 169; reinvention as historical suburb, 168, 169; sociopolitical role of, 11; workers' movement in, 19; workers' resistance against Fascism during WWII in, 168. *See also* Pirelli
Bicocca historical suburb project. *See* historical suburb project
Bicocca Technocity. *See* Technocity
biennio rosso, 46
Bigatti, G., 54, 55
Bigazzi, D., 62
Bjornerud, Marcia, 1
BMW, 141
Boccioni, Umberto, 23–24
Bolchini, P., 83, 84
Bolshevism, 47, 55, 82
bonum facere practice, 61
Borgo Pirelli (workers' village), 9, 46, 58–59, 63, 78, 161–62

Breda, 36, 37, 69
Bridgestone, 140
La Brusada (the Burnt House), 35, 39, 78

Cafagna, L., 62
Cantone, Eugenio, 25
capital: changes in nature of, 143; diversification, 168; under Fascism, 53–56; fears of working-class movement, 47; global dynamics of, 138, 167, 172; industrial land mobilization as financial asset, 7; land revanchism and, 12, 82, 108–11; land's transformative role in accumulation of, 168; plans to produce skilled labor force, 98; social spaces returned to, 7; speculative capt, 150; use of land as lever by, 12; workers' village to mitigate conflict over, 168. *See also* accumulation of capital; capitalism; land revanchism
capital accumulation: crises in, 5, 11, 12, 81; demand for overturning of, 98; global, 4–5, 139, 167; industrial land as, 13, 15, 117, 118, 153; institutionalization and, 62; land revanchism and, 12–13; strategies of, 3, 119–23, 168; transition to new forms of, 4, 5, 82, 154, 168
capitalism: about, 2; evolution of, 168; high-tech capitalism, 7; land's transformative role in capital accumulation, 168; phases of global finance capitalism, 169; shift in class struggle around, 168; speculative capitalism, 7, 145, 148; Technocity as high-tech, 168. *See also* industrial capitalism
Cavallari, Alberto, 60
CEAT, 85
CGIL (Confederazione Generale Italiana del Lavoro) (trade union), 83, 87, 89, 90, 92, 113
Christian Democrat Party, 73, 82, 83, 84
churches, 38, 61, 164
CIP (Compagnie Internationale Pirelli), 50, 52
CISL (Confederazione Italiana Sindacati Lavoratori) (trade union), 83, 90, 92
Citroen, 109
city planning, 34–37, 80
class consciousness: class struggles over land and, 41–44; CUB and, 89, 91; forging of, 6, 8–10; industrial land and, 45–46; industrial paternalism and, 61–64; loyalties and, 47; as spatially grounded, 3–4

INDEX 195

class homogeneity, 9, 46, 59, 97, 161

class issues: assetization of industrial land and, 2; class conflict in industrializing era, 7; class identity formation, 9; class struggles over land, 7, 9, 12–13; contemporary class struggles, 169; documentation and, 170; lived dimensions of struggles, 169; nineteenth century struggle over land, 167; production of space and, 2, 6, 8–9; research on, 170–72; shift in class struggles, 168. *See also* Italy's Stalingrad

CLN (Comitato di Liberazione Nazionale) (National Liberation Committee), 10, 62, 67, 69, 73

CNR (Consiglio Nazionale delle Ricerche) (National Research Council), 125

Cofferati, Sergio, 113 ˙

Comitato di Liberazione Nazionale (CLN) (National Liberation Committee), 10, 62, 67, 69, 73

Comitato Unitario di Base (CUB), 88–93, 102, 113

Communist Party, 70, 73, 74, 82, 83, 89, 92, 97

Communist-Socialist coalition, 82

Compagnie Internationale Pirelli (CIP), 50, 52

competitors: CEAT, 85; Continental, 140–41, 144; Dunlop, 49, 109, 110, 120, 140; Firestone, 39, 49; Goodrich, 39, 49; Goodyear, 39, 49, 103, 112, 140; Michelin, 49, 53, 68, 85, 103, 108–9, 112, 140; Sumimoto, 140*tab.*. *See also* tire industry

Conca Messina, Silvia A., 27

Confederazione Generale Italiana del Lavoro (CGIL) (trade union), 83, 87, 89, 90, 92, 113

Confederazione Italiana Sindacati Lavoratori (CISL) (trade union), 83, 90, 92

CONFINDUSTRIA (General Confederation of Italian Industry), 125

Consiglio di Gestione (CDG), 75

Consiglio Nazionale delle Ricerche (National Research Council) (CNR), 125

Conti, Ettore, 55–56

Conti Affair, 141

Continental, 14, 140–41, 144

Corporativismo, 9, 45, 54, 57–60

Il Corriere della Sera (periodical), 18, 26, 54–55, 89

Crespi, Cristoforo, 38

CUB (Comitato Unitario di Base), 88–93, 102, 113

Cuccia, Enrico, 142

Cultural Center, 10–11, 68, 78–80

Daimler-Benz, 141

Dalla Costa, 97

Danusso, Arturo, 76

decaffeinated urbanity, 16–17, 155–56, 161–63. *See also* financialized land

Declaration of Intentions Protocol (*Schema di Protocollo di Intesa*) (*Protocollo*), 115

deindustrialization, 12–13, 108, 114, 125, 169

design: for Bicocca Technocity, 131, 150; decaffeinated urbanity, 16–17; of historical suburb project, 157–58, 159, 163; importance of, 8, 59; paternalistic principles and, 39

disciplined labor: importance of, 7, 28, 31, 59; industrial age and, 30; of Italian discharged soldiers, 7

diversified products, 24, 52, 115, 149*fig.*

documentation, 7, 18–19, 170

Donegani, Guido, 56

Dunlop, 49, 109, 110, 120, 140

economic issues: economic geography, 173n4; economic value added (EVA), 143; national economy after Fascism, 73; regional economics, 173n4; understanding of global economy, 170; use of land as financial asset and, 168

Einaudi, Luigi, 54–55

ENEA (National Agency for New Technologies and Sustainable Economic Development), 125

entertainment spaces, 150, 160, 162. *See also* art spaces; theater

entrepreneurs: *bonum facere* practice, 61; city planning and, 36; class conflict concerns of, 27, 31, 32; cooperation with workers, 33; EVA production by, 143; Fascist party and, 55–56, 58; industrial capitalism and, 27; industrial paternalism and, 34; as investors, 25; labor discipline concerns of, 29; land financialization and, 44; paternalism and, 62; philanthropy of, 26; solidarity network, 8; solidarity network and, 41–42; workers' rights and, 54. *See also* Conti, Ettore; Crespi, Cristoforo; Pirelli, Giovanni Battista; Pirelli, Leopoldo; Rossi, Alessandro; Silvestri, Giovanni

196　INDEX

Ethiopia, 56
ethnic issues, 42, 169
Eureka moment, 13–14, 118–19, 120, 121.
　See also financialized land
European Periphery, 171
EVA (economic value added), 143

factories: Corporativismo and, 9; factory
　management, 10; living memories of, 19
Falck (company), 56, 69
Falck, Giorgio Enrico, 56
Falck family, 143
far-left groups, 12, 82
far-right groups, 12, 82
Fascism: bans on strikes and workers' meet-
　ings, 54; Corporativismo, 9, 45, 54,
　57–60; entrepreneurs and, 55–56, 58;
　forced welfare under, 57–60, 61; indus-
　trial land's sociopolitical role under, 10,
　67; industrial paternalism and, 16,
　45–46, 47, 61–64, 127, 139; Italian
　industry under, 53–56; national economy
　after, 73; Pirelli's distancing from, 76;
　resistance against, 44, 69–70, 88, 162,
　168. See also anti-Fascist resistance; Mus-
　solini, Benito
Fascist Industrial Confederation, 57
feminist movement, 3, 6, 11, 16, 81, 90,
　96–99
FIAT: Agnelli and, 55, 56, 57; Fascism and,
　57; industrial action at, 93, 100; as living
　laboratory for radicalization, 99; loan, 52;
　Michelin and, 109; Operaismo movement
　and, 96, 99–100; Pirelli partnership,
　109; SISI and, 83–84. See also Agnelli,
　Giovanni
Filcem CIGL, 144
finance: about, 7–8; global dynamics of capi-
　tal, 167. See also global finances; land
　financialization
financialization: capital switching from
　industrial production to, 147; disembod-
　ied nature of debates on, 170; as lived
　process, 7, 14–16, 167, 170, 171,
　174n5; research on, 170–71. See also
　land financialization
financialized land: as asset, 7, 14–16, 118–
　21; global dynamics of, 167; as no-man's
　land, 16–17, 155–56, 164–65; produc-
　tion of, 14–16. See also land
　financialization
Firestone, 39, 49
flexible peasantry, 7, 23, 27–29, 41

Fordism, 16, 83, 127
Frassati, F., 69
Fumagalli, Fabio, 144

Gappisti (guerrilla group), 69, 174nn1(ch3)
gender issues, 9, 169
General Confederation of Italian Industry
　(CONFINDUSTRIA), 125
gentrification, 169
geographical space: financialization of land as
　process in, 167; financialized land as,
　167, 170; production and trade locations,
　48; urbanization and, 122, 130
global issues: of capital, 138, 167, 172;
　financialized land as, 167; global capital
　accumulation, 4–5, 139, 167; global
　economy, 132, 170; global finances, 5,
　167, 169, 170, 172; Global North, 49,
　171; Global South, 42, 171; global tire
　market, 50; producers, 140; regenera-
　tion, 169; shift in global alliances, 138,
　170, 172
Global North, 49, 171
Global South, 42, 171
Goodrich, 39, 49
Goodyear, 39, 49, 103, 112, 140
Gorz, A., 114
government: fundamental role in conversion
　of Bicocca of, 170; tire industry and, 84
Gramsci, Antonio, 70
Great Bicocca. See historical suburb project
Greece, 71, 171
Guizzi, Chiara, 53

Haila, A., 122
Hangar Bicocca (art gallery), 17, 152, 156,
　162
Harvey, David, 154, 165
healthcare, 9, 32, 46, 164, 172
hierarchy: of buildings, 39, 59; disciplined
　labor and, 7, 30; importance of, 10, 59;
　of loyalties, 46, 47, 63
highway network, 84
historical suburb project: architect, 150,
　151; design of, 157–58, 159, 163; local
　authorities and, 152–54; Nassi and, 159;
　neoliberalism and, 16; Pirelli and, 132,
　138, 149–52; redevelopment as, 15;
　Technocity project and, 147–49; working
　class and, 161. See also Arcimboldi
　theater; Hangar Bicocca (art gallery);
　Milano Bicocca University
Hot Autumn of '69, 113

INDEX

housing: at Bicocca, 69; flexible planning regulations and, 151; high-end apartments, 161, 163; in historical suburb project, 16; industrial paternalism and, 38, 41, 61; at Krupp plant, 34; labor unrest and, 31; Pirelli's commitment to, 79; urban development in Milan, 37; as welfare provision, 9, 32. *See also* Borgo Pirelli (workers' village)

IACI (Iniziative Agricole Commerciali Italiane), 148
IACP (Istituto Autonomo per le Case Popolari) (Institute for Social Housing), 58
Imprese Electtriche Conti, 56. *See also* Conti, Ettore
industrial action. *See Operaismo* movement
industrialists: entrepreneurs and, 55–56; paternalism and, 61; struggles over industrial labor, 7; support for industrial democracy, 55. *See also* Pirelli, Giovanni Battista
industrial land: as an asset, 7, 13–14; assetization of, 2, 4, 17, 43–44, 133, 169; Bicocca as production site, 168; collective ownership perceptions of, 9, 45, 64; as cultural space, 75–80; forging of class consciousness and, 3–4, 6, 9, 44, 45, 61–64; material and symbolic roles of, 3, 6, 8, 10, 12, 63, 108; production of, 14–16; radicalizing social claims over, 11–12; sociopolitical role of, 8–9, 10; as unproductive asset, 23–26, 43–44
industrial paternalism: aestheticization of spaces of production and, 38–41; class consciousness and, 42, 45; end of, 86, 143; under Fascism, 45–46, 127, 139; feudalism and, 42–43; impact of, 61–64; international examples of, 34–35; lack of state intervention and, 47; Pirelli and, 8, 16, 35, 86, 90, 126, 155; rise of, 31–33; solidarity networks and, 42; spaces and, 41; Taylorism and, 35, 39. *See also Corporativismo*
industrial production: crises in, 11; crisis in, 7; expansion of, 28
industry: about, 7–8; commodity production, 14–16; downturns in, 168; industrial democracy, 55; industrial discipline, 8; industrial labor, 7, 7–8; industrial trade unionism, 168; layoffs, 168; restructuring, 168. *See also specific industries*
Iniziative Agricole Commerciali Italiane (IACI), 148

IRI (National Institute for Industrial Reconstruction), 56
Istituto Autonomo per le Case Popolari (IACP) (Institute for Social Housing), 58
Italian Communist Party (PCI), 92, 97
Italian Road Initiative Company (Società per lo Sviluppo Delle Iniziative Stradali Italiane) (SISI), 83–84
Italy's Stalingrad, 11–12, 16, 81–82, 88, 100, 155. *See also* industrial land; radicalization

Keil, R., 162
Knight Frank & Rutley, 148
Krupp, Friedrich, 30, 34

labor force: creation of disciplined, 28; Fascism and, 54; higher education institutions and, 98; low-cost labor force, 28; morphing of, 4; skilled labor force, 98; struggles of industrialists over, 7; students as members of, 98
labor militancy, 11, 12, 81, 101, 103, 107
labor movement: collective labor agreements, 33; under Fascism, 53–56, 62; paternalism and, 41–43; strategies of, 87; weakening of, 12, 13, 82. *See also* strikes; unionism; workers' movements
labor relations: Bicocca and, 168; challenges for, 86; contracts and, 62; difficulties with, 54; evolution of, 168; mediating, 43; productive modernization and, 97; restructuring of, 7; Technocity project and, 111; workers' village to mitigate conflict in, 168; Zanetti on, 146
land: as catalyst, 8–10, 13; contemporary alliances over, 169; local class struggle over, 167; as reclaimed from workers, 12–13, 168; as space for political action, 10–11; as stronghold of workers' resistance against Fascism during WWII, 168; symbolic function, 168; transformative role in capital accumulation of, 168; as unproductive asset, 23–26; workers, 10–11. *See also* peasantry; space
land financialization: in Bicocca, 167; class issues and, 167; documentation and, 7, 170; as geographically grounded, 167; as historicized process, 167; as lived process, 7, 14–16, 167, 170, 171, 174n5; research on, 174n4; as socially embodied, 167. *See also* Bicocca; financialization; financialized land

landowners, 123, 168. *See also* Pirelli

land revanchism: assetization of land and, 13; capital accumulation and, 12–13; capital and, 12, 82, 108–11; completion of, 119; defined, 7; Eureka moment and, 13–14, 118; industrial production crisis and, 7; as lever to reclaim power, 12–13; by Pirelli in Bicocca, 168; transition to high-tech capitalism and, 7, 117; unmaking the working class and, 12–13, 107–8, 133; as violent act, 12; workers' movement and, 7. *See also* land revanchism

layoffs, 12, 15, 81, 85, 133, 138, 139, 144, 146–47, 168

Le Case Popolari e le Città Giardino (periodical), 36

Lewis, R. D., 34

life histories, 18–19, 170

lived financialization research, 170–71

livelihoods: displacement of, 172; financialization of, 169

Lösch, August, 173n4

Lotta Femminista (Feminist Struggle), 97

low wages, 7, 31

loyalty: factory loyalty, 9, 44, 47; hierarchy of, 10, 46, 47, 63; industrialists' loyalty to city, 76, 78; industrialists' loyalty to Fascists, 57; industrial paternalism and, 45–46, 47, 63; multiplicity of loyalties, 10, 46–47, 63; place loyalty, 28, 117, 131–32, 142–45, 152–53, 168; working-class consciousness and, 47

Lupo, G., 164

manufacturing suburbs, 34

Marelli family, 143

marginalization: of Bicocca's historical residents, 160–61, 162; of radical workers' organization, 113; of workers, 19; of working class, 169

Marx, Karl, 30, 43–44, 96

Marzotto, Gaetano, 38

MCI (Milano Centrale Immobiliare), 138, 148–49, 149*fig.*, 156

means of production: management's resuming of control of, 74; turning flexible peasantry into, 28–29; workers' appropriation of, 10–11, 16, 63–64, 67–68, 73, 81, 155; workers' return of, 80

Mediobanca, 142, 143

methodology, 17–20, 170–72

Michelin, 49, 53, 68, 85, 103, 108–9, 112, 140

Milan: about, 1–2; Bicocca reinvented as historical suburb of, 168; evolution of, 168; General Master Plan, 128–30; industrial district northeast of, 8; industrial land at Bicocca, 167; industry of, 167; mixed-use spaces for, 19, 156, 164, 168; post-Fordist development and, 123, 124*fig.*, 131, 139, 152; riots, 8, 32, 34; wildcat strikes in Milan, 11, 81; working class of, 167. *See also* Bicocca

Milano Bicocca University, 17, 19, 112, 125, 151–52, 156, 157, 163. *See also* students

Milano Centrale Immobiliare (MCI), 138, 148–49, 149*fig.*, 156

Minoletti, Fondo Giulio, 78

mixed-use spaces, 19, 156, 164, 168

Mocera, Gianmario, 144

modernization, conflict and, 26–27

Modrone, Visconti di, 25

Molotch, H., 123, 130

Montecatini (company), 56. *See also* Donegani, Guido

Montenegro, A., 52, 54, 56, 71

Morgan Stanley Real Estate Funds, 145, 149

Mumford, Lewis, 30

Municipal Urban Policies Framework (*Documento di inquadramento delle politiche urbanistiche comunali*), 130

Murray, F., 116

Museo delle Industrie Pirelli, 53

Mussolini, Benito, 8–9, 45, 47, 53–56, 57, 68. *See also* Fascist party

Myrdal, Gunnar, 114

Nassi, Giovanni: on 1970s crisis, 102–3; Bicocca historical suburb project and, 159; on CUB and Red Brigades, 102; on housing for workers, 58; on land as means of accumulation, 120; on land development, 147–48; on Leopoldo Pirelli, 112; on managerial roles, 18; on Pirelli transport plans, 37; on Technocity project, 129–30

National Agency for New Technologies and Sustainable Economic Development (ENEA), 125

National Institute for Industrial Reconstruction (IRI), 56

National Liberation Committee (Comitato di Liberazione Nazionale) (CLN), 10, 67, 69, 73

National Research Council (Consiglio Nazionale delle Ricerche) (CNR), 125

neo-Fascist groups, 12, 82

INDEX

neoliberalism: business/city rapport under, 153; government's role in, 170; historical suburbs and, 16; mainstreaming of, 114; workers as underclass, 13

Nervi, Pier Luigi, 76

Nitti, Francesco Saverio, 61

no-man's land, 16–17, 155–56, 164–65. *See also* decaffeinated urbanity

Olivetti family, 143

OND (Opera Nazionale Dopolavoro), 57

Operaismo movement, 6–7, 11, 16, 63, 81, 88, 89, 96–99, 101, 155

Opera Nazionale Dopolavoro (OND), 57

Partito Socialista Italiano di Unità Proletaria (Proletarian Unity) (PSIUP), 72

paternalism. *See* industrial paternalism

PCI (Italian Communist Party), 92, 97. *See also* Communist party

Pellegrini, Bellavite, 56

Piano di Lottizzazione, 130

Pirelli (company), 56; about, 1–2; diversification of, 24, 25–26; in financial capitalism, 168; financial debts, 103; first factory, 30; founding of, 25; in high-tech industry, 168; land revanchism in Bicocca by, 168; management team, 18, 19; Milan and, 24; in real estate, 168; Research and Development unit, 54; as tire-manufacturing company, 168; as transnational holding company, 168; use of land as financial asset, 168. *See also* Bicocca; Compagnie Internationale Pirelli (CIP); Pirelli & C.; Pirelli family; Società italiana Pirelli (SIP)

Pirelli, Alberto (son of GBP), 25, 39, 47, 48, 49, 50, 52, 55–56, 60, 69, 71, 72, 73–74, 76, 78

Pirelli, Giovanni Battista: acquisition of Bicocca, 8, 23; on company control, 50, 52; concerns about class conflict, 27, 31; concerns about loyalty, 33; concerns about strikes, 32; concerns about worker discipline, 30, 31, 33; death of, 52; early life and schooling, 25; employment of discharged soldiers, 7; expansion by, 52; family home of, 25, 78, 164; founding of Pirelli (company), 23, 25; international advertizing campaign, 26; on international expansion, 48; parents of, 25; philanthropy of, 26; political involvement of, 26; purchase of Bicocca, 35; rubber prod-

ucts company, 7; sons of, 39, 47, 52; on strikes, 32; struggles with industrial labor, 7; support of small-scale enterprises, 30, 31; welfare provision and, 33, 34; on workforce, 44. *See also* Bicocca

Pirelli, Giovanni (grandson of GBP), 71–72, 73, 75, 99

Pirelli, Leopoldo (grandson of GBP), 71, 102, 103, 108, 109, 110–12, 125, 132, 140–42, 143–44, 150, 152

Pirelli, Piero (son of GBP), 39, 47, 52, 71, 72, 74, 75

Pirelli & C., 50–52, 52, 149*fig.*

Pirelli factory: arson incidents, 102; number of workers at, 8; strike hours, 101, 102; strikes at, 32, 74, 90, 91, 92, 94, 99–100

Pirelli family: CEOs from, 14, 142–43, 144; legacy of, 60; memoirs of, 18; Milan and history of, 78; negotiations with, 144. *See also* Compagnie Internationale Pirelli (CIP); *specific Pirelli family members*

Pirelli Group: finances, 145*tab.*; national market base of, 83–84; real estate and, 148; structure of, 51*fig.*, 52, 149*fig.*; workforce, 54

Pirelli management: after WWI, 10; collaborative management, 72–74; restoration of corporate power, 10, 68, 72, 74–75

Pirelli Real Estate (Pirelli-RE), 15, 37, 138

Pirelli SpA, 102, 121, 142, 149*fig.*

Pirelli Tower, 25, 76–78, 84, 94, 100, 109–10

Pirelli Village, 63. *See also* Borgo Pirelli (workers' village)

Pirelli: Vita di una azienda industriale (Pirelli: The life of an industrial company) (A. Pirelli), 76

political action: documentation and, 170; land as space for, 6, 10–11; role of government, 170; Silvestri on entrepreneurs and, 56. *See also* radicalization

polyvocalism, 18

Ponti, Giò, 76

Popular Front, 82

population density, 9, 46, 59

post-Fordist development, 16, 123, 124*fig.*, 127, 131, 139, 152

power relations, 113, 116, 170, 171, 172

producers: displacement of, 169; industrialists as, 36; key German automobile producers, 141; top global pneumatics producers, 140; working class producers, 169 production: "Albania" (Bicocca recycling site), 147; class struggle around, 168; decrease in, 103; expansion of, 8; financialization of space and, 169; of high-tech tires, 112, 150; industrial commodity production, 14–16; industrial restructuring in Bicocca of, 112, 147, 168; local class struggle over, 167; production of land as financialized asset, 14–16; *Protocollo* and, 115; tire production removed from Bicocca, 119; units at Bicocca, 54. *See also* means of production

Progetto Bicocca SpA, 13, 15, 58, 119–20, 121, 138, 147, 148–49

Progetto Passante: Documento Direttore proposal, 123

Proletarian Unity (Partito Socialista Italiano di Unità Proletaria) (PSIUP), 72

Protocollo (*Schema di Protocollo di Intesa*) (Declaration of Intentions Protocol), 115, 117, 119, 123, 125

PSIUP (Proletarian Unity) (Partito Socialista Italiano di Unità Proletaria), 72

Quaderni Rossi (Red Notebooks), 89

radial tires: advances in, 103; Michelin and 108–9, 112; recycling of, 103, 108

radicalization: of industrial trade unionism, 168; of social claims, 11–12. *See also* political action

real estate: industrial land as real estate asset, 4, 14, 15, 16, 118–19, 138, 148; as part of Pirelli Group, 148–49; production of value, 170; redevelopment and, 147; regrouping of real estate activities, 148–49; value extraction, 169. *See also* Progetto Bicocca; Technocity

Recruitment Control Commission, 74

Red Brigades, 101–2

redevelopment: on "Albania" site, 147, 148; of Bicocca, 15, 116; economic returns from, 148; of Milan, 123, 128, 130; negotiation for, 113; no-man's land and, 17; Progetto Bicocca SpA and, 119–20, 147; real estate prices and, 147; social history eradication and, 156, 164; *White Paper for the Redevelopment of Abandoned Industrial Areas* (*Documento direttore delle aree industriali dismesse*), 126. *See also* financialization; historical suburb project; Technocity

redundancies, 11, 14, 62

regeneration, 133, 169

relocations, 107, 115, 125, 153, 169

La Repubblica (periodical), 18, 143

Rerum Novarum dogma, 61

resistance. *See* anti-Fascist resistance

retread sector, 103, 108

riots, 8, 32, 34

Rivista Pirelli (periodical), 10–11, 60, 68, 78–80

Rossi, Alessandro, 29, 38, 61

rubber: Dunlop rubber company, 109; high-tech production of, 14; imports, 56; international demand for, 68; international price of, 103, 108; Pirelli and, 7, 24, 25, 26; plantations, 48–49, 50, 168; production of, 39, 40, 48; production units, 54; product units, 146; recycling of, 147; synthetic rubber, 49, 56; vulcanization, 100

sabotage, 11, 70, 81, 93

SAIGIS (Società Italiana per la Gomma Sintetica), 56

Sappisti (guerrilla group), 69, 174nn2(ch3)

SAQINM (Società Anonima Quartiere Industriale Nord Milano), 36, 37

Scalfari, Eugenio, 143

schools: at Bicocca, 9, 46, 59, 60, 69; industrialists funding of, 27; at Krupp plant, 34; Montessori nursery school at Bicocca, 36, 164; as welfare provision, 8, 38, 41, 57, 60, 86. *See also* Milano Bicocca University; University of Milan

Secchia, P., 69

Silvestri, Giovanni, 55, 56

SIP (Società italiana Pirelli), 50, 52

SISI (Società per lo Sviluppo Delle Iniziative Stradali Italiane) (Italian Road Initiative Company), 83–84

Smith, Neil, 98

socialism, 32, 47, 61, 116

social issues: claims over industrial land, 11–12; land as social space, 6, 8–9, 168; land financialization as lived process, 7, 14–16, 167, 170, 171, 174n5; reclamation by Pirelli in Bicocca of, 168

Socialist Party, 72, 73, 82, 83

Società Anonima Quartiere Industriale Nord Milano (SAQINM), 36, 37

Società Italiana per la Gomma Sintetica (SAIGIS), 56

INDEX 201

Società italiana Pirelli (SIP), 50, 52
Società per lo Sviluppo Delle Iniziative Stradali Italiane (SISI) (Italian Road Initiative Company), 83–84
Il Sole 24 Ore (periodical), 18, 145
solidarity network, 8, 9, 41–42, 45, 70, 88
Somalvico, Anna, 60
space: aestheticization of spaces of production, 38–41; as class conflict, 41–44; in economic analysis, 173n4; financialization of, 169; land as social space, 9, 168; mixed-use spaces, 168; production of, 2, 6, 8–9; real estate value extraction of, 169; as reclaimed from workers, 12–13, 168; relocations, 169; social and working space, 8, 9, 169; solidarity network and, 8, 9, 41–42, 45, 70, 88; solidarity spaces, 9; spatial organization, 8, 41, 59; symbolic forms of appropriation of, 11. *See also* land; land revanchism
Spain, 48, 68, 171
Special Zone Z4 legislation, 128, 129
speculative capitalism, 7, 145, 148
speculative real estate, 14–15, 119–20, 121, 138, 149–50, 152, 168
Strade Ferrate Meridionali, 36
Strategic Plan for Milan, 156
Strategy of Tension, 12, 13, 81–82, 100–102, 108, 113. *See also* Years of Lead
strikes: anti-Fascist protest strikes, 70; avoidance of, 27–28; bans on, 9, 54, 55; during *biennio rosso*, 46; as class conflict, 14, 138; at FIAT, 99–100; improvised strikes, 90, 91–92, 93; labor movement and, 47; in Milan, 32; *Operaismo* movement and, 99–100; over salaries and welfare demands, 32; at Pirelli factory, 32, 74, 90, 91, 92, 94, 99–100; at Pirelli Tower, 100; punitive measures against, 32; socialism and, 32; strike hours, 101, 102; trade unions and, 113; wildcat strikes in Milan, 11, 81
student movements: Bicocca and, 16, 81, 96–99; Pirelli CUB and, 90–91; workers links with, 11. *See also Operaismo* movement
students: Bicocca and, 6, 17, 19, 162, 163; in social labor force, 98. *See also* Milano Bicocca University
Sumimoto, 140*tab.*

Tadini, Francesco, 74
Taylorism, 8, 35, 39

Technocity, 12–13, 15, 40; abandonment of, 138, 149–50, 152; architect, 150, 151; capital/land relationship and, 117; design competition for, 131; flexible planning regulations, 127–30, 139, 150, 152; global economy and, 132; as highly contested, 111–14; high-tech industrial sector and, 139, 168; land use for, 168; post-Fordist development and, 124*fig.*, 131, 139, 152; Progetto Bicocca and, 138, 147, 148; proposal, 108, 110, 111, 124*fig.;* publicity campaign for, 132; redevelopment plans for, 117, 121, 125–27, 147–48; regrouping under MCI of, 148; University of Milan and, 125; value of assets developed as, 120
technology: about, 7–8; crisis of, 103; high-tech capitalism, 12, 105; innovation, 12–13; investment in, 103, 109; research in, 109, 112, 117, 125, 129, 151
terrorist acts, 12, 70, 82, 100–102. *See also* Years of Lead
textile industry, 29, 32
theater, 17, 38, 150, 152, 156, 157, 164
timeful analysis, 1–6, 17, 18, 19, 63–64, 172, 173n4
Timefulness (Bjornerud), 1
tire industry: auto industry and, 84; global market, 50, 53, 103, 108, 139–41, 144; high-tech tires, 110, 112; highway network and, 84; mergers, 109; oil production and, 103; Pirelli in, 12, 25, 37, 54, 144, 146, 168; retread sector, 103, 108; rubber plantations, 48–49, 50; SIP and, 52; state protectionism and, 84; vulcanization, 100. *See also* competitors; production
Tosi, Franco, 38
trade unions: anti-Fascist liberation movement, 73; CGIL (Confederazione Generale Italiana del Lavoro) (trade union), 83, 87, 89, 90, 92, 113; CISL (Confederazione Italiana Sindacati Lavoratori) (trade union), 83, 90, 92; CUB and, 88–89, 89, 93; in factories, 32; Fascism and, 54, 70; labor contracts, 88; leaders of, 19; national trade unions, 100, 101, 113; opinions contesting, 97; paternalism of, 90; persecution of unionists, 75; Pirelli and, 112–13, 115–16, 119, 144, 146, 168; representation, 73, 74; solutions suggested by, 91–92; state as ally against, 82; UIL (Unione Italiana del Lavoro) (trade union), 83, 90, 92. *See also* unionism

202   INDEX

traditional elites, 4, 5, 7, 131–33, 137, 153–54, 169
traditional labor, 87, 91–92, 154, 169
traditional unions, 88
Tronti, Mario, 98

UIL (Unione Italiana del Lavoro) (trade union), 83, 90, 92
underclass: creation of, 111–14, 168; term usage, 174n3; workers shift to, 13, 168
Unim, 149
Unione Italiana del Lavoro (UIL) (trade union), 83, 90, 92
unionism: industrial trade unionism in Bicocca, 168; internal division of unions, 12; state's role against, 82; trade unionism in Italian factories, 32. *See also* CUB (Comitato Unitario di Base); trade unions
L'Unità (periodical), 18, 70
university complex (Milano Bicocca), 17, 112, 129*tab.*, 130, 150, 156, 161. *See also* Milano Bicocca University
University of Milan, 125, 151
university students, 156, 163
urban economy, 7, 15, 122
urbanization, 24, 122, 150–51, 169

Vicari Haddock, Serena, 123, 130, 164
violence: between capital and labor, 27; industrialists use of, 6–7, 47; of land revanchist, 4, 7, 12, 13, 15, 82; of Milan riots, 32; of Mussolini's government, 54–55; of protests, 100; of Red Brigades, 101; Strategy of Tension, 12, 13, 81–82, 100–102, 108, 113; Years of Lead, 11–12, 13, 81–82, 100–101, 108
Vitruvio, 148
Volkswagen, 141
vulcanization, 100

wages: agricultural workers search for extra wages, 28; cuts in, 11; delays in regulation of, 62; feminist movements and, 97; fight for increases in, 89; fixed wages, 29; low wages, 7, 27, 31; repressing of, 83; strikes and increases in, 94; student wages, 98
welfare provision: Bicocca and, 35; *Corporativismo* and, 9, 45–46, 57–60; crèches, 8; expansion of, 8; health services, 8; industrialists and, 27, 33; industrial paternalism and, 61; Pirelli's legacy and, 76;

political elites and, 33; schools, 8; spaces dedicated to, 8; as workforce pacification, 8. *See also Corporativismo*
Wilson, D., 162
workers: anti-fascist resistance of, 10–11; attire and manners of, 8, 40; Bicocca as village for, 168; education of, 29; histories as added value, 169; industrial restructuring and, 168; layoffs, 168, 169; militant workers, 168; negotiating class power of, 168; pacification of, 8; from peasantry to industrial labor, 7–8; in Pirelli-Bicocca area, 18–19; punishment measures against, 147; relocations, 169; resistance to Fascism during WWII by, 168; retired workers, 60; shift to underclass, 168; social activities for, 8; social spaces of, 7; solidarity network, 8. *See also* disciplined labor; housing; retired workers
Workers' Commission (*Commissione operaia*), 47
Workers' Concordat, 33
workers' meetings: ad hoc meetings, 91, 93; bans on, 9, 54
workers' movements: industrialists use of violence against, 47; Milan riots of May 1898, 32; weakening of, 7. *See also* labor movement; strikes
work ethos, 28, 31
working class: concept of, 169; under Fascism, 54; industrial world victory over, 82–83; as marginalized group, 169; *Operaismo* and, 97, 98; reclaim power from, 12–13; shift to underclass, 13, 111–14, 168; unmaking of, 107–17, 133. *See also* land revanchism; unionism; workers
World War II: anti-Fascist resistance during, 6, 10–11, 16, 63, 67, 155, 168; Bicocca during, 68–72; corporate power restoration after, 72–75, 82; Pirelli during, 56; workers' resistance against Fascism during, 168. *See also* anti-Fascist resistance; Fascism; Mussolini, Benito
Wright, E. O., 114

Years of Lead, 11–12, 13, 81–82, 100–101, 108. *See also* industrial land; radicalization; Strategy of Tension; terrorist acts

Zanetti, A. M., 146

Founded in 1893,
UNIVERSITY OF CALIFORNIA PRESS
publishes bold, progressive books and journals
on topics in the arts, humanities, social sciences,
and natural sciences—with a focus on social
justice issues—that inspire thought and action
among readers worldwide.

The UC PRESS FOUNDATION
raises funds to uphold the press's vital role
as an independent, nonprofit publisher, and
receives philanthropic support from a wide
range of individuals and institutions—and from
committed readers like you. To learn more, visit
ucpress.edu/supportus.